Once More unto the Breach, Dear Friends

Once More unto the Breach, Dear Friends

Incomplete Theory
and Complete Bibliography
of Irving Louis Horowitz on
the occasion of his 75th birthday

Compiled by Andrew McIntosh,
Patrick Ivins, and Deborah A. Berger

Aldine Transaction

A Division of Transaction Publishers
New Brunswick (U.S.A.) and London (U.K.)

Second updated printing 2005
Copyright © 2005 by Transaction Publishers, New Brunswick, New Jersey.

Library of Congress Catalog Number: 2004051745
ISBN: 0-7658-0274-0
Printed in the United States of America

Library of Congress Cataloging-in-Publication Data

Horowitz, Irving Louis.
    Once more unto the breach, dear friends : Incomplete Theory and Complete bibliography of Irving Loius Horowitz on the occasion of his 75th birthday / compiled by Andrew McIntosh, Patrick Ivins, and Deborah A. Berger.
        p. cm.
    ISBN 0-7658-0274-0 (paper : alk. paper)
    1. Horowitz, Irving Louis. 2. Horowitz, Irving Louis—Bibliography. 3. Sociology. 4. Political science. 5. Learning and scholarship.
    I. McIntosh, Andrew, 1967- II. Ivins, Patrick. III. Berger, Deborah A.
    IV. Title.

HM479.H67H67 2005
301'.092—dc22

                                                            2004051745

Table of Contents

PREFACE

· ·

Let me start with a painful confession: I am by no means certain whether these random essays coupled with a systematic bibliography constitute a proper sense of self-esteem or what Immanuel Kant called an unpleasant "craving for honor". Given the complex nature of the vocabulary of motives, I have elected the statements, and the publication record, to speak for themselves. There are no encomiums provided, no communal celebration, and no grand gathering. If I can boast of nothing coming close to the master of Königsberg's *Critique of Pure Reason,* I can at least try to emulate his commonsensical distinctions. As he informed us, everything should be subject to the free and public examination of reason grounded on itself and confined to itself.

More specifically, rather than unduly burden friends and colleagues to make public statements on my reaching the age of 75, which is after all a biological roll of the dice and hardly qualifies as a day for collective celebration, I decided to pick out a few relatively recent publications. Half of these statements concern areas that are near and dear to me. Some have been written during the past decade for various ceremonial occasions or since publication of the wonderful *festschrift* offered to me put together by Ray C. Rist in *The Democratic Imagination* in 1994. The other half is connected to my role on *Society* magazine, *Transaction* publishers, and the crossover world of publishing and professing the social sciences. I hope that my friends appreciate the contents while graciously ignoring this display of promotion.

I am honor bound to say plainly that this is not intended to be a sequel to *Daydreams and Nightmares.* It is not an autobiography in any legitimate sense of that word, but simply my personal reflections on areas of work that I have been involved with over the years. It is more a manifestation of concern with the status of various parts of the social science field, not so much as a critic but as a participant. If an academic spends a lifetime on one subject, he or she is identified as a specialist. If one covers several subject areas, however related, he or she (in this case me) becomes magically transformed into a generalist—a frowned upon status in the best of circumstances. For my part, neither specialist nor generalist has

much cachet. The joy of scholarship is in the process. The horrors of scholarship are in the presumption that the world comes to a pinnacle with a system, design, or path to discovery.

One reason for not writing an autobiography is the almost inevitable consequence of converting self-reflection into self-serving. The emphasis on self not only reduces the worth of the other, but too often conflates the cares and concerns of the larger world with the careers of oneself. In the social sciences, an area of modest achievement at best, this has led to a series of disastrous autobiographies that can barely be read. Too frequently, works in this genre waiver between pomposity and aggrandizement. Modesty is not a virtue that often afflicts social scientists. There are, of course, marvelous exceptions–two of which Transaction had the good fortune to publish: George C. Homan's great book, *Coming to My Senses*, and Robin Fox's flinty *Participant Observer*. But being dubious about the capacity to rise to such heights, I prefer to offer brief statements made during the course of my recent life, related to tasks and traditions with which I have been connected.

To the three young people who edited, printed, designed, and corrected a most complex bibliography–Andrew McIntosh, Patrick Ivins, and Deborah A. Berger–each of whom have enough to do without this chore, goes my last gratitude. It would be impossible to thank each person who assisted or advised me on such a large bundle of writings. In any event, they know who they are. But as a whole, they offer testimonial to the community of scholarship that exists, and transcends differences, arguments about contents, and even concerns about format and publication strategies. Social science is indeed a culture wrapped in an institution known as the university. The one exception to this blanket appreciation, is Mary E. Curtis, who has been with me since we met in the fall of 1967 (when she was a student of mine at Washington University in St. Louis). I doubt that there is a serious (or for that matter, a frivolous) piece of my work that she has not looked at and made better. What more can I possibly add to this brief Preface–except to hope that the values of this set of essays combined with a full-scale bibliography exceed its transparent vanities.

Note to the Reader

With the exception of the first and ninth chapters, an asterisk next to the corresponding entry in the bibliography indicates the derivation of the chapter. The two exceptions are herein published for the first time. They were originally delivered as lectures. The relevant source information is contained at the conclusion of these two chapters. I have been emphatically reminded to note in conclusion that my date of birth is September 25, 1929.

Irving Louis Horowitz
Hannah Arendt Distinguished University Professor Emeritus
Rutgers, The State University of New Jersey

1

PREDICTING AND REMEMBERING
· ·

When I was initially contacted by the head of the DeWitt Clinton High School Alumni Association to speak before the fiftieth annual class reunion in 1997 my first thought was to say no. Not that I had any negative feeling about my High School Alma Mater but when he asked me to speak with a "Clinton Perspective," I was foolish enough to think my erstwhile fellow-student (who is now dean of the Touro Law School) meant our current President, William Jefferson Clinton, not DeWitt Clinton High School. I told him I would think about it. It was 48 hours before the light bulb turned on, and I understood the years to slow one down after all.

Still, after making all the proper apologias and declaring myself available, questions remained: just what was the Clinton experience, and how does it relate to the youngsters one sees in the hallways and classrooms of the High School today. DeWitt Clinton celebrated its one-hundredth anniversary in 1997, which makes it no small matter, at least symbolically, to be a member of the 1947 graduating class, fifty years ago. I would be at a school founded in 1897, addressing an audience of peers in May 1997—100 years later—who had graduated fifty years ago. I have enough superstition about numbers, as those who know me well can attest, to be strongly intimidated by the event and its meaning.

I am a sociologist. My task and theme for this occasion, I decided, was what, if anything sociology can contribute to an understanding of that which distinguishes the Clinton graduates of January 1947 (there was also a graduation class in June of that year) from those of 1997. Obviously I knew a great deal more about the former. But going into the classroom every semester at Rutgers does allow me to engage students who are only a year or two removed from being graduates of Clinton and other New York area high schools, albeit a year or two later down the pike. Applying what I have learned from my students at Rutgers to a consideration of my own student days gave me perspective on what has changed, and what remains the same.

One major quality that 1997 graduates of DeWitt Clinton have in common with those of 1947 is a great sense of the importance of upward mobility, or in plain English, moving up the socioeconomic ladder beyond their parents. This is a fast fading phenomenon in middle class America, a world in which children now aspire to do as well rather then better, but it is a cement which binds the poor to one another and to the dream of America as a land of opportunity.

The high school graduate, and I daresay college graduate in suburban America must wonder what can be aspired to that has not already been achieved by their parents. But Clinton graduates of fifty years ago and those today have few such worries. True enough, African American, Puerto Ricans, and a variety of other new immigrants have flocked to New York City, and they have different cultural backgrounds than the Jewish, Italian and Irish youngsters who dominated the Clinton of a half-century ago. They share a foreground filled with hope and opportunity and a sense of unlimited potential rather than fixed stratification as what matters in the souls of the young.

If I may venture an outrageous hypothesis, it is possible that young people coming out of a high school like Clinton may score better on tests, and show lower rates of so-called deviance than they do in schools in areas where high school graduation is a ritual on the way to emulating and perhaps falling short of achievements that have been registered by parents and elders. I learned that Clinton is recognized and rewarded for being one of "America's Best Schools" in 1997. Perhaps this may prove a harbinger of things to come, a world in which inner city youngsters realize the ambitions of the nation, and do so with greater pride and less cynicism or despondency than their fellow teenagers in suburbia. Let us hope so.

But there are other characteristics of being young in urban America besides stratification and moving on a success ladder. These are more troubling, and cast a dark shadow over the silver lining. The most important of these is personal identity. There is so much talk about identity crises today that it is probably wise to spell out what one means in flintier, less fuzzy, rhetoric. The young of 1997's graduating class share a uniquely modern cultural formation. They are unsure about male and female roles, uneasy about the risk of deadly diseases such as AIDS, and they are profoundly unaware of the relationship of sex to human affection.

Such concerns are common to high school graduates of the present era whether they are suburban or urban, rich or poor, native or migrant. Such concerns are the core consequences of an adult, parental generation that has changed the valuation base of human relations. The young of today know more, even as they may care less. They know what the human body actually looks like without having to search old issues of the National Geographic for photographs of far away tribes. They have sexual intercourse as a property of the biological ability to do so; they need not challenge theological edicts that deny the body. Young people today seem to look upon the private life as a realm that is far more significant than public life or community service. Were this not the case, a host of politicians and retired militarists would not need to convince them to consider the values of volunteering.

But for those in the inner city high school, in DeWitt Clinton high school, identity crises are not middle-class cultural meanderings or searches for excitement. They are a function of the hard realities of broken and damaged families, a world in which divorce is the norm, violence is a commonplace way adults relate to one another, and the experience of sex is far more commonplace than the achievement of love. And in this one must be frank and say that in these respects life in 1947 was far easier on the young. I will not say better. The inhibitions and fears that existed among traditional families imposed constraints from which the parents of the new Clintonians tried to escape, alas with such frightening and fearsome success.

The concerns of the moment are less over what kind of family life is best for the young, than whether any sort of family life can be detected, at least one that can insure the safety and well being of the young. To think that the federal government will replace the family as a source of comfort and well-being is as preposterous as it is malevolent. Indeed, it is the totalitarian dream to have the leader become one with the father, and the state provide the dispensations that were formerly the prerogative of the family. This ideal of government as big parent in the sky was barely noticeable in 1947. It may have been a concern among those who realized that the conduct of warfare lodged such enormous power in the hands of a central authority that in an era of peace, the objectives of such centralized power would shift, but not diminish.

But all that talk of government is an abstraction, far removed from the quotidian world of the high school graduates I saw about me in 1997. In the absence of stable personal relations, of a well-crafted sense of personal identity, government becomes simply a repository of goodies. Government provides jobs as well as norms for the society as a whole, but especially its young, and increasingly success and failure become images centered on governments rather than persons. Failure results when a government does not deliver rather than when a person fails to achieve. This is a large-scale change in the fault-lines of American society. How the graduating class of Clinton handles it will go a long way to determine the peaceful or violent future of this society.

The Clinton graduates of 1947 had in common with those of 1997 a peculiar hybrid of marginality, what might best be called cosmopolitan parochialism. In the world of then Mayor Fiorello LaGuardia's New York, we all had a stake in the city, but it was limited to the city. Who would need more than Mecca, and who knew (or cared) what lay beyond Mecca. New York was the capital: of culture, of the arts, of theater, and also the much loathed business and commerce.

The students of 1947 sensed the proximity of aspiration and reward. The American dream was conflated into New York dreaming. And while DeWitt Clinton had as many students with "strange" names as it does at present, the commonalty of goals dwarfed any sense of difference. These shared aspirations created a sense of stake in the City of New York, which made of it the permanent, final place, rather than a way stop on the road to elsewhere. That at any rate is how graduation seemed to us in 1947.

Whether the sheer ease of movement has created a weaker sense of place, or a weaker sense of place has stimulated higher relocation, the fact is that America on the move translates into cities with a very high sense of transience. New York is a gateway city into the country, and as such it is especially prone to such ecological shifts. If in the old days the movement was from Manhattan to Brooklyn to the Bronx (as was the case with me and my family), the newer patterns might be from New York City proper to Chicago and on to Los Angeles.

The new realities of rootlessness are well captured in a recent column in *Newsweek* by 26-year-old Jennifer Crispin. "I am not from anywhere. But that's as much a part of my identity as a hometown is for other people. I am a person who is not from anywhere . . . I am from nowhere, and I am from everywhere. That's the way I like it." (*Newsweek*, May 26, 1997) I can hardly imagine a Clinton student of fifty years ago making such a declaration of deracination, much less doing so with a sense of pride. Indeed, I recollect that when fellow students moved out of the neighborhood, they left us with a sense of void, not to mention loss.

So in this third area, graduates of 1997 not only differ from, but also suffer in comparison to those of 1947. For in the absence of physical rootedness, it is hard to create the foundations of moral rootedness. That the attempt is even made already represents a triumph of the search for spiritual community in the absence of the existence of actual communities. The neighborhood of old places with settled and secure values, has become the 'hood of the present, a place of physical pain and spiritual loss. I suspect that the youngster who makes the train ride from Mosholu Parkway to home is embarking on a more perilous course than most of us knew a half century ago.

It is simply a pleasant fiction to think that one is from everywhere, when the reality is that such a person is from nowhere. Without roots there can be no identity. Being free of all sanctions, all norms, and all faiths may seem to be a heady experience in the short run. But in the long pull of time, such "freedom from" conflicts with "freedom to" create, freedom to learn, freedom to care. Roots provide not such spiritual comfort but material safety - the safety net of one's own family, clan, and yes, friends. Roots tell us where we have come from, which may turn out to be as important as where we are heading.

The Clinton graduate of 1947 was blessed with the conceits of a stable world of rights and wrongs, goods and evils, beauties and ugliness. I fear that the graduate of 1997 is cursed with the anguish of having to plow through a dense forest to work out for himself or herself all of the above sets of moral antinomies. But if frankness must prevail, the quest in 1947 may have been far easier on the mind; while the goals for the 1997 graduating class is far more intriguing, closer to the marrow of the stuff of life than to the life of stuff their elders have so assiduously accumulated and cultivated.

An address to the fiftieth year reunion of the graduating class of DeWitt Clinton, May 10, 1997, DeWitt Clinton High School.

2

SCHOLARLY PUBLISHING AS THE WORD MADE FLESH

. . . .

In *The Gospel According to St. John* we are told that in the beginning was the Word (1:1). But a little later, we are also notified that "The Word was made flesh, and dwelt among us . . . full of grace and truth (1:14). This conversion of the word from the divine to the human, so deeply rooted in the Judeo-Christian heritage, was something that I so took for granted that its biblical origins did not have to be recited to me for the enticements of words to take root in my soul.

Publishing and professing came together early in my life. Still, neither came easy, nor were doors flung open at the mere mention of my name. The written and the oral always seemed linked as two ways to escape from the bondage of life. They were intimately related activities—loves might be a better way to say things. I never could appreciate the Socratic emphasis on the oral tradition as something above and beyond the literary tradition. To be sure, were it not for Plato writing down this dialectic of discourse, we would be bereft of the very emphasis Socrates sought to instill.

Thus it was that my first venture into business was publishing scholarly books. It all seemed so natural, so perfect. But between abstract love of learning and the concrete act of manufacturing and selling a book is a huge gulf—one that I had to traverse. But where to begin, what to do for capital, how to acquire titles, where to set up shop, and when to launch this enterprise that the world definitely was not awaiting-these concerns could not readily be resolved by appeals to divine support or inspiration.

The first task, and doubtless the easiest, was to identify a proper name for the new launch. I settled on Paine-Whitman Publishers. It had a nice and serious sound. It called forth a hero of the American Revolution, albeit one born in England, Thomas Paine; and one of our greatest poets, Walt Whitman. The figures were indigenous radicals, stood in opposition to the conventions of their respective eras, and were quintessential democrats. In an age defined by McCarthyism at one extreme and Stalinism at the other, this seemed a happy choice. And it was.

The selection of a name, like dreams of glory, is a long way from the realization of ideas on paper. But if ever anyone entered the world of publishing ignorant of all the processes that enter into the final result, the book itself, that person was myself. I was so infatuated with the meaning of the words on the paper, even the smell of the book itself, that how a book is made, or who even to call for some advice, did not enter my calculations. I did have one secret geographical ally: the world of Fourth Avenue in lower Manhattan. There inside the space of one mile, could be found the best used book shops in the world, or at least outside of Paris, substantial printers and binders of small editions, headquarters for a plethora of small, independent journals, and free-wheeling intellectuals and would-be academics ready to declare and declaim on everything and anything. If publishing and printers ink ever had a special perfume, the aromas of Fourth Avenue and lower Broadway provided the necessary first whiffs.

It was such a comfortable environment. Nearly everybody was young. And there was an absence of the sort of pretense and good form offered at Ivy League in New York-Columbia. I am convinced, in retrospect, that the reason so few Jews made it through the Columbia University system had less to do with overt anti-Semitism or racism, so much as the cult of manners parading forth as civility. In any event, manners was hardly a problem on Fourth Avenue and Tenth Street in the 1950s.

If it is true that publishing is, as the Association of American Publishers used to trumpet, an accidental profession, I am that illustration of an accident, par excellence. But in a curious way, behind every accident is a necessity of choice. And the interests which I manifested in publishing, were driven, on the negative side at least, by my experiences as a philosophical deviant and no less, a permanent political outsider. Neither in the past nor present was I comfortable with movements, especially those that self-designated as "mass movements." But looking upon others quizzically is a sure way to be removed from the great and empty battles that cost so many people so much suffering. Politics is like war: necessary struggles that in retrospect turn out to be expensive in victory and often bitter in consequences. One pays a price for heroic images of being a lonely individualist warrior in a world of collective decisions and decision-makers. But it did stimulate an intense belief that the answer was publishing. For one thing that I had imbibed from theology and philosophy alike: the word mattered. Paper mattered, books mattered. In an unreal world, in a world in which the ordinary norms of social life were hardly extant, words came to matter even more.

The enlightenment belief that people would read the truth and respond to the truth in their practices was still with me. Indeed, this insane belief in the power of words linked the much-hated theologians with the philosophers of nature. Yes, of course, interests determine attitudes. This lesson I learned early on from Marx's *German Ideology.* The good books of Marxism and philosophy alike preached a world of redemption, one could be saved through good words, and right thoughts. Thus, what we mock in religion, its redemptive power, a power derived word accepting the word of the Lord, was very much present in my life but as a secular force. The word as Reason rather than word as Faith was to be my salvation. I did not entertain the obvious possibility that the reason of revolution was the momentary reflection of the faith of revelation. My Jewish origins made possible this faith in words. My Christian environment made necessary some translation of all this into works. And thus started the quest for a publishing vehicle-the drive shaft of personal redemption and public notoriety.

What gave substance to this quest was the state of publishing at least as I knew it: people like Angus Cameron were being dismissed from Little, Brown as editors tinged with communism, while the most incredible rubbish was being published by the Communist Press. International Publishers was not simply the vehicle of awful trash, but it sounded worse in English than in the original Russian—given the nature of the languages, and no less, the availability of alternatives. Imagine a list in which Stalin, Beria, Molotov, vied with William Z. Foster and Eugene Dennis as the greatest "thinkers" of the century—my how that word was terribly abused at the time. Every dictator fancies himself a philosopher. The zealot wears a world view as a badge of fanatic honor. Anyhow, I made the acquaintance of Mr. Cameron as a result of a review which I wrote in *Mainstream* of *Giant in Chains* by Barrows Dunham. It was a quite decent book on the philosophical implications of violating the busing codes in the South, on what happens to the morality of people when a bus is more than a mode of transportation but a definition of racial separation.

In our one meeting, I mentioned to him what must have seemed like an adolescent cry in the night: what is one to do to reach an audience. He listened with remarkable patience. I presume he had the time to do so after his dismissal (and before he entered a publishing partnership with Carl Marzani). His answer was quite simple: "Go into publishing. The price of admission is cheap, prospects for reaching lots of people are great, and the feeling of doing something worthwhile very real." I did not need too much prodding. With a career in philosophy just about over before it began, a marriage wrapped in fanaticism and going nowhere, and work prospects confined to the non-lethal-like bookkeeping, as George Washington Plunkitt might have said, I saw my opportunity and seized it!

The one thing which Mr. Cameron did not inform me of was how to acquire the capital needed to start a publishing house! I guess in his editorial capacities at Little, Brown such plebian concerns were of small consequence. From my experiences in my father's hardware stores I had learned something amazing: there was a world of borrowing and another world of credit. But even before such financial considerations, one needed a name and a business address. These were the fun parts. For the name, I selected Paine-Whitman Publishers. It was an amalgam of Thomas Paine and Walt Whitman. This was done to establish the American character of the Arm, its serious intellectual purpose, and its populist ideological concerns. In truth, I still like the name Paine-Whitman Publishers—and for the very same reasons! So many publishers take the names of the founders: McGraw, Wiley, Jovanovich, Knopf, and what have you. As an act of conceit, this ranks high on the list. Publishing started by using the name of the printer, since the printer was responsible for the seditious word. But by the mid-twentieth century, this became a literary affectation. Proof that a Mr. Simon and a Mr. Schuster once existed.

Now that I had invented a distinguished progeny, linking Thomas Paine from the eighteenth century, Walt Whitman from the nineteenth century to the yet-to-be-discovered Irving Louis Horowitz from the twentieth century, what next? An address of course. I could not afford a place on Madison Avenue or any other Avenue for that matter. But for the munificent price of $4.00 per month at 1170 Broadway, I had the privilege of having an answering service, a mail drop, and two pleasant, bleached-blond Jewish sisters who stepped out of a Diane Arbus photograph, yet who had a wonderful sense of business, and would actually call me if anything special seemed in the works. What a bargain! In addition, the two sisters liked me-and would even carry my "rent" when I was late with my monthly tariff! The eighth floor at 28th Street was not a pretty picture. Behind a reasonable facade were the remants of a sweatshop industry in decline. But the building was in the midtown area, and close to Peerless Willoughby's where I was working at the time in the accounts payable department. While I drifted in and out of various jobs, they were all in this area of the city. I made sure they were, since Paine-Whitman was the love of my life, even as it became the bane of my life as well.

The next step was to establish a credit rating. This worked easily enough at some levels, poorly at others. For supplies all the way to bindery and warehouse in, I was able to call forth my father's hardware store accounts. Many knew the name Horowitz, and even if my father had gone out of business, his credit ratings were good—no bad debts. So the name Horowitz had a cachet. It enabled me to establish a credit line at Chas. H. Bohn Bindery, and the Brooklyn Battery Warehouse was willing to bill and ship-especially since they did a great deal of work for the Bohn bindery. In the world before Dun dc Bradstreet, credit ratings were established more informally than they are at present. There were few checks, and the desire to sell and move merchandise and services was very high. I am astonished in retrospect how few vendors asked what, if any, the relationship was between Horowitz the piano player and Horowitz the retail hardware operator. I confess not to have aided much in the process of enlightenment.

That left one piece of the puzzle: getting the books, and then getting them into composition and printing. This was aided and abetted by my hanging around the offices of *Science & Society* and *Partisan Review* in New York. Both used a firm called The Liberal Press. They did hot lead composition, printing, but farmed out the binding. I had become a presence at the printers—with little else to do. I read the proofs for various reviews and articles I did for *Science & Society, so* I got to know the Italian owners of The Liberal Press. They knew me well enough to know how little I had, but somehow, believed that what I was doing with Paine-Whitman was not that much more strange than the work at the aforementioned magazines.

The owners warranted that if I could come up with $400 in cash, they would carry a small run edition of a book for the remaining $400. The title I already had: the article and papers of Samuel Bernstein-an old curmudgeon, independent thinker, and senior editor at *Science & Society* at the time. The title for our first Paine-Whitman venture then was *Essays in Political and Intellectual History.* Actually, it was badly named: it was in fact, Studies in French Revolutions from 1789 to 1871. The book might have done much better under such a solid and accurate title—but with such a heavy philosophical background, and proposed list, I chose the more general and the more abstract title. I learned this was a foolish decision, a lesson from which I have profited many times:

when in doubt, be concrete as to title. Stay away from titles that start with "Essays In" and end with "Intellectual History" But auto-didacticism is not necessarily a good way to learn, simply the only way open to me at the time.

Well now, how to raise $400! I was between jobs, which was a plus in giving me time to work on my first title, but bad from a fund raising point of view. I then went to a bank, I believe the Manhattan Trust as Chase-Manhattan was then known, and made application for a loan. I asked how long it would take for processing, and was told that it was a matter of checking references and credit ratings. That I had no job was bad, that I had no outstanding debts was good. So as a job reference I gave the number of a little used telephone close to my apartment, and made up some sort of corporate name; I also gave the name of Paine-Whitman, and instructions to my answering service that if a call came in about me from the Bank, it was to be transferred to home. Since one needed to be able to provide at least two phone references to be checked out for a loan, this device was important.

God smiled. On the morning after I filed my application, a call came to the public telephone. I answered, gave a fictitious name as a resident of the fictitious firm, and assured the voice on the other end that Irving Louis Horowitz was good for a $400 loan and much more. This having been done, I ran home, and sure enough in mid-afternoon, a call came through, transferred from the service number at Paine-Whitman, asking about the status of the "firm," its assets, and the assets of the same Horowitz. Obviously, this too checked out. The necessary reassurances were given. The following day, I received a call at home to assure me that the loan had been approved, and that I could come in for the check. To say that I was ecstatic is putting it mildly. This was more money than I ever had at a single time. And unlike fellowship and tuition remissions, it was actually spendable in any shape or fashion I decreed proper. That this all came about through a hoax, rather than through hard work, did not endear banking capitalism to my mind. The matter of repayment was yet to come. But at least the stage was set for the production of the first Paine-Whitman title. In the beginning may have been the word, but before the legendary word came the compositor and the printer. This was an important lesson for me as to the true nature of God. His first-born son may have been a carpenter, but his second son was a member of the International Typographical Workers Union.

The New York City ambience of the mid-1950s was critical to the success of Paine-Whitman. Where else could one find in one ten block area the offices of *Partisan Review, Science & Society,* and *Dissent.* Certainly no other part of America could boast such a plethora of printers and binders. In 1990, one can look in vain for binderies located in the city limits. But 35 years ago, New York City was the center of printing and publishing, and not just the editorial headquarters for publishing conglomerates. In this sense I was blessed by the accursed City of New York.

Samuel Bernstein was not so much a prototype as the guinea-pig for my venture into publishing. First came the contract. I knew nothing of this world, so I simply took the contract I had signed with Coleman-Ross, the publisher of my very first book, *Giordano Bruno* in 1952, and modeled the agreement for *Essays in Political and Intellectual History* after that effort. In retrospect I realized it was not a bad contract to use as a model, since it guaranteed the publisher all sorts of things and left the author with practically nothing. I guess what was done to me at the receiving end could thus be used at the giving, or not so giving, end. The contract signing was actually a very pleasant experience. The Bernsteins invited me to supper at their Upper West Side apartment. We had a good meal, drank wine, which made me very drowsy, signed the agreement (which Rose, Sam's wife, "witnesseth") and we were on our way.

Now it should be realized that, poorly chosen title notwithstanding, Samuel Bernstein was very well known, if not well liked, by his fraternal colleagues in French political history. So there was an audience for the book among specialist historians, revisionist Marxists, and assorted readers of the journal which Sam co-edited. All of this may seem proof of my business acumen, but in fact, it was all an accident of place and time. Sam had a manuscript. I knew it to be of high quality, we were both marginal to the communists, and no straight-ahead university press would touch Sam's work. I also had the advantage of Sam's editorial skills. Copy editing was second nature to Sam because of his work at *Science & Society.* Alas, so too were author alterations! Like Balzac, the work was largely rewritten on galleys. I saw my typesetting bill at The Liberal Press increase by $200 and a snarling Sam Bernstein who paid no attention to pleas for moderation. Still, we got beyond the galley stage, and were able to move into printing the book with relative dispatch. I was there every day the book came off press-signature after signature, in eight page folios, using miniature rather than big presses.

It was all so beautiful, so perfect, so clean, but flat sheets are not bound books. Close but no cigars. I took the initial sheet to Chas. H. Bohn. They prepared an estimate, which I was not in a position to turn away or spurn, since they alone had extended me credit. The flat sheets were sent down to Spring Street from Fourth Avenue-a trip of three blocks, not thousands of miles. Since Liberal Press knew of Chas. H. Bohn, they were sufficiently impressed not to insist on immediate payment for the author alterations portion. Now that the job had been printed, they too had a vested stake in everything working out well.

The dust jacket—initially without lamination, and hence easily scratched and damaged—was modeled after a simple design of the times. The printing was done at the Bohn warehouse. The physical product was bound and jacketed in roughly one month. All still very much a mystery, but I called my friend at the bindery. I went down to Spring Street where they were located, and saw the first advanced copies of the book. It was a beautiful sight— a magical mystery tour brought to fruition. I was the first to lay eyes on the bound book. After delivering a few to Bernstein at 20th Street, where the office of S & S were located, I came to the slow, very slow realization, that I was the proud owner of one thousand copies of a single book-without the means or the talent to sell a single one of them!

So fixated had I become on the production process that the act of making public, of publishing, simply eluded my attention. This was a big lesson which I have always remembered: there is a big gulf between the printing and selling of a book. To publish, the act of making public, is very different than the act of printing. I also realize that authors, even revolutionary ones like Sam Bernstein, could hardly care less about copy one thousand. Only copy one, only the artifact he held in his hand and placed on his curriculum vitae sheet actually mattered. It was not long before euphoria turned into fright. After all, one could fool the Manhattan Trust Bank once, but not twice. And by this time, the first payment was coming due, and I was without a job, but with a wife and two infants!

I should say in frankness that although the stress and strains of a less than perfect marriage had already begun to show through the facade of everyday life, Ruth helped me in every way possible. She did copy editing, helped with the billing, made supper for prospective poor authors. Ruth did not especially appreciate my expenditure of valuable time on Paine-Whitman. It was clearly not a way to support a family in any style. Ruth objected that a part-time activity had pre-empted my energies—and that the real victims of this hubris were the children: Carl and David. In retrospect she was probably right in her assessment. But publishing is the sort of business equivalent to writing poetry. It is done because seemingly no other way of life can offer a satisfactory alternative. Ruth did not object too strenuously, since Paine-Whitman, as a cottage industry, enabled her to do something constructive without leaving the house. And the titles themselves certainly appealed to her own intellectual ambitions and beliefs.

But for the moment, the problem was not domestic tranquility but the lack of publishing skills. Having created my own problem I had to find my own solution. This was not so easy. There were no lists of radical historians to send out news about the Bernstein book. Indeed, the only keepers of such lists were probably the FBI, and they hardly were in a mood or a position to share this information with a fledgling publisher! Anyhow, marketing was not only a foreign world but one requiring hard domestic cash. Having spent every cent I had on the production of the book, there was no money left.

Well, not quite. There was the ongoing salary just enough to feed Carl and David and Ruth in the modest style of poor West Bronx denizens. What to do? My next step was to print up an invoice, containing all the basic information on the Bernstein title, including the dollar extensions. The top spaces were left free to fill in with the customer's name. Ah, but who were the customers?

In searching out the answer to this question, I discovered that Paine-Whitman was not a trade or text publisher, but a professional publisher! Our market was the libraries. I borrowed a list of national libraries (one could actually borrow reference items overnight in the mid-1950s from local branches). Then I developed a strategy of sending out single copies to libraries, one hundred at a time. I did not have enough money for a more extensive mailing of the book.

I sent books to the top one hundred libraries in terms of funds allocated for book purchases, without regard to whether the libraries were state, city, or local, public or private-just overall dollar expenditure. Each book was accompanied with an invoice, addressed to the head of special collections; or if there was no such designation, that person or of lice most likely to be in a position to approve a purchase. Keep in mind too that in the days before the big jobbers, the Baker and Taylor organizations that provide librarians with programmed purchasing, such purchases were actually made by individual librarians.

To make an already long story a bit shorter, the mailing proved slow but successful. Fourth class mail is slow in being received, and processing small vouchers for payment also slow, especially when there is no offsetting purchase order. So for the first several weeks, I was in great pain—thinking that not only had I spent everything on a book I had no means to market, but then I had turned around and given the book away to big libraries which had absolutely no obligation to purchase the book, or even return it for that matter.

By the fifth week, my quiet desperation eased; at least twenty checks in payment for the book arrived at my mail drop place. Another twenty or so came in the following week. Then a trickle of payments arrived over the next month or so. When the dust settled—and it took two full months to do so—we had "sold" seventy-five to eighty copies of our first title. And nearly all the rest were eventually returned by the libraries who declined to purchase the book. Those who declined the book sometimes expressed deep anger that the mails were being used to send solicitations and invoices in this way. I empathized, but was not in a position to take on such a postal cause with any militancy.

It was now time for the second round, that is, sending out one hundred additional books and invoices to those on the reference list of major libraries. Now the rewards were lower—perhaps sixty purchases and forty returns—and the letters of protest a trifle more stinging. Still, I had now sold approximately 140 copies of the book-or more precisely, been paid for them. This was just enough to pay off the bank loan. Which I did in a lump sum. Doing so, I lowered my interest payments and established a credit "line" at "my" bank. Well, it was not actually my bank. I decided to do the banking for Paine-Whitman close to the Broadway mail office I had opened. It turned out to be the Greek-American Bank of New York, later renamed the Atlantic Bank of New York. But strong credit references among bankers are transferable!

I then went back to a third and fourth round of mailings based on my original formula. And these netted me perhaps another sixty sales which translated into roughly 200 copies sold. The problem now is that I was running out of libraries with big budgets for research books or books with titles that began *Essays In Political and Intellectual History.* The costs were increasing vis á vis the returns. There had to be a better way. Still, I could not afford real marketing. But I was able to send out copies of the book for review purposes—to leading scholarly journals of social and intellectual history. Each of them was accompanied by a personal letter—a plea for a review for the first title by a new publisher. Whatever the reason, the reviews did start coming in, and much faster than today, perhaps because the ratio between scholarly texts and scholarly journals was healthier.

Many of the reviews were highly critical of Bernstein's Marxist perspective, his romanticizing of French cutthroat leaders like Marat, and his inability to sustain an argument. Bernstein moved rather to highlights like 1789, 1830, 1848, and 1871—the usual for such theorists—and ignored the real history that goes on between momentous events. Still, even the critical reviews acknowledged that Bernstein was a good and conscientious scholar, that he had his notes and references in order, and that even his ideological proclivities were at least couched in decent rhetoric. In short, the book was not a failure-at least in intellectual terms. And before one can even address commercial success and failure, such feedback is critical.

Further, because of Sam's role at *Science & Society* we were able to get the publication to design an advertisement for the book, which they placed in a variety of issues. And at a time when this may well have been the only Marxist forum of opinion, the advertisement was seen by several thousand subscribers that the journal did build up over the years. I do not recall any other space advertisement for this title. I can hardly imagine where the money to pay for it would have come from.

In any event, real orders actually started to come through. I imagine that at least 150 orders were received between the fourth and ninth month after publication. That was fine, but it still left me with an inventory of 600 copies and not enough money to launch additional titles. I should add that proposals too started coming in. What Irving Howe said proved true in my case: "I do not know whether books are written to explain socialism, or socialism is an idea that had to come in order to satisfy a craving to write books." But whatever the causal spin, I was sitting with proposals as well as a manuscript of my own, *Claude Helvetius: Philosopher of Democracy and Enlightenment,* that awaited publication.

Without too much digression from the publishing theme, the fact is that I had developed a deep sense of writing the history of western philosophy from a naturalistic basis. It was to be an answer to Bertrand Russell, Joachim Windelband, Father Coppleston, and a variety of such books that I felt badly neglected the radical tradition. My Bruno dissertation had been published by Coleman-Ross Publishers in Boston in 1952 and the Helvetius was to be the next item on that agenda. I should add that such a vision got me into all sorts of deep troubles at Columbia. While the philosophy department resisted the encroachments of McCarthyism through the front door, it managed a foothold through the side door. Appointments became increasingly conservative, and the old guard took refuge in technical aspects of their specialties. The kind of proposal I had set forth was okay for well-established scholars, but was considered less than satisfactory as an undertaking by a young man in his early twenties. But that is another story. Still, since my book became part of the Paine-Whitman story, I take the liberty to at least broach the subject of Columbia philosophy at the start of the 1950s.

Before we turn to other books, we still had the problem of Bernstein and the unsold inventory of *Essays*. What I did next was to get directories of overseas libraries-especially those with hard currencies. I sent out 200 or so copies of the book to libraries in England, France, Germany, Italy, Spain, Australia, Canada, etc. and enclosed a note: "This title is sent for your purchase. In order to ease the task of payment, you can forward a check or cash in your national currency. Francs, Marks, and Pounds are welcomed." The idea came to me because Perreira and Sons was right next to my Greek American Bank. They would cash any foreign convertible currency for a small fee. And with my bank account number that fee was reduced. The results were excellent. Hardly any copies were returned. Nearly all were paid for—most in national currencies, and surprising, often with cash and not check. This was after all a postwar environment in which books were scarce, and much small business still done on a cash basis. So not only did one title establish Paine-Whitman as an American publisher, but as an international publisher as well!

In real terms, this final selling effort established Paine-Whitman on a reasonable footing. At least I had no need to go to the bank for an additional loan. Indeed, my money started earning interest (I had opened a savings account) and I was in a position to produce the second book, using the same model—but with some refinements learned along the way. Everything from manuscript preparation to maintaining a cash receipt journal had been accomplished—and as long as I did not overreach, I had a successful formula for publishing a small, independent list. As I was eventually to learn, it was also a formula for stagnation, for rotating small cash reserves, rather than building a strong list of titles and a business as well.

The formula worked best as long as it was a part time activity, or more bluntly, as long as I had a position, however remote from my loves and interests, that generated the bread needed to feed a family of four. Paine-Whitman was no longer a cash drain, but neither was it a cash supplement. And every waking hour was a torment between trying to write an essay or an article that might make me famous and catapult me into an academic job market, or doing the mailings and editing necessary on one of several titles. In short, the tensions of being both publisher and professional were early impressed on me. It is somewhat jarring to think that such considerations remain very much a part of my life today.

Before leaving the subject of book contents, I should like to run down the list of Paine-Whitman titles. They were few. But each taught me a valuable lesson about publishing as a whole. And what I am about to say is not a comment on the quality of the books we did, so much as the character of different aspects of publishing. For I realize now that every title published is a reflection of the intelligence or lack thereof, of the publisher as well as the author. The question of editorial judgment starts the process of publishing. But the actual reception of the book and its sales verifies or disconfirms that judgment. Publishing in this way is a cruel taskmaster. Publishers always prefer to emphasize success in a review of books published, but with a tiny list, one can and must review failures as well.

One must be honest. Mixed motives drive the world of ideas no less than instincts. Although I started with the Bernstein volume, my goal was to establish my own work in the history of philosophy as part of the corpus of present-day thinking about philosophical history. I essentially did not succeed in this. Although I published my Helvetius volume (which did not go anywhere), and the *Idea of War and Peace in Contemporary Philosophy* (which was a much more modest book in intellectual design, and, was received very well by at least a segment of the professional journals), neither fared all that well in the marketplace. At least not at first publication.

The Idea of War and Peace was in fact reprinted in England in the early 1970s, and has continued to receive some critical attention. It shifted the focus from the individual level that is the "great figures" of thought, to the probelmatique as it were. The work had a present-day theme rather than a thesis about a past figure. But in the 1957 period, with the exception of potboiler communist books like those written by John Somerville and Howard Selsam, the subject of war and peace was nonexistent in American thought and in England. While it deeply preoccupied great thinkers like Bertrand Russell, the quality of his writings on social themes was so far beneath that of his writings in logic and epistemology that they were dismissed by the professional crowd, and indeed were used as evidence that philosophers should not meddle about in murky international waters. *The Idea of War and Peace* finally convinced me that the problem was not necessarily what I was writing about, but in the audience I presumed to be addressing. The book was published just before my first trip to South America, and marked a distinct turning point from philosophy to sociology, via the Mannheim tradition of the sociology of knowledge.

The Idea of War and Peace had a life outside of English. It was published in a fine edition in Spanish, and it was also published in Poland by a very distinguished house. I suspect that the funds for that Polish project came from the United States Information Agency. The positive view of Lenin, in a larger context of twelve to fourteen other major figures, nearly all from the democratic vistas, gave it potential to slip through the Polish censors. Its publication in Spanish was part and parcel of my easy gravitation to people at Buenos Aires University, who also had one foot in the publishing door. And to my astonishment, this was nearly everybody of consequence. So here I was with a realization that translations matter-and that scholarly books are not nearly as time bound in this regard as trade books. To be sure, our Bernstein book was sold for a special library edition in the 1970s, long after the firm had ceased to exist as an ongoing entity. The matter of rights is not simply to be ignored or discussed as an afterthought. A book is a property—and yes, a private property. Its value is determined by market forces frequently long after the date of publication. These were not easy lessons for someone professing anticapitalist values while trying to pry open the capitalist secrets.

Our second non-Horowitz title was by Stanley W. Moore. That title was aptly enough named *The Critique of Capitalist Democracy.* It was actually not a bombastic book as the title suggests, but a textually rooted (almost Talmudic, if one dares say this of a rock-ribbed Protestant) analysis of Marx, Engels, and Lenin on the structure of capitalism as such. It was written in a lean, positivist mode. During the 1950s, Stan had been professor of philosophy at Reed College in Oregon. He was living in New York as a result of his dismissal from his post for failure to sign the loyalty oath concerning membership in the Communist Party. Anyone who knew Stanley would appreciate the irony of this. He was about the last person who could work and play well with others. I seriously doubt he could attend more than one meeting of an organization, any organization, without being bounced out for conduct unbecoming a member of society. Still, here he was in New York with a manuscript—and a good one.

Stanley was also a remarkable capitalist for all his blather about critiquing the system. He could dissect a contract with a scalpel-like skill I have never equaled, nor have seen anyone else equal. His essential approach was to advance the publisher all composition and printing costs, and in return have the rights reverted to him in five years (the duration of the McCarthyist emergency as it turned out), after which he was able to place the manuscript with a large, commercial publisher. He also made a good deal giving him a relatively high royalty rate. So with Moore I entered the world of negotiating a contract based on relative risks and participations. The scheme worked well. The book did well, and amazingly after five years, the book was reverted to Moore, who then did take it and have it published by another house—I believe it was Cambridge University Press.

My own participation in this book was fiscally modest. The proprietary lessons were not lost on me. But neither was the fact that an arrangement between author and publisher was negotiable and not cast in stone. Such things as royalties and returns could be bargained and bartered, all with a sense of fairness. To be sure, an imperial style ill suited a publisher with three titles on his "list." I left the imperial style to Stanley W. Moore—certain as he was in theory of the collapse of capitalism, but shrewdly no less certain in practice of its long range survival—or at least long enough for him to profit from his own brainchild!

For our next venture Paine-Whitman selected a new edition of Marvin Farber's *Foundations of Phenomenology*. It is still recognized as a classic in the study of Edmund Husserl as well as in phenomenological theory. The book has been out of print for several years. Roy Wood Sellars, who wrote the introduction to my *War and Peace* book strongly recommended me to Professor Farber, as did Abraham Edel, my mentor. Farber himself knew me well enough to assign a few reviews to write for social theory texts in *Philosophy and Phenomenological Research*. Farber's book presented a special set of problems: it was a big book physically, and costly to produce. And I determined early on that the book needed a new preface by the author if it were to be successful. This is something I have retained to this day in the various classics series at Transaction: a book does not to come out a decade or even a century later unless it merits a superior new opening statement. If one cannot interest a single scholar in such a task, then one cannot expect to elicit any sort of reader interest. Once again, with this book we had a title written by a serious journal editor-and this helps a great deal in the post publication marketing of a scholarly work.

We tracked down the printers of the original version of *Foundations of Phenomenology*. They were located in Belgium and proved extremely helpful. All costs of manufacture were lowered, the typeface for the new opening statement by Professor Farber was made, and we had established a sufficient credit line with the printers to buy us six months of credit at a very modest cost. Paine-Whitman produced 1000 copies of this book—in cloth—and supplied the scholarly market which magically expanded to meet our supply. And for the first time, we were able to make a strong profit on a text. Indeed so strong and continuous was the demand for the book that after Paine-Whitman ceased publication, the State University of New York bought up the rights and did a third printing-and also sold out its printing.

At about the same time, we were contacted by Routledge and Kegan Paul about taking on a book by the British scholar John Lewis on *Marxism and the Modern Mind.* Dr. Lewis was an urbane and decent gentleman, who edited *The Marxist Quarterly* in London. Again, this was a scholar with whom I had established contact in my efforts to somehow network myself within an independent left position. Lewis's publisher in England was Routledge and Kegan Paul. Later on, Norman Franklin, its acerbic publisher, would issue my own *Radicalism and the Revolt Against Reason.* In the meanwhile, not a single one of twenty publishers to whom the Lewis book was shown, had reciprocated any interest in the book. We were able to make an arrangement on relatively favorable terms.

Here I learned a tough lesson about co-editions: having only United States rights on a short run edition by a British scholar is a tough way to make a living or to sell a book. Indeed, to my chagrin, wherever I went, even in the United States, I saw the Routledge edition and not the Paine-Whitman edition. In this way, I was introduced to the technique of "buying around," that is to say, the American jobbers would buy from the British publishers at a lower net cost, and supply the domestic, i.e., American market in this way. This is probably the only book we published in our short happy career where we sent our invoices only to be told that the book was already on the shelves. This experience has left me with a bad taste for importing books from England. The costs of doing business can be very high when tiny markets are divided and subdivided. And the international role of wholesalers has increased rather than diminished over the years. Still, the book sold in sufficient quantities to at least not lose money—unless one factors in the costs of labor, in which case, all of our Paine-Whitman titles lost money!

The Struggle For Madrid by Robert G. Colodny was in the area of military history—a footnote to the major works in the area but still well worth issuance. My problem was a severe lack of knowledge in the area of what had been done or what was needed. I learned a vital lesson: the need for outside expertise or referees, for advice of a sort that one could not self-generate. Indeed, the further a field one travels intellectually, the greater the need for others. All of this is obvious of course. But given the experiential rather than rational way of learning common to scholarly publishing, all of this had to be experienced by myself for myself.

As I think about these decisions thirty years after the events, I begin to see that there is a link after all with childhood, a sort of primitive instinct for self-reliance. My behavior was not Emersonian in that it did not reflect a theory of individualism, so much as Nietszchean, a reflection of a practice in which little quarter is given or asked. But in the review process that is what one does: ask for a quarter, a saw-buck's worth of information.

Happily, in relation to the Colodny book, all sorts of people and lists were around—veterans of the Abraham Lincoln Brigade and people who could provide first-hand knowledge of the competence of Colodny's analysis. This was a bit dicey, since the lists were sought after by the FBI no less than myself! The problem of lists was settled by having the veterans' organization do the mailing on the Colodny book on my behalf—a technique which has now become standardized.

Returning to an author and asking him to make changes was yet another experience—one that made me quite frankly nervous, since bypassing the external referee was perhaps a latent function of going into such self-publishing in the first place. The Colodny book did well. There was a mini-revival of interest in the Spanish Civil War; the membership lists of the Abraham Lincoln Brigade became available for the purposes of selling this book, and the military history buffs resonated well to a text with well designed battlefield charts. Increasingly, book by book a certain sophistication was beginning to take hold, a sense of publishing as more than the first copy, or more than ideological conviction. I began to dimly perceive publishing as a valid activity, a hard business that required no external validation. Publishing provided a tradition and offered a challenge in its own right, apart from purely scholarly considerations.

Another work by a good social scientist published by Paine Whitman was Manuel Gottlieb; *The German Peace Settlement and the Berlin Crisis.* His argument was rather controversial, but not unusual for losers in battle to use: the reparations agreements in the post-war settlement were so severe as to provoke continuing crisis and struggle. Indeed John Maynard Keynes had used a similar line of reasoning in the description of post-World War One agreements. And indeed, Professor Gottlieb was an economist, who had practical experience on a variety of U.S. commissions addressing the reparations question. That West Germany recovered so remarkably well and East Germany did so poorly was a function of United States' leniency on the one hand and Soviet stringency on the other. And with the Marshall Plan the United States was able to shore up Western economies as such; something that the economic weakness no less than political blindness of the Soviets prevented from happening.

Gottlieb wrote an important book, but it was poorly written. It was technically competent, one that any university press would have been proud to add to its list. But in doing this work, a whole new set of considerations entered my mind with respect to the causal linkage between formal presentation and professional competence. Gottlieb himself was a modest man, a decent man. He had converted from Judaism to Episcopalianism after his wartime duties. And while he continued to teach economics, his affections were clearly with theology by the time I got to know him toward the end of the 1950s. At a supper we had in New York, I kept asking him questions about Keynes and he kept answering in parables about Jesus. This book never did find its proper audience, or better, I was never able to reach the public interested in the subject matter of the book. This latter formulation I owe to

Jeremiah Kaplan, who constantly reminds his listeners that a marketplace is what a publisher locates through hard work, not something simply residing in prefabricated lists.

The final work which Paine-Whitman issued was a good deal later than the others; indeed the book was published after the decision to suspend the firm had already been made. C. Wright Mills died in March 1962. One work which he left unpublished was the much-disputed dissertation, *Sociology and Pragmatism.* All sorts of questions about this work were raised-most dealt with in my 1983 volume for Macmillan, C. *Wright Mills: An American Utopian.* One item of particular importance here is that the work had been shown and offered to a myriad of publishers over the years by Wright—without apparent success. Indeed, looking at the manuscript left little wonder why there was so much resistance. Simply put, it was a technical mess, and Wright himself either refused or became disinterested in doing the necessary clean-up work. It took six months of hard work to do the technical editing-indeed, technical is too modest a word in this case. But the result was important Paine-Whitman did a book that was important, by a writer who was important. And the thrill of seeing a lengthy two-page statement on *Sociology and Pragmatism* in *The New York Review* solidified my romance with publishing.

All told, Paine-Whitman published ten titles in its brief four-year history. Of these, each one turned a small profit (as long as the costs of labor were entirely discounted). Seven of the ten were translated into major European languages. Rights were sold to five of them (three on a term basis and two outright). Eight of ten either remain in print, or have been absorbed into lists of other scholarly publishers. This is no effort at flag waving or boasting. Rather, it speaks to the special nature of the times, when publishing outlets were fewer and academics more concerned with their work than turning out potboilers. It also needs to be said that most of the books were philosophical. Those did best. The books on topical matters, like *The German Peace Settlement and the Berlin Crisis* or *The Struggle for Madrid: The Central Epic of the Spanish*

Conflict had the best initial sale, but relatively little follow-up or durable interest. Again, this is offered not as a model for others, but only as a record of what took place-often behind the back of the publisher, namely myself.

In our brief history, Paine-Whitman also became acquainted with the world of vanity publishing. Indeed, I was astonished by the number of proposals we received, small as we were, offering financial support for the publication of a book. For the most part, these were so absurd as not to merit even second thoughts from a serious publisher. And size and sobriety have little to do with each other in publishing.

But one title did come in, *The Social Psychology of Religious Experience* by Prynce Hopkins that did merit a second consideration. I confess that without a stipend to support publication we would not have done this title. But it did have the elementary merits of scholarship, and was written by a highly educated, if eccentric, queer English duck. In a sense, the cash granted for this book was more than made up in extra editorial costs. It must have taken me three months to completely re-edit this work and make it presentable. Dr. Hopkins was no Emile Durkheim or Max Weber, but at least he read those major figures, alas not with a sufficient understanding that could translate into anything new.

The experience with accepting money from an author to publish confronts the publisher with a bundle of problems pros and cons: the money can be used to put out an otherwise non-publishable good title, the money can offset losses on older titles, the money can simply be viewed as a reward for doing good works! Conversely, acceptance of funds does color decision-making. The essential nay is turned into a halting, quivering yea—and that involves much work and little emotional pleasure. Further, a list is known by its highs and its lows, and given human nature, more often by the latter than the former. *The Social Psychology of Religious Experience* was definitely our low point. May Dr. Hopkins rest in peace and with the sure knowledge that his money was sorely needed and deeply appreciated by the Horowitz family—children included.

We also put out Ludwig Gumplowicz's *Outlines of Sociology*. A pioneering text, perhaps the first real text in sociology, one that I still greatly admire for its courage and forthright treatment of race, nationality, and ethnicity in large-scale contexts. Gumplowicz was the father of conflict theory a major figure in social theory, as such. He understood conflict in all its riches: class conflict, race conflict, ethnic conflict. If he was rather oblivious to the ways in which a society achieves, or at least strives for consensus, he can be forgiven. The Europe of the late nineteenth century offered few illustrations of nations, tribes or peoples getting along. The Gumplowicz text, nicknamed "Gumps" by my colleagues was a prime example of a minor classic. To be sure, if other "conflict theorists" tended to trace their lineage to Marx and Simmel, my own publishing activities compelled me to offer Gumplowicz in evidence.

This was Paine-Whitman's first and only entrance into the world of "classics"—a world which Transaction has since carried to considerable heights. The problem with "classics" is in the definition of same: Who is a classic author? How old does a book have to be for such a designation to stick? Does every work of a classic author merit the designation? Is it really the book or the field that defines longevity? That is to say, can an empirical piece of research achieve the same set of heights as a work on general philosophical themes? God knows that *Outlines of Sociology* did not answer such big questions. It was just something I liked. One might well say beware of vanity unchecked by the judgment of others. But then again, one might say that the judgment of others, or better, the collective other, will usually lead to non-publication.

The decision to terminate Paine-Whitman was not taken lightly. Nor was it made without deep regard for that handful of authors who had placed their work at my disposal. It was a sacred trust, not a profane disposal. I did meet with a few book jobbers and smaller publishers, showed them my one and only catalogue, but decided against a fire sale. I remember one such meeting at the home of C. Wright Mills' widow in West Nyack. She had been an illustrator for children's books prior to meeting and marrying Mills, and as a result, she got to know a variety of publishers. One of these was interested in the Paine-Whitman list. But the offer was something like 25 percent on net sales with payment made after the sales.

While I realized that academic obligations and the start-up of obligations for being the social science editor for Oxford University Press—I followed Robert A. Nisbet in this role—would prevent any further evolution of Paine-Whitman, I decided that the interests of authors and publishers alike were best safeguarded by the slow, but at least continuous sales of those nine titles already published. And it was a sound decision that met with the approval of the authors. They too were changing with the circumstances. Colodny received a senior position in the history department at the University of Pittsburgh, Stanley Moore went to work in the philosophy department at Stevenson College at the University of California in Santa Cruz. Manuel got a good post at the economics department at the University of Wisconsin, I had returned from South America and had a variety of academic posts at Bard College, Hobart, and William Smith, and finally at Washington University.

Paine-Whitman was an emergency publisher which perished when the political emergency came to an end. It came into being to satisfy a special niche: non-communist left-oriented books—too scholarly for trade publication and too risky for standard university press books. The 1960s were so remarkably different from the 1950s in terms of academic fates and fortunes that the structure of independent publishing itself had to change and accommodate such changes. People like Frederick Praeger appreciated such changes, and were well positioned to take advantage of new opportunities.

Those Paine-Whitman titles that were neither sold nor licensed to other publishers were maintained in inventory, and when Transaction became independent in its move from Washington University to Rutgers University, they were shifted to the Transaction catalogue, where they continue to survive, if not exactly thrive. I think that all of our authors were indebted to Paine-Whitman for the act of survival. I have often thought that this maintenance of the list was rewarded by supportive authors in the more affluent period that followed the age of McCarthyism. It took real courage to confront real enemies. Our band of authors had that quality. I think we served them as well as might be expected, with an amateurish passion for publication underwritten by a professional sense of scholarship and humane letters.

So often professional publishing is viewed as a response to "market forces" or new fields of research. But this is not always the case. For me, as I have tried to show, the entrance into publishing was a function of a terrible polarity in the 1950s-between McCarthyite values that were dominant on the right, and a terrible Stalinist paralysis that had gripped the left, and would not let go despite the death of the tyrant in 1952. In some curious way, Transaction has continued to negotiate between such political poles—although Transaction had the advantage of social science as itself a paradigm of work and thought, and even more profoundly, a rooted rather than rootless academic class. But again, that takes us far a field. It is enough to conclude with a sensibility about scholarly publishing that gives it a unique dimension; for whether it is the discovery of polymers in applied chemistry or the search for an empirical framework in social philosophy, what drives the world of professional publishing is the idea of the new. This is also the reason why firms cease publishing; the new becomes established, becomes part of a mainstream, taken on by other well-known publishers.

I look back at this brief episode, this lost footnote to an abortive publishing venture, with great joy. Each of the titles published remains firmly etched in my mind. Perhaps if pressed I could describe the circumstances for a handful of books which Transaction has published. But more than 2200 plus titles later, routines do set in, and one forgets, if indeed one ever remembers the special circumstances involved in the issuance of each and every book. Paine-Whitman taught me that behind each book is a real person who writes for, one hopes, a real audience which reads. That sense of the individual behind the product remains very much at the core of my sense of what makes professional and scholarly publishing different and special.

Scholarly publishing is a one-by-one affair no less than a one-on-one affair—and that goes for every stage in the process of publishing. Those who cut invoices in the fulfillment process, or who sit in small retail shops awaiting the next customer, know this well. Those of us who fancy ourselves publishers probably know this least well—or at least lose that cutting edge which unites scholarship and commerce in the strange world of the book. For every bulk purchase order there are individual readers, and for every big check there are a lot of small checks along the way. Everything goes back to the long gray line connecting reader to publisher. Sever that line at any step of the way, and the act of publishing is reduced to rubble.

Paine-Whitman was a tiny Actor in publishing, and never became more. But I would like to think that it played its part in overcoming the academic terrors of a timorous decade, somewhat akin to the lonely figure standing in front of a row of tanks at Tiananmen Square. At least it was such for me: rejections and denials plagued me for most of the 1950s. But in the tiny world of Paine-Whitman where I was sovereign, things were different. Publishing was a world of pleasures and affirmations. It most assuredly was a personal training ground for my work to come at Transaction.

Paine-Whitman never did make the big jump from charisma to organization. It never did employ people, not even a secretary. It was doubtless an extension of personal vanity, and vanity is often defined as a sin. But I rather believe that vanity, when directed toward some higher purpose, can also have a divine element, like Whitehead's description of creative madness. It is all based on a positive myth that words matter, and that once transmitted they have a life of their own. This is where my brief memoir on Paine-Whitman must conclude; for if in the beginning is the word, then in the end there ought to be a return to the purity and perfection of silence—at least a moment of silence before the world of Transaction emerged.

3

THREE WORLDS OF DEVELOPMENT:
35 YEARS LATER

· ·

To be given the opportunity and the honor to reflect on one's work is itself a statement of durability. As in mathematics so too in the social sciences, it is not always a question of asserting whether one is right and wrong, and in which areas, instead one engages in a discovery of the process of deduction and induction; that is how we have arrived at the present moment in development theory. If we were uniformly right about important issues, then the world would cease to offer the chances for discovery and mystery. If we were in turn always wrong about these same issues, then an exercise of reexamination would be, to put it mildly, an embarrassment.

What complicates matters in social scientific self-examination is that truth and error is more than a function of checking theories against facts, but determining what a fact "on the ground" actually is. There is a constant need to move beyond a rationalistic tradition of model building in development that prefers to revise facts and adjust realities rather than alter inherited theories. However, the ubiquitous nature of change as such compels care. Great events, often unanticipated by researchers, necessarily alter great theories.

Thus, the Iranian Revolution of Khoumeni in 1979 once and for all settled the issue of the reversibility or irreversibility of development. Alas, the former turns out to be correct. When the long evolution of the Persian Empire can be brought up short and subjected to the edicts and practices of the Moslem faith, then we must acknowledge the reversibility of development, at least as a process of secularization and modernization. And with the collapse of the Soviet Communist Empire a decade later in 1989, we also come face to face with the reversibility of economic systems. The doctrine of the transformation of capitalism into socialism collapsed in a heap—despite the best efforts of dogmatists to save the theory while damning the system.

Having said this, we are still faced with the need to make sense of the world both as it was and as it is. For this is what "theory" amounts to: making sense of the universe, not building castles in the sand or models in the sky. We must all strive to determine what has actually endured in developmental terms, not just these past thirty-five years, but throughout the twentieth century. Then we must consider what has changed in this block of time. Finally, let us try to determine how our thinking about the world has affected the process of development as well as how the process of development itself affects what we think about development. For the word denotes change in an upward direction. And this is a painful process, not simply a moral equivalent for sugar, spice and everything nice.

The most startling continuity in developmental terms is consistency where economic might and political authority are located. We have experienced two world wars and countless lesser wars, not to mention short-term strikes and battles. These have resulted in the slaughter of untold millions of innocent people as part of military conflagrations. Despite this, we are left with amazing continuity. Western Europe, Japan, England, Russia (whatever its system) and, of course, the United States remain the major players and powers worldwide. One may disagree with V.I. Lenin's Imperialism with respect to the nature of power, but surely not with the physical location of power either now or one hundred years ago.

What has changed are first, the ratio of power and might among leading developmental powers. The United States now ranks in the forefront of most major measures of development, with Western Europe and Japan just behind. But the power of the defeated military powers in World War Two, Germany and Japan in particular, is not only diminished or curbed, but has increased exponentially. So we can put to rest another dogma, that victory or defeat in battle always transforms itself into a realignment of economic potency. This most certainly is not the case. It is more nearly the case that in conflict among the major powers, victors and vanquished alike manage to benefit in material terms at least.

It is the case that warfare brings about a repositioning among the major powers. This occurs in import-export games, for example, and also brings to the fore the potential of new players in the game of development. One can say with some confidence that nations as widely varied in social structures as China, Brazil, Canada, Australia, and possibly India and South Africa, may join the major powers—either as antagonists or as allies and even satellites. It is clear that the size of the developed in relation to the developing or underdeveloped club is growing, and they have certain national characteristics I did not anticipate in earlier writings.

Nearly all members of the developed nations club share certain characteristics. First, they are large either in natural geography or in amalgamation such as a European Union. Second, they have immense natural resources as well as human resources at their disposal. Third, developed nations have a large preponderance of their population living in or about urban and industrial centers, coupled with a constantly diminishing agrarian sector able to produce increasing amount of food to support the population. Fourth, they are committed to high technology in the form of communication and transportation, to the point where the struggle for control shifts from production to information as such. Fifth, they have vaguely democratic political systems which allow for the expression of public opinion without public punishment, and which do not thwart innovation or invention. Finally, in developed nations the edges of poverty and opulence are controlled by a Welfare State, one with the power to curb the natural propensities to aggrandizement of the Commercial Civilization.

This is a somewhat different picture, a different snapshot of the world than that which I offered in Three Worlds of Development.

It is one that reestablishes a place for nation building at the expense of world systems. It is one that locates power in limited middle range areas such as food production, health and welfare, education and culture, and life span. Such realities move us away from more abstract considerations such as capitalism, socialism, and feudalism on one side, or open market versus planned regimes on the other.

This does not imply that such larger considerations are not factors. Clearly they are, but their relative importance has diminished as human needs rather than social orders have assumed a front and center position in development.

There is still life in the Three Worlds model despite what I said in my opening remarks. For example, the First World, comprised largely of the United States, United Kingdom, Western Europe, and Japan, remains indeed first. Indeed, these nations have gained in relative power and stature over the past thirty-five years. In this, I would say that my chapters on the First World of United States development might need some cosmetic surgery and fine-tuning, but remain essentially quite accurate. Development permits the evolution of economic accumulation of wealth and political civil liberties. Trade unionism emerged as an independent force serving labor as professionalism services the elites of an advanced society. Even the criticisms launched in the first world chapters, such as the poor response to the needs of the underdeveloped world, have been largely confirmed over time. My unsentimental view of the First World under American leadership might be subject to dispute, but not the essential profile of what development requires. Above all, a population is needed that can be rapidly mobilized for essential socioeconomic goals, one highly skilled in the management and manipulation of material goods and essential services. Nations of the First World also have a sufficient political cohesion to identify and pursue precisely defined goals.

When I deal with the Second World of Socialist development, the issues become both more fascinating and more confusing. Obviously, the collapse of the Soviet Empire places at risk any evaluation based on the continuation of Communist authority in

Russia. Still, certain patterns describing my second world chapters remain very much in evidence thirty-five years later. My forecast of a gradual shift, under the impact of industrialism' from a strictly coercive Stalinist totalitarian regime to a far less coercive authoritarian regime under Khruschev and Brezhnev was accurate. This movement later permitted the rise of a Gorbachev opening to the West. The continual fascination of developing regions with the Leninist State Model, and with the concentration of political power in development policies, also remains characteristic. In the post Communist epoch, it is perhaps even more so, as the memory of the genocide and murders of the communist regime recedes. Finally, as I forecast, the power of nationalism was far greater than the theory of permanent revolution as a touchstone for measuring Soviet Communist life—and even more, post Communist life in Eastern Europe. The rhetoric of communism emphasized internationalist goals; the conduct of Soviet policy never wavered from serving national interests. This is not exactly news. But the pretensions of Soviet ideology never cease to cloud the heads of even the best of analysts. Those who prefer disconnected theory also seem to have a propensity for inherited ideologies.

My treatment of the Third World elicits the most acute need for reflection and self-reflection. Happily I had discounted world systems theory from the start, so I was never trapped by the absurd idea that one can determine and define patterns of global development by sitting in Washington, D.C. or Wall Street. Such crude neo-Leninist theorizing only stymied actual examination of the Third World, and substituted caricature for character, ideology for analysis. At the same time, I also avoided the pitfall of so-called modernization theory, which upon inspection was little more than the assumption that the entire world can be indexed to the production of automobiles and consumer goods as the cardinal text for development. So much is lost in terms of cultural variability at the level of demands and aspirations, that I found modernization doctrines woefully inadequate in either predicting or explaining the nature of development. Indeed, my own approach was and remains to emphasize the uniqueness the special properties of the Third World, in part as an effort to insure some sort of close reflection on actual conditions in such regions. I hoped to direct thinking away from what in the mid-1960s was already a tendency to assume that world systems theory would be the whipping post to dissolve capitalism and hence magically permit the rest of the world to flower.

My emphasis on the structural infirmities of "Thirdness" carried with it penalties and problems of its own. For example, I assumed that proclamations made as a series of conferences in Bandana, New Delhi, or Belgrade were more than a loose series of demands. In point of fact, as the decades wore on, it became increasingly clear that what the Third World had in common was animus toward the First World more than any united vision of development. These world gatherings may have announced a third way, but could not elucidate a third system. My views of thirty-five years ago are best reflected in what has evolved as the post Maoist Chinese model. The Chinese have combined a Leninist model of hard state control with a Keynesian model of a soft economic landing. And while some nations within the Third World have taken steps to adopt such a formula, most others have chosen not to do so. This formula of communist power and capitalist market is at best a glass half full or half empty— depending on one's sentiments about such a fusion of Lenin and Keynes. But it is hardly an occasion for joy, since the growth of such nations has been uneven when adopted and unhappy when not.

State Capitalism and State Socialism each have had major successes in Asia. But whether we are talking of India, which has undergone a remarkable and scarcely noticed growth in the past twenty years, or China, whose growth has been well reported, the emphasis has to be on the State more than the Economy. The successes of the developmental process have come along with a limited political openness to the population—dependent voluntary associations remain few, freedom of speech curbed, free trade unionism recognized more in rhetoric than reality. In short the costs of development and the requirements of development have been unevenly distributed, and in a world in which the egalitarian model is central, the Asian miracle is a volatile as well as vulnerable miracle. In any event, neither India nor China pays much attention (if indeed they ever did) to the Third World. Certainly, it is far less important to their thinking than their role as trading partners with the advanced powers.

Latin America exhibits the most interesting example of a middle class, with an urbanized area established alongside a free market economy. Unlike Asia, its state system is historically weak. It is subject to the norm of illegitimacy rather than legitimacy, made so by powerful military caciques that have seized power from democratically elected regimes, only to themselves falter repeatedly at the level of economic performance and social organization. As a result, constitutional regimes have emerged in Chile, Brazil, and Argentina, now joined by Mexico. There has been corresponding growth in the overall economy, which must be considered a major development in the real evolution of this region of a fragmented Third World.

The growth of investment by the native bourgeoisie within each of these countries and the growth of investment by overseas actors and agencies has refurbished the key nations of Latin America. Thirty-five years ago, five years deep into the Fidel Castro seizure of power in Cuba, it appeared that dictatorships of the Left and the Right would become the norm. It also appeared that the overall economy would continue to be the victim of forces beyond the control of the populace. While such patterns of chaos and unchecked violence do exist in Colombia, Peru, Venezuela, and parts of Central America, the large nations of the region have shown the path to genuine development spearheaded by the private sector. The populism from above, characterized by Getulio Vargas in Brazil in the 1930s, Juan Domingo Peron in Argentina in the 1940s, and a string of PRI figures in Mexico spread throughout the century, is now largely a style of the past. Such charismatic leaders stimulated the process of urbanization and industrialization, but it took legitimate constitutional figures to bring economic development to social and human fruition.

In Africa we find the deepest problems. The end of colonial rule did not correspond to the end of colonial formations. Nations created by artificial geographic requirements for symmetry of the division of spoils degenerated into chaos as ethnic and tribal chieftains crossed borders to reclaim ancestral rights and punish long standing weaker and in some cases stronger ethnic groupings. Nationalism became linked to sectionalism, regionalism and tribalism—a condition it must be noted just as common in Yugoslavia as in Ethiopia. Small wars fought by small men with small arms became the norm through much of sub-Saharan Africa and parts of Eastern and Southern Europe. Powerful Moslem factions in North Africa decimated regimes to become a force in Central African affairs. As a series of Amnesty International reports have made clear, traffic in children and even the re-emergence of slavery became normative if not typical. The data on disease, starvation, and lack of education in Africa reveals an appalling breakdown in the basic rights of people to normal lives. Periodic forced migrations have served to slow to a halt the process of normalization, of a legitimization that might permit economic development to move forward. Blaming the long gone British, French, and Belgian colonialists has become more a pastime than a serious form of analysis—akin to blaming parents for the sins of the adult offspring. These matters of record are embarrassing, but must be spoken of. They make clear that political policy and moral forces are hardly a monopoly of old victims. Too often these old victims of colonialism manage to seek and destroy new victims of nationalism.

While much of Africa has been bypassed in the development race, there are some bright spots. Apartheid in South Africa ended with a multi-racial society coming about. Enterprise flourished in smaller units such as the Ivory Coast. It must be said unequivocally, that models of military socialism have been dismal failures even in potentially wealthy areas such as Nigeria. Natural wealth has been plundered and human capital siphoned off of development projects. The government-to-government aids programs often serve to institutionalize and rationalize those dangerous situations. The plight of Africa is also linked to worldwide patterns of

racial concerns about migration. Hence, the persistence of dictatorships in the new nations of Africa has had a deleterious effect on
any impulse to economic assistance from the wealthy nations. Patterns of investment are largely rooted in the extractive industries
where costs are relatively low and profits based on quick turn around
rapid. As we enter the new millennium, Africa lags far behind
Latin America and Asia (nevermind the highly advanced economies of the West) in areas that matter: economic size, purchasing
power, and international trade. It has the lowest gross domestic
product, highest debt and debt service, and highest dependency
on the agrarian sector. Crippling epidemics such as AIDS find
sub-Saharan Africa at the forefront of a statistic hardly to be en-
vied: death by unnatural causes.

There is today no unified Third World, and not even a coalition
of nations developing common regional patterns. National formations in development, types of development, and consistency of
development are not matters of prior edicts of historical infallibil-
ity, or of peculiar inheritances. It is now evident that the issue of
development is increasingly one of policy not history, decisions
not determinism. The export of formulas, whether of planned economies, free market economies, or third way mixtures are always subject to cultures and to traditions. One can design the most perfect
tax system imaginable and it will fall on its face (as it has in Russia) simply because the idea of expropriation, which I point out in
Three Worlds of Development is the essence of a tax, does not take
root in a population. And it does not because there is no trust in
leadership and no faith in the honesty of those who rule. In this,
my earlier concerns with Weberian problems, which are with issues of legitimacy, organization, bureaucracy, and administration,
remain critically important features in the study of development.
They largely, but not entirely, move beyond Marxist problems of
class stratification and workplace exploitation.

Looking at the process of development in such broad stroked
global terms has some serious weakness. The foremost is that so
many developments at the micro-economic and micro-sociologi-
cal levels fall through the net of analysis. There are amazing ex-

amples of developmental projects that work, such as population relocation for the purpose of installing new energy supplies in China. And there are varieties of cooperation on foreign policy matters that occur on a daily basis amongst Third World nations at the United Nations. Indeed, as I noted in Three Worlds of Developments, the United Nations might well be said to serve as the fulcrum of the Third World as such. But overall, what one finds is a strange paradox at the end of the century. There is a rationalized marketplace operating within a common set of rules, regulations, and standards, but there are huge chunks of the underdeveloped world existing outside of such patterns of rationalization. Perhaps that is in itself a major cause for the persistence of underdevelopment.

There are widespread themes and variations on this revised model of development, but little evidence of a return to a bipolar world of politics or a triangulated world of economies. Ours is a world in which the impulse toward egalitarianism now reaches into the deepest part of the world order, and in which concerns for individual persons rather than social systems come to dominate private and public aid agencies alike. At the other end, one must note the rise of a ferocious series of nationalism, continuation of military hostilities at low levels of intensity, and genocidal patterns of conflict in which the line between civil and military authority has been blurred beyond recognition. This is neither a pretty picture nor a hopeless one. But it is an entirely credible photograph of a world in flux.

In a universe of technical and social extremes, the neat taxonomies of even the recent past seem shabby, and the need for serious policy seems remarkably elusive. We go on with our analysis and our work, not in joy and celebration, but in a fuller recognition of the size and shape of tasks ahead. We need to be at home in a world of episodes and chapters rather than ideologies and sentiments. We need to be informed but not constrained by past histories. We need more bottom-up policies and fewer top down impositions. The moral and normative basis of decision-making should remain firm. The political posture should remain open ended. The economic capacity should be adjusted to human needs. But this tension in the affairs of the human world between what should be and what is here and now defines the normative condition for people who dedicate their lives and energies to developmental goals.

4

EDITING *SOCIETY* FINAL THOUGHTS, LAST HURRAHS

· ·

So let me offer a few personal remarks on stepping down as editor-in-chief of *Society*—a last hurrah as it were—at the operational level. I will try, with mixed results I am sure, to avoid being avuncular—a criticism that I regret to say is on target. Some of these points have been discussed in passing, but it might not be a bad idea to highlight a few of them. I should add that my choice of the word operational is intentional, since decision making must ultimately reside with the editor and his associates.

Society is a publication that is the common property of all the social sciences, old and new. While its origins are deeply embedded in the sociology of the early 1960s, and a vision of public relevance, it has from the outset aimed to broaden its base to include all serious people—as writers and readers alike—who reside within the various fields of social research. You will need the will to resist the temptation to fall back on individuals you know, and continually reach out to innovators less well known.

Society seeks to be a user friendly organ. By that I mean our publication is written by specialists in various fields, but for larger publics who may not have the technical skills or special interests that are serviced by strictly bounded professional journals. Indeed, I have never been quite sure whether to identify *Society* as a journal or a magazine—so I have taken to simply identifying ourselves as a publication of record for important new work, and for providing a forum for scholars to give expression to their strongest public concerns.

Society is a national, and increasingly an international publication—like Transaction as a whole. It is important to reflect that fact in the choice of contributors no less than selection of topics. While this may seem an utterly transparent point, the fact is that every editor is subject to local pressures. This was true in our founding period at St. Louis, continued to be the case in the New York metropolitan area, and it might be even more so in the Boston metropolitan area, which boasts several hundred fine institutions of higher learning. Being a telephone call away from an editor is a temptation for an author and a potential torment for an editor. Even with good intentions, this factor can play havoc on decision-making.

Society is not the theoretical property of any one approach or any single agency doing social research. There is a level of performance quality in an article that must be weighed apart from grand theory or good morality. Were this not the case, political ideology would be an open sesame; private virtue would assure highest quality. If a social science publication is to justify being read for what it is, then it must do so apart from specific commitments to "isms," even of the loftiest sort. Our publication has always been strongly rooted in current events, especially social and political events. This is not an entitlement to "mouth off," but a responsibility to bring to bear upon that which social science can bring to the table of public discourse.

A publication such as *Society*, while always encouraging the widest possible participation, cannot simply substitute ascriptive features for real achievement. In recent years, thought police techniques have been introduced into social science scholarship by sponsoring agencies: making sure that women are represented on every professional panel, making certain that racial minorities alone are allowed to comment on books about them, making sure that certain topics are avoided because they tread on inherited religious or ethnic sensibilities.

The list of extra-academic requirements are now legion; and at the other side, taboos are endless. But at the end of the day, one is left with boring orthodoxies that confirm prejudice rather than creative responses to hard issues that remain vexing. If the world were a struggle between good and evil, then the need for a *Society* would be obviated. But as long as we inhabit a human planet in which the struggle is between one set of goods and another set of goods, it is best to avoid a priori joys of self-righteousness.

We are in a new epoch; one in which academic struggles have become simplified—perhaps too much so. No longer is the conflict in social science between liberalism and conservatism, nor quantitative versus qualitative styles of work. Standard paradigms within which academics work are still there for the taking. But in this new epoch it is now clear that the struggle is between social science as such, and those who in the name of "culture" proclaim the death of evidence, experience and empirics as sources of wisdom in sociology, political science, economics, psychology, anthropology and related disciplines.

There is some mysterious, or at least hard to define, realm at which the values of social science and those of a free society mesh. It may be best expressed as simply the right to speak freely and intelligently on major issues without fear of sanction or censure. In this sense, *Society* has never wavered, and I hope never does, in its faith in a free press. Being right should be encouraged, being wrong should be exposed. But that is not the same thing as being vindictive or mean-spirited. In the realm of ideas, creative mistakes may count for more than prosaic truths. And while these sentiments turn out to be fine line distinctions, they somehow do factor into editorial judgments.

Editorial work is a sure road to divided opinion as to your worth! After all, you will be nay saying at least as often as yea saying, and probably a good deal more so. And even the people to whom you publish one time around, may turn out to be the same people whose work you reject the second time around the track! So editing is hardly a popularity contest. The chief editor of *Society* is indeed a position of modest power and influence; and if you do your job well, even some modicum of respect. But affection will be a hard commodity to come by. Happily, we can select objects of love from the entire range of humanity, and not just a handful of social scientists.

I suspect that you knew my sentiments on all of the above before this. Still, putting them down on paper gives me some comfort, leaving my post with a proper sense of closure. You know from your experiences as editor of *The American Sociologist* (a task you performed with admirable skill) that I never interfere in editorial judgments that are not mine to make, or for which you will bear responsibility. On the other hand, as long as you need and request my support, it will be there for you. If you do your job unflinchingly, this same sentiment will motivate the best and the brightest within the social scientific community to bring their work to you—and to *Society* readers—for publication.

5

SOCIAL SCIENCE AS A
MORAL CALLING

. . . .

Oddly enough, as I reflect upon the meaning of this gathering, what one close colleague has called a tribal affair, my thoughts turn to those no longer with us. Foremost is the loss of Aaron Wildavsky and Ron Serge Denisoff, contributors to *The Democratic Imagination*, the work being honored this evening. Mind you, this loss is during the first month in which the book is actually published. For that matter, the loss of more than half the contributors to *The New Sociology*, now thirty years old, including special people like Rose Goldsen, Alvin Gouldner, Ernest Becker, and Erich Fromm, among others, is a fact that does not escape my attention as tribal leader, at least for this evening.

I am led to think of those who cannot be with us because they are no longer of this world. Nonetheless, these people were mightily important for my being here this evening. I do not want to turn this into a morbid event of reflections on death, but neither can I forget the efforts of so many on my behalf over the years. The scholars who come readily to mind are Gino Germani; Rizieri Frondizi; and Jose Luis Romero, who made my time in Buenos Aires downright exhilarating; while people like Enrique Butelman, founder of Editorial Paidos; Jorge Grisetti, of Siglo Veinte Uno; and Orfila-Reynal, of Fondo de Cultura, offered living proof that scholarly publishing and actual scholarship are entirely consonant.

I am also compelled to acknowledge how important to my life were the rescue efforts of people like Paul Radin, Philip Rahv, and

Herbert Marcuse at Brandeis; its program in the History of Ideas in the late 1950s was brilliantly crafted. Gerard DeGre's support of me as his replacement at Bard College when he left for South America on a Fulbright; George Walsh (who happily is very much alive), Maynard Smith, and Louis Hirshorn at Hobart & William Smith were likewise excellent companions in a small school setting who did great work. While I was at Washington University there was Alvin W. Gouldner, whose vision for a public role of sociology was an essential component in the very start of Transaction; Merle Kling, who fought like a tiger to support us during some dark fiscal days in the early 1960s; and Jules Henry, who knew better than anyone else that the push toward departmental specialization had costs no less than benefits. These were just a few of the people who made a defining impact on my life. Without pushing this theme too hard, I often remember the extraordinary contributions and support to the very survival of Transaction made by Herbert Blamer, Oscar Lewis, and Harold Lasswell at a time when the existence of Transaction hung in the balance. It would be impossible to pass over twenty-six years at Rutgers University in silence without mentioning, above all, my huge debt to Mason Gross and Edward Bloustein, two presidents whose styles were radically different from each other, but whose substantive concerns were identical: transforming a decent college into a great institution of advanced learning. Even the current president, Francis Lawrence, with whom my contact has admittedly been limited, has offered his support in a way no less vividly than to place his intellectual efforts on quality control in higher education with Transaction Publishers.

Sadly, while many of the aforementioned people are no longer with us, all of this should teach us a sense of the culture that nourishes us—and the need for renewal of that culture—by doing likewise for those who come after us. We may all be the offspring of the intellectual greats with whom we choose to identify, but in truth, these grand figures of a dim past are filtered through our imaginations by the real figures of an immediate past—so immediate that it seems like the present. Happily for me, and all of us, grand scholars like Robert K. Merton, Eli Ginsberg, David Riesman, and Abraham Edel are very much of the present. So it is too that younger scholars like William Helmreich at the City University of New York, James E. Katz of Bell Labs, Ray Rist at George Washington University, Jeanne Guillemin of Boston College, Howard Schneiderman at Lafayette College, and Martha Crenshaw at Wesleyan University—to name but a few people linked with The Democratic Imagination—are also very much of the future. This thought pleases me very much. That Transaction has two such special people in Scott Bramson and Mary E. Curtis, both of whom were educated at Washington University and have been with me at Rutgers University for more than a quarter century, offers further evidence that the renewal and redemption of culture is very much with us, very much what we are about.

On a ceremonial occasion such as this, one should impart wisdom, or at least a summing up of secret lessons of living that might help others. Fortunately for this extraordinary gathering, I am terribly lacking in wisdom these days, and hence, what I have to offer at this level can be short and sweet, or long and bitter, as the case may be. Every public presentation, however ceremonial, entails a set of decisions: should one be serious or humorous, strong or timorous, emphasize public policies or private lives? Does one offer personal reflections disguised as moral homilies or, for that matter, moral homilies disguised as autobiography? This occasion entails precisely such considerations. Given the ostensible reason we are gathered—to celebrate a changing of the guard at the organizational end, and publication of a festschrift in my honor at the professional end—the necessity for choosing an appropriate theme and approach is transparent.

After due deliberation, I have decided to speak to you, hopefully with some new wrinkles, about the assault within sectors of the academy on the autonomy of science and social research. This assault is made in the name of righting ancient wrongs, but all too often this is a thin disguise for wronging ancient rights, such as subtle denials from a variety of circles, that all human beings are created equal and endowed by their Creator with inalienable rights as a result of their humanness. Such rejections can be made in the name of the biological superiority of one group or person over another, or as in now more common view that all human differences are somehow hierarchical and therefore unjust. For the extremists amongst our ranks, usurping the work of God has become routine behavior.

Professional activities and publishing chores are constantly bundled. Transaction has made this bundling inevitable. On any given day a librarian in Burundi will ask for book donations because one or another ethnic tribe has burned his institution to the ground. An economist in Havana will request access to a specific book or journal in a land where hard currency exchanges are virtually impossible outside the black market. A sociologist in California will inquire how to handle his humiliation in having to make a public apology to students and faculty for the "crime" of sexually harassing a female professor, when what he claims to have done is engage in old-fashioned vigorous debate. A psychologist from Canada appeals for help in responding to a granting agency that charged that an application deals too much with the Holocaust in a proposal dedicated to the suppression of memory in a totalitarian context. A black prisoner will write eagerly for copies, any copies, of SOCIETY in a closed environment in which library budgets are entirely absorbed by legal texts. We must receive at least 100 such requests annually. Then there are rejections from reputable journals and magazines of advertisements for books that seem ideologically risky despite their scholarly content. These everyday requests and rejections are reminders that however we are born, we do not always remain equal. It is one thing to prattle about constitutional safeguards, but quite another to actually exercise free speech in a forthright and vigorous fashion.

The needs and constraints on others serve as a steady reminder that the celebration of purely personal fulfillment is fatuous as a goal unto itself; one that can lead to the degradation of the human spirit. It does this by converting a goal into an operating principle: cowardice—or as Dennis Wrong notes in his concept of "over socialization", a reticence to speak frankly and deal fairly with dangerous themes. It maximizes the idea of personal safety while undermining the idea of public service. Utilitarianism becomes a confused cluster of ends in which the pleasure principle is conflated into the normal desires for happiness. Speaking plainly becomes a risk rather than a reward.

My lifetime concern is a world of learning that serves as an umbrella between professing and publishing. In the world of learning, the supposedly genteel universe of discourse that embraces such arts as teaching, writing, and publishing, the reduction of value to utility has had especially disastrous consequences. By locating so many academic awards and emoluments in consensual behavior instead of authentic, and perhaps conflicted behavior, we generate conformity rather than encourage creativity. The pursuit of success is too easily reduced to a quiescence that may yield a deep sense of personal unhappiness, displeasure with ourselves for yielding to powers and authorities that deprive us of the joys of everyday life.

The efforts to right historic wrongs quickly, of men playing at God, and to assign blame for such wrongs to those closest at hand and most vulnerable, hardly are new or unique to American society. The first half of the century bears witness to the utter corruption and decimation of science and social research in Germany under Hitlerism, Russia under Stalinism, and, closer in time and space, a series of lesser tyrannies imposing an iron will over the course of learning. Indeed, most human rights annuals identify roughly 20 out of 200 nations that practice a thing remotely identifiable as free speech. While it is not axiomatic that dictatorships equate to anti-science, there is evidently a strong propensity to harness science toward totalitarian ends, and when this is not possible, to destroy that which cannot be harnessed. In a nutshell, dictators often have legitimate complaints. What they invariably lack are plausible solutions. A quick perusal of the Nazi and Communist prototypes makes clear this gulf between complaints and solutions. It may also help set the stage for the context and magnitude of the present day American dilemma with respect to science and learning in general.

The Nazis were largely correct in their pre-rule days by pointing to the bitter consequences of World War I reparations, the disincentive to a normal, healthy economy under Weimar, and its encouragement, through a policy of managed economic bribes, of a disastrous inflation that sapped the strength of a new democracy and made possible the rise of a brutal dictatorship that bridled a runaway inflation by a tight reign over labor and industry alike. This was a concern enunciated by John Maynard Keynes in *The Economic Consequences of the Peace* and not just reducible to a piece of Nazi doggerel.

What Hitler and his cohorts failed to understand is that the foreign enemies were as nothing compared to the demons from within. The New Third Reich was sapped of its strength long before the Allied invasions in 1944. The Nazis created a house divided against itself by turning German against German—by identifying science with racial purity; by the expulsion of the likes of Einstein and Freud from its scientific academies; by appointing university officials based on their racial backgrounds and party loyalties; by the mobilization of physics to pure war aims; by converting medical science into racist eugenics; and the harnessing of social science to demographic efforts to seek and destroy Jewish communities for the goal of mass murder. In the denial of the autonomy of science, one found the end of the Nazi era in its very beginnings; in the structure of its heartless ideology. Totalitarian regimes have the capacity to harness scientific work to practical, if destructive, ends. Less well appreciated is how dictators frustrate the processes of discovery and invention, and as a result, seriously erode the very regimes they seek to perpetuate.

Max Weber well understood this process of totalitarian ruled how science becomes anti-science for supposedly noble ends. The process of incubation was well advanced even before Weimar Germany, much less Nazi Germany. Time has dulled our memories of speeches made in 1918, but it has not dulled the sharp blade with which Weber spoke—fifteen years before the ascending power of the Nazi behemoth.

"It is said, and I agree, that politics is out of place in the lecture room. It does not belong there on the part of the students.

. . . Neither does politics belong in the lecture room on the part of the docents, and when the docent is scientifically concerned with politics, it belongs there least of all." To take a practical political stand is one thing, and to analyze political structures and party positions is another. When speaking in a political meeting about democracy, one does not hide one's personal standpoint; indeed to come out clearly and take a stand is one's damned duty. The words one uses in such a meeting are not means of scientific analysis but means of can-vassing votes and winning over others. They are not plowshares to loosen the soil of contemplative thought; they are swords against the enemies: such words are weapons. It would be an outrage, however, to use words in this fashion in a lecture or in the lecture room. . . . To the prophet and the demagogue, it is said: "Go your ways out into the streets and speak openly to the world," that is, speak where criticism is possible. In the lecture room we stand opposite our audience, and it has to remain silent. I deem it irresponsible to exploit the circumstances that for the sake of their career the students have to attend a teacher's course while there is nobody present to oppose him with criticism. The task of the teacher is to serve the students with his knowledge and scientific experience and not to imprint upon them his personal political views.

That such a notion of science as a vocation gave way to politics as a passion only fifteen years later in Nazi Germany in no way weakens the impact of Weber's message. That betrayal of truth was in no small part responsible for the collapse of the Third Reich as such.

The same is the case for the Soviet era in Russia. Speaking before the First Conference of Russian Industrial Managers in 1931, Joseph Stalin outlined the tragic history of old Russia. He dramatically, and quite properly, pointed out that "the history of old Russia is the history of defeats due to backwardness. She was beaten by the Mongol Khans. She was beaten by the Swedish feudal barons. She was beaten by the Polish-Lithuanian squires. She was beaten by the Anglo-French capitalists. She was beaten by the Japanese barons. All beat her for her backwardness." What Stalin failed to understand is that his policies toward science and culture would perpetuate that tragic history in the new Russia, the Russia of Soviet power. Social class and not personal ability came to determine scientific promotions. As a consequence, the history of the USSR is the history of defeats due to a different sort of backwardness. Russia was beaten by the very communist system that presumably was to overcome backwardness. She was beaten by a regime that substituted a specious theory of environmental adaptation in place of the science of genetics. She was beaten by a regime that allowed appointments in mathematics only to party loyalists. She was beaten by nationalistic theories of language that destroyed prospects for social commitment beyond those of ethnicity. She was beaten by a regime that promoted individuals for loyalty to party instead of fealty to science. She was beaten by a regime that rewarded individuals for proletarian purity instead of scientific integrity. She was beaten by a regime that punished minorities for excellence in research that resulted in autonomy of behavior. Finally, she was beaten by a regime that purged and executed those who dared to disagree at all. Russia could overcome the Nazi hordes, but it could not overcome its own Communist ideologies and actions. The search for "the new man" ended in the demise of old tyrants.

Early on in the history of Soviet rule, the great Nobel psychologist and physiologist Ivan Pavlov dared to express the unbridgeable gulf between science and ideology. In his address to a Marxist-Leninist cadre in 1923, when it was still barely possible to express plain truths, Pavlov stated to an audience of youthful communist loyalists that when you enter science you will find that science and dogmatism are entirely different things. Science and free criticism, these are equivalent. But dogmatism is not suitable. There is no need to bring up examples. How much was avowed truth? Take for example the indivisibility of the atom. Years have passed, and nothing has remained of this. And all science is saturated with these examples. And if you respect science, as it follows that you become thoroughly acquainted with it, then in spite of the fact that you are communists, or members of workmen's schools set up by the Soviets, if you acknowledge that Marxism and communism are not absolute truths, that it is only a theory in which there may be part of a truth, but in which there is perhaps no truth, then you will look on all life with freedom of view, but not in slavery.

The victory of the proletarian, partisan theory of "science" cost the lives of many thousands of scientists and academics in a futile effort to preserve a system intellectually dead on arrival. Worse yet, it cost the lives of millions of people who, in the name of a dogmatic ideology, were ill equipped and poorly led in what the Russians still refer to as the Great Patriotic War. As if external enemies were not sufficient, the Soviet leaders engaged in the massive destruction of its own peoples in a genocide unequalled and perhaps only paralleled by the Nazi leaders.

While I would not wish to affirm an analog of current American social and political life with that of the Nazi German and the Soviet Russian regimes, certain parallels are ominous, and the risks dangerous. Once again, we find a corruption from within that is either ignored or dismissed. It is written in an old Jewish proverb that "the urge to forget prolongs exile, the secret of redemption is remembering." In this case, to remember—at least the horrors of our own century—will help us better understand our own nation in this moment of time. For while in each of the aforementioned dictatorial systems, the political parts of government made frontal assaults that led to the serious decomposition of the intellectual life of those nations, in the case of the United States, it is the other way about: the higher academic communities have set themselves up as the vanguard of the people, offering clarion calls ranging from curbs on the Bill of Rights to demands in the selection and hiring of personnel by quota, based on considerations of gender, race, and class—quite apart from knowledge or talent.

Once again, we find the assertion of well-intentioned people arguing the need to right historic wrongs immediately, in the American case, by asserting theories of affirmative action—creating setasides for socalled minority businesses that rarely trickle down; shifting the base of appointments and promotions from intelligence to experience; adopting quixotic ethnic standards for federal promotions—standards that treat successful minorities as majorities; making university appointments on the basis of gender identity rather than simple talent; encouraging the public display of private sexual preferences through awards, emoluments, and special placements in institutions of higher learning; and, if all else fails, by changing the grading structure on Standard Aptitude Tests to calm the fears of the public with respect to a failing American educational system.

We have reached a point of inversion that passes into perversion. In the recent past, segregation was viewed, and properly so, as an enemy of democratic norms; we now have demands for re-segregation as part of the arsenal of multiculturalism. The separate but equal doctrine, which was the law of the American land in the late nineteenth century and then fearlessly overcome by the middle of this century, is again being touted as an answer to our problems in the late twentieth century. In short, rather than permit the pendulum of progress to come to rest on a consensus, American society witnesses a greater separation and suspicion among races, classes, genders, and religions than in recent memory. We seem to have come full circle; starting the century with separatism as a way of life, compelled to develop integrationist patterns by a series of wars and depressions, and now, in the full flower of affluence and world leadership, being urged to again return to segregation, this time rallying about the flag of pleasantries such as cultural flowering and self-realization. For every achievement in erasing large inequalities we seem to have two demands to generate smaller inequalities. While world resources and supplies may be finite, demands and grievances appear to be infinite.

This shifting ground from equities to biases, however anti-democratic, is at least tolerable as long as it does not effect the vitals of a society. But when the very core of science itself is invaded, indeed polluted, by attacks on science for its maleness, its inability to infuse experience and experiment with love and feeling, we have a return of verstehen theory, to subjectivity, with a vengeance. We start a process of artificial selection that makes science hostage to fashion and social science an active participant in its own decimation. When a legal system is mobilized to support new forms of favoritism in the name of righting historic wrongs, the very soul of American industry and society is sapped, and prospects for American democracy become bleak and stark, the reverse of the intended outcome.

Such words may not sit well with academics who genuinely want to advance causes deeply held, or seek redress for past wrongs by accelerated means, and who feel less than sanguine about a system that historically has invoked genteel or harsh prejudices to prevent everyone from fully participating in its bounties. This is not a call to reaction, or to set the clock back; not an argument for conservatism in politics nor constraint in morality, for to do so would be to perpetuate the very wrongs that American democracy is dedicated to overcome. But such historical wrongs cannot be overcome by yielding to social demands in an arbitrary and capricious manner; or by anointing theories as ultimate truths in the face of everyday realities to the contrary. I do not believe for a moment that a race of people who have given us, in sociology alone, the likes of a W. E. B. DuBois, Booker T. Washington, James S. Johnson, E. Franklin Frazier, and now William Julius Wilson and Charles V. Willie, will tolerate, much less abide, patronizing placebos from a white table. The constant din at the fringes between white supremacy or black superiority or for that matter, black supremacy or white superiority, does little to put American society on the road to equality. We need to address policy potentials to alleviate inequities whatever may be their historical sources or current angers.

The task of liberal society is to permit all to gain a place at the starting gate of the struggle to achieve the just, but different ends of each and every person; it is not to guarantee a place at the finish pole for each and every person. A race that ends with everyone arriving at the same time at the finish line in a dead heat is fixed. A society that ends with everyone standing on the same spot is just plain crooked, or just plain dead. The lack of innovation, incentive, or invention is more injurious to the survival of a system than foreign armies standing at the gates. This much the United States can, and should, learn from the Nazi German and Soviet Russian experiences.

Equity, like inequity, is an endless process, not a thing. Rights are won; new wrongs are located in the process. This is the way of the world. This is the way of all flesh. Demands are infinite, supplies are finite. The good society must find ways to bring public needs and private rights into some sort of harmonious framework. It is the role of science policy and research to help calibrate the relation of equity to liberty. But when science itself is infected with ideological demands on one side and ascriptive regulations on the other, the aims of the good society, the democratic society, are permanently crippled. We make our society vulnerable to the very forces of political extremism that we have spent the century overcoming in foreign lands. Unpleasant as it may be to contemplate, the slope from Aryan Science to Proletarian Science to Race or Gender Science is not only slippery, but hard to climb out of in a peaceful or painless way.

The lessons of twentieth-century history are clear enough; the capacities of people to understand that history is less in evidence. We would do well, each in our own way, each walking in the path of science and social science, to maintain the banner of quality in research and integrity in knowledge. We have seen the consequences of a science for society in which color blindness is replaced by color determination; racial equity is replaced by racial bigotry; religious freedom is replaced by religious fanaticism i universal fairness is replaced by clannish bias; and simple civility is replaced by gangsterism in personal relations. I intend no lecture on policy. Those will evolve naturally enough once the dangers to democratic society are perceived. Indeed, perhaps we need a moratorium on new policies to fully absorb those already enacted into laws. If we fail in this shared mission, days and nights of celebration for books with titles like *The Democratic Imagination* will themselves become rare and subject to dissolution—along with its celebrants.

I would like to leave you with the words of the late Robert Cooley Angell—sociologist, socialist, and American. In reading remarks he authored in 1941 under the rubric of *The Integration of American Society*, I could not help but be astonished by the change in theme as well as tone that has taken place in our intellectual life over the past half century. The words of Angell—along with hosts of other Americans like Robert E. Park and Robert MacIver, or Europeans like Karl Mannheim and Thomas Masaryk, to name a few—sound not only old fashioned, but downright quixotic. To those who have been dismissive, and even abusive, of my assertions about *The Decomposition of Sociology*, I dare take the liberty of reciting the admonitions of at least one old-fashioned mid-Westerner. Angell notes that there is some connection between the danger of social disintegration and the rise of free-standing groups. The latter have disrupted an older type of moral community and have not been able to foster the development of an equally strong one of a new type. This accounts for two shortcomings from the viewpoint of societal integration: the tendency to emphasize non-common interests, and the tendency to nullify common values through differences in perception of the existing situation. . . . In a society in which most needs can be satisfied with money, one cannot ignore the importance of lessening disparities of property and income. Such lessening cannot be achieved abruptly without running the danger of killing our democracy. But once a start is made the gains should be cumulative. A reduction in property and income differentials should breed more understanding, and more understanding should bring into the area of discussion programs aimed at further reduction. . . . No one expects that they would easily agree upon particular solutions, but they could at least canvass alternatives with mutual respect. . . . In a country where the standards are as materialistic as in the United States, many will continue to regard improve-ment in technology as the main line of progress. They will not realize that such improvement does nothing to strengthen the foundations of our society. The supreme test of democracy will be the promptness and the intelligence with which we meet this challenge.

While we may hope and pray that those charged with social policy and social practice are up to the tasks defined for us a half century ago by Professor Angell, this is neither the time nor place to offer palliatives. For our part, for my part, the continuing struggles that define our public needs happen to be the same struggles that bring private pleasures—or, if you will, the fulfillment of life, liberty, and the pursuit of happiness. If we fail, if we fall prey to the gods of totalitarian tyrannies and reductionist fanaticisms, then the sciences, and here I include the social sciences, will be nothing more than instruments serving deadly masters. This sort of political positivism must be resisted with all of our human hearts as well as human resources. That the outcome is actually in doubt should remind us all of the urgency of this struggle. If we bury our collective heads in the academic sands and claim to have achieved personal pleasure in so doing, we will have failed of our private values no less than public responsibilities. The democratic imagination—in small letters—is comprised of two parts: the willingness to engage in public discourse without being humiliated or liquidated, and a respect for truths that compel us to change our minds—also without being humiliated or liquidated. Being wrong should be corrected, not punished. Being right should be an occasion for quiet reflection, not raucous celebration on the dead bodies of victims. May the democratic system of the United States of America survive this terrible time of testing. Let it not be said that we grieved for our age, but lacked the vision to find solutions to its problems.

An address delivered at a dinner honoring publication of *The Democratic Imagination*, on the occasion of the sixty-fifth birthday of Irving Louis Horowitz. The affair was held at Scanticon Conference Center, Princeton, New Jersey, on September 23, 1994.

6

GAUGING GENOCIDE

· ·

The study of the arbitrary taking of life is not exactly equivalent to being a pioneer in the invention of a new learning field or even the discovery of a new way of bottling old wine. Indeed, to be a "pioneer" in the study of collective death says much about the dark side of this extraordinary century, and about the vanity of those who attempt to make sense of it all. Perhaps it would better if we admitted that what we "study" is not an "area" but the culmination of a century in which invention has been matched, discovery by discovery, by the machinery and technology of death. Genocide is not an area of study that can be bracketed within well-defined boundaries. Such concerns are the common property of humanity. It is no less a characteristic of our age than welfare. The twentieth century has mastered the art of destruction and construction. These are not exactly specific areas of study so much as facts of life that we all share in common.

Still, I confess to serious concern with the dark arts of mass murder. I came to the study of genocide in an attempt to define a primary social indicator that can help provide sociology with a quantitative equivalent of voting for politics and money for economics. In doing so, in seeking some quantitative, that is numerical, measure for the quality of life unique to our times, I hoped to contribute something positive to the sciences of mass emancipation, and not just the anti-sciences of mass destruction. These remarks are not intended to summarize my *lebenswerke*, only to provide the private undercoating that makes possible a contribution to the public enterprise.

I grew to young manhood at the start of World War Two. Because of deep family roots in Russia on both my paternal and maternal side, my first interest was in the fate of the people of the Kiev Basin during the Second World War, where most of my family remained. I followed the course of the war on a daily basis. My room was filled with maps and pins detailing the movement of Wehrmacht troops on one side and Red Army troops on the other. Seeing the film *Alexander Nevsky*, the great Russian nationalist classic directed by Sergei Eisenstein, formed my imagery. Evil was blue eyed and blond and adorned in white, Good was etched in darker, Slavic colors of the Russian defenders of the faith. I have never have forgotten this reversal in values between black and white. Having grown up on a diet of Westerns at the Sunset and Luxor theaters in Harlem, New York, where I spent my childhood, violence and death were my constant companions, but so, too, were the wonderful and varied life of a unique and fascinating neighborhood. Living at the edge was the denominator, shared by us all. More of these early experiences were detailed in my autobiography *Daydreams and Nightmares* (Horowitz, 1990) and need not be labored further.

My earliest memories were of war overseas and war in the streets, not of state power and mass murder. Indeed, although I had a keen sense of being Jewish, having been largely among the last generation educated in the Yiddish culture of the secular socialist Workmen's Circle and Sholom Aleichem schools at the fringes of Harlem, my focus was less on the tragic fate of the Jewish communities of Europe than on the participation of Jewish communities of American and Russia in the struggle for democracy and anti-fascism. In retrospect, this may appear naive and even foolish. In the context of the times, 1941-1945, this seemed a natural posture for a very young Jewish teenager. My greatest linkage to the Jewish community was a basketball court at the Jewish Center in Flatbush, Brooklyn, where the Horowitz family moved after leaving Harlem. It was my religious friend from Harlem, Arthur

Grumberger, whose family migrated from Budapest, Hungary, who first alerted me to the tragedy that was befalling the Jewish People. Having been reared in Jewish socialist (Workman's Circle schools), the emphasis was less on European Jewry than American class wars. It was Arthur who introduced me to religious ritual and observance. He shared with me his Hebrew School texts, and was, in fact, my first teacher of the Hebrew language. And while this did not especially "stick," the sense of the Jewish people as a universal people, and the special condition of Jews in the interwar period of 1918-1938 became part of my intellectual arsenal, if such it could be called. My heart was not hardened to my people's suffering, but I was terribly unaware of the magnitude of the war against the Jewish People that was being waged, and, alas, won by the Nazi regime at the same time as it was clearly losing the war against the Allied Powers. Genocide does not take place in hot house isolation from other aspects of social life and political struggle. It is a function of legal, ethical and cultural disintegration.

My writings on genocide reflect the circuitous route of an obviously misspent childhood and youth. After two early theses efforts in the history of European thought, specifically on the dialectical tradition in Italian Renaissance and French Enlightenment thought, done under the supervision of the great Jewish scholar, Paul Oscar Kristellar in 1952 and 1953 at Columbia University, I wrote my first serious and independent work, *The Idea of War and Peace in Contemporary Philosophy and Social Theory*. The effort had scarcely a word about genocide or the Holocaust. It was the seeming potential for nuclear annihilation that was of paramount concern in that volume. In the mid-1950s, the American nation, indeed the entire world, was gripped by the fear of a nuclear holocaust. Everything, from films on the makeup of a post-nuclear assault to books on stages in the processing of such warfare, became common grist. For the first time, the American public came to believe that a third world war would be fought on American shores as well as European capitals. Despite this, my summary of major figures of our century, from Alfred North Whitehead to John Dewey in philosophy, and from Vladimir Lenin to Mohandas

K. Gandhi in politics, was thought by some to stray too far beyond the path of linguistic philosophy and logical positivist methods that held sway in the Anglo-American world of the 1950s.

With the early 1960s, my work moved from an interest in conflict and its resolution to a more focused emphasis on anarchism and violence. The heating up of the war in Vietnam seemed the proper time, and still does, for a natural extension of my thinking about the metaphysical foundations of war as such. Along with the noted social psychologist David Riesman, I helped found the Committees on Correspondence and a monthly bulletin alerting the academic and policy communities about the dangers of the pending expansion of the South East Asian conflict. It also was fueled by the academic shift from philosophy to sociology as a career path. It was in such a congruence of practical and academic considerations that the issue of genocide came into any sort of focus. In such works at *Radicalism and the Revolt against Reason* (Horowitz, 1961) and a large-scale anthology on *The Anarchists* (Horowitz, 1964), I described the issue of genocide as mass murder by state authorities; and saw this as a source of anarchist rationalization of violence against government officials. It also became apparent to me that the anti-statist forms of terrorism cut in multiple ways: some toward radical reconstruction of society, others toward reactionary reconstruction of earlier societies. On either side, the Jewish question became a litmus test for social theory. So whether dealing with one or another variety of radical approaches to the German condition, the situation of the Jewish people became a problematic rather than a given. To study war and conflict in modern times was to look closely at the German contradiction between education and barbarism, rationalism and mysticism. My earliest concerns saw Jews as part of the revolutionary movements within German life, as part of the class structure identified with the "interests" of other radical groups, but not on Jews acting in their own behalf. Hence, everyone from Karl Marx, Werner Sombart, and Theodore Herzl came into play by the mid-1960s. To study the Holocaust as a concrete expression of human behavior meant to also look at National Socialism as a specific manifestation of German behavior.

By the close of the 1960s, my interests in war, conflict, and genocide was given a large boost by an invitation to serve as visiting professor at the Hebrew University in its American Civilization program. That trip had a profound effect on my sense of the magnitude of the Holocaust. I met some survivors and some children of survivors, and realized that Israel as a modern State had itself risen out of the ashes, the charnel house of a wartime Europe. I spoke with people who lived in towns and cities from whence my parents came, and saw firsthand evidence of broken bodies, and even bent spirits that seemed to be a common if subdued legacy of all Israel. Indeed, some of my closest friends and colleagues were from Hungary and Romania, with untold infirmities that made my own hair-lip and cleft palate pale in comparison. Some were induced from their concentration camp experiences, others that limited movement or impeded speech. The number of such people on my first visit moved and disturbed me. But more pointedly, these colleagues went about the business of living without self-pity. They nearly all had wives and children and large families at that. The tragic sense of Europe played against the canvas of the liberating sense of Jews reborn in the Old World and new State of Israel. All of that weighed heavily on my mind.

Even before that, a decade earlier as a matter of record, in a demographic study of the Jewish communities in Buenos Aires in 1958-59, I was forced to recognize that the issue of Jewish survival was bundled with the issue of the Holocaust, of the genocide committed against the Jewish people by the fascists in the most obvious sense, and then by the Stalinists in only a slightly more covert sense, i.e., socialism as a struggle against Zionism. But even as backdrop in my book *Israeli Ecstasies and Jewish Agonies* (Horowitz, 1974), the sense of genocide remained a distant backdrop to what appeared to me to represent a more urgent set of considerations as exemplified by the title. So it was the actual contact with Israel, remote and transient though it may have appeared at the time, that provided a perspective on genocide in particular and conflict in general, sorely lacking in my earlier work.

On a practical level, I became involved with the struggles of the Jewish people to survive Stalinist and post-Stalinist power in the Soviet Union. I became a fervent advocate of the idea that the struggle of intellectuals was far different than simple identification with political parties and partisan enterprise. Intellectuals in the conduct of their research and work must take a cue from atomic scientists: to struggle against the misuse or abuse of their specific contributions to the century by forming appropriate voluntary associations. Together with a handful of extraordinary people ranging from Hannah Arendt at the New School for Social Research, Daniel Bell and Eli Ginzberg at Columbia University, Andrew Hacker and Milton Konvitz at Cornell University, Ithiel de Sola Pool and George Wald at MIT and Harvard respectively, to name some of the better known figures, and with a particular bow to the extraordinary leadership in this effort taken by Hans J. Morgenthau, we formed the Academic Committee on Soviet Jewry—one of several specialist groups mobilized by largely Jewish agencies, to ward off what was felt to be an impending disaster for the Jewish people of Russia. Our mission in the late sixties and early seventies, if such were it called, was to assist in the migration of Jewish men and women of letters to Vienna, Rome, Jerusalem, and points West. It was an amazingly successful mission which, combined with other efforts on behalf of Soviet Jewry, paved the way for the massive Jewish migrations from Russia to points West in the 1990s. The support, albeit belated, from the American Jewish Congress, provided an organizational platform that extended our efforts from the university to the political realm. We established contact with important figures in Soviet academic life and linguistics, mathematicians, physicists, and musicians, and developed networks for their early emigration and resettlement in Israel and to a lesser extent Europe. It was an effort that extended up to and through the toppling of Communist power in Russia. This is not said in boast, for our committees probably did too little rather than too much. But it was a mechanism by which we translated a concern for a new holocaust into a practical effort of saving lives. For this chance to participate, I shall be forever grateful.

A strong leitmotif in my work, terrorism, provided an essential piece of the puzzle before I attempted a direct investigation of genocide. In the late 1960s and early 1970s, I conducted a series of seminars for the Council on Foreign Relations on terrorism. Our working group, under my direction, developed a variety of scenarios when terrorist acts were likely, and more important, the sources of such acts, that is, from state or anti-state elements in a society. My interest in terrorism derives from the same intellectual background as my interests in genocide—that is, from political sociology as a field for studying the interaction of state and society. Only now, with the publication of my volume entitled *Behemoth: Main Currents in the History and Theory of Political Sociology* (Horowitz, 1999) have I been able to provide a fusion between various strands in the political processes that bring together the story of violence with that of specific assaults on subjugated peoples. As my work moved from a study of terrorism as a series of actions, to issues of legitimacy and power on one side, and profiling the terrorist and above all, to the victims of terrorism and terrorism's impact on the larger society on the other, the various strands initially seen by myself as separate and distinct came together. By 1980, I began to see some semblance of a general theory of genocide come into focus. By the close of the millennium, this general theory was completed. It became the grounds for the fourth edition of *Taking Lives: Genocide and State Power* (Horowitz, 1997), virtually a new book, and as mentioned above, *Behemoth*. The title, based on the Hebrew word, *Behemah*, or huge, unruly, beast, was hardly accidental. It was a shorthand way of bringing together discrete strands in my earlier thinking.

Only when I started work on *Foundations of Political Sociology* at the start of the 1970s did the issue of genocide come into sharp relief. In studying the sources and systems of National Socialism and International Communism alike, it became apparent that the State under totalitarian control exercises its power, not in connection with or on behalf of a social class or strata, and not even with much regard for the nature of the economic system, as is repeatedly claimed from Marx through Lenin, but as an independent actor as Max Weber uniquely understood. My primary evidence became the condition of the Jewish people throughout twentieth century Germany. Under the Weimar Republic, it was clear that Jews formed a substantial part of the working class in membership and leadership alike. They were active players in the economic expansion of Germany since emancipation. But it was not only that Jews were hence a target from Left and Right perspectives alike, but from the State apparatus, the regulatory mechanisms for the maintenance of social order from the top down. The historic strategy of maintaining a "low profile" in alien environments back-fired. Unbridled from considerations of functioning social classes or even economic rationality, the State ferreted out its victims, and "cleansed" the nation of its "enemies." In the process, it satiated the feeding frenzy of its Aryan citizens. The Jews were both victim and explanatory device for the Nazi State. Only the fortuitous death of Stalin, and the aborting of the so-called "Doctor's Plot" of Jews against the regime, prevented a similar outcome from evolving in the Soviet Union. The State was the epicenter of genocide because it was the root of terrorism and totalitarianism alike.

What made this a hard lesson to learn was the need to rethink the relationship of fascism to communism, to see them both as "right" and "left" aspects of totalitarianism. With the aid of the classic tradition in political sociology, especially the work of Max Weber and the no less classic, neo-Kantian tradition in legal phi-losophy as exemplified by Hannah Arendt, it was possible, nay necessary, to rethink fundamental fault lines. The process became simpler once the unitary character of anti-Semitism in Germany and Russia under its dictators became evident to all but the blind. In my case, the strange crossover careers of Hitler and Stalin made it necessary to further understand that these regimes were based on maximum terror, on taking lives.

I have tried to make a fundamental contribution to the litera-ture on the Holocaust: in the areas of social stratification in which Jews were either absent or poorly represented, most particularly in the bureaucracy and the military. Jews thus became vulnerable as scapegoats for whatever went wrong in the political establishment.

The overestimation of the role of economy, combined as it was with the underestimating of the role of the State as an instrument of policy, created a dangerous situation that was to enable demagogues and extremists to lay the blame for whatsoever went wrong at the feet of the Jews. They could be blamed for being bourgeois exploiters of people, and at the very same instance, blamed for being rabble-rousing agitators goading these same masses to anti-government protests and riots. A deep source of genocide in general and of the Holocaust in particular, is the ability of the holders of state power to demonize a group, expose their vulnerabilities, and isolate them from potential allies and supporters. By their estrangement from the levers of state and military power, the Jews, for all of their vaunted historical capacity to survive adversity, found themselves in an impossible situation: without legitimization and without the means to defend themselves. The search for sociological and objective rather than psychological and subjective sources of genocide became a prime mission reflected in my book *Taking Lives: State Power and Mass Murder* (Horowitz, 1980).

What pushed me in this direction was the twin exaggerations of genocide studies: on one hand, the personal narrative which explained survival techniques and torture better than the systematic destruction of people; on the other hand, theological discourse that presumed teleological explanations for Jewish tragedy as something "fore-ordained" by a turn away from Talmud and Providence. My personal no less than professional need was to make sense of genocide as part of the theory of the relationship between the behemoths of state and society, that is, a function of the system of governance that not only permitted but mandated racial warfare and religious hatred. The study of the Holocaust also stimulated in some a notion of quantification in the measure of the quality of political and social orders. Thus, my work in this area was self-perceived not simply as an exercise in memory recovery but an exploration in social scientific method and theory.

We have too long taken for granted the nobility of science and social science in and of itself. But it now becomes clear that a vast army of psychologists, physicians, lawyers, demographers, and even anthropologists maintained their loyalty to the Nazi government. Indeed, a huge and unexplained anomaly is how the Holocaust could be conducted by that nation boasting the highest levels of education, the most advanced institutes of research, and cultural traditions that were linked to emancipation and enlightenment. So it becomes evident, to me at least, that the task of social science and social research does not stop with the collation of data or the presentation of theories. It does carry a moral component. But that component can only be exercised by intellectuals and academics acting as a class for and of itself, not as lap dogs for any particular political power or social ideology. To be sure, the perfume of power, the exhilaration of standing in the national limelight defined by others, was and remains itself an element in genocidal practice, no less than critical research. The search for the fine line between science and values is endless. But the pursuit of genocide by totalitarian regimes sharpens that line. I mean by this that the thin line between the taking of life and all other forms of mischief of which statist regimes are capable, even the best of them, thickens the line. My work has increasingly come to rest on distinguishing varieties of anti-democratic regimes from the unique regimes that have practiced genocide. This may not be a pleasant distinction, but it is a useful one as a guideline through the dark voyages into state power.

My primary aim in this field has been to show genocide as part of a general theory of violence; or more broadly, the capacity of unbridled state power to utilize violence against a specific group in order to secure and maximize its own autonomous realm of operations. Once seen in this light, the study of genocide is an extreme end of the continuum involved in war and peace studies. The breakthrough here was made my dear friend, R. J. Rummel, of the University of Hawaii. He has demonstrated, in method and theory, how anti-democratic states are the unique carriers of the poison of genocide. And conversely, that democratic states are the societies that embody anti-genocide premises and principles. In my capacity as editorial director at Transaction Publishers, we were able to promote his work and indeed publish his final six books. This kind of work, when combined with studies of terrorism and violence of earlier researchers like E. V. Walter of Brandeis University and Walter Laqueur of Georgetown University, provides a framework to bring genocide studies back home, that is back to the world of social science research—where they stand the best chance of being understood and basically overcome. Genocide is not only a problem of power, it is a fact of numbers; and social scientists should know how to count and interpret "raw data."

To permit the study of genocide to become the exclusive domain of theologians and psychoanalysts is to return such studies to self-inflated and not always accurate memoirs of events now considerably long past. This is not to deny the place of a theologically centered and autobiographical witness literature; it is to note that such efforts are starting points, not ending points of sound scholarship and social research. It is difficult to speak of matters of death and mean-spirited brutality in clinical and objective terms. But to do otherwise is to remove this enormous characteristic of the century to the realm of the personal, the unspeakable, and ultimately, the mystical. Whatever else social science is or should be, it must always be in the realm of what one can rationalize and generalize. There are altogether too many social scientists quite pleased to avoid confronting the issue of genocide as a critical test of the very worth of the social sciences. That cannot be permitted, not only as a matter of human responsibility, but as a matter of improving the analytical ground on which we share a common ground. The preservation as well as presentation of human life is a sociological imperative.

In this regard, one of the major efforts I have made in relation to the study of genocide is the publication of outstanding works by others that illumine the field. Transaction Publishers has in the course of its 37-year-plus history published a fundamental series of works on the Armenian genocide, including efforts of Ephraim K. Jernazian, Richard G. Hovaniassian, Anny Bakalian, Jacques Derogy, and Vakhan Dadrian. We have published the collective efforts of the aforementioned R. J. Rummel, itself a landmark in the study of genocide and its relationship to contemporary totalitarian regimes from China to Russia; major works by Jewish and Israeli scholars on genocide in comparative geographical as well as ideological contexts, including the work of Israel W. Charny, Donald J. Dietrich, Iwona Irwin-Zarecka, William Helmreich, and Daniel Elazar. More recently, we have published works on the medical and legal aspects of genocide by Kurt Jonassohn, Howard Adelman, and Mark Osiel that extend the boundaries of our understanding of the relationship of professional life, moral standards, and legitimizing devices that the State has at its command in the conduct of annihilation. In short, in recent years, my concerns have turned from a personal effort at scientific analysis to publishing the best and the brightest scholars working in this area. Having said this, I should make clear that my publishing activities were not uniquely focused on genocide, but on the social sciences as a whole and of which the study of state power and state terror is a part. But it is precisely that phrase, genocide as part of the fabric of social life, which sets our publishing house as unique and distinct in the field of international social science.

In the early 1980s, I also became heavily involved in the efforts of the Armenian National Assembly, more directly as a member of the board of the Zoryan Institute. Although my understanding of the Armenian genocide was relatively weak in the early 1970s, my references to its similarities and antecedents to the Holocaust were evident. And I began to write increasingly on such continuities and discontinuities, especially as issues about the uniqueness of the Holocaust came to the fore. While I recognize the special features of the Nazi assault on the Jewish people, I also felt that it was dangerous to exaggerate the uniqueness of the destruction. The rising tide of interest led to an expansion of victimology as an ideology, one that displaced real analysis with the mantle of self-immolation—a dangerous form that substituted sentimentality for analysis and personal narratives for systematic study.

My later work on the Armenian condition, which was later to involve a trip in the mid-1990s to Yerevan in Armenia and Moscow in Russia, provided a comparative framework—one that emphasized prospects for survival and growth of a victimized people without basking in the sunset of defeat. By going to Armenia, I was able to appreciate the degree to which the people of that nation and ethnicity had moved considerably beyond reflecting on the past, and were attempting to fashion a democratic state in a hostile environment—not entirely unlike the Israeli effort to fashion a Jewish state in a Moslem world. Here, too, was an ancient civilization coupled with a modern state. And here also was a religious entity surrounded by Islamic theological-political structures. There are, to be sure, profound differences in levels of economic development. It is one thing to have a British mandate, quite another to be of a decaying Soviet empire.

The more I examined the issues, the more it became evident that the business of genocide involved more than professional examination. It entailed a set of personal decisions. Indeed, I say without fear that my three major "passions" of research in foreign policy—Israel, Armenia, and Cuba—involve a basic struggle for human decency. Small nations are often litmus cases for big issues. And even though the dictatorship of Fidel Castro is in no way commensurate with the horrors inflicted by Nazi secret service agents or Turkish military officers, it is of a piece with the general consideration that to struggle against genocide is to struggle for democracy. I realized through personal involvement that nation-building imposes its own strict rules of survival, and that having been victims of genocide is no sure guarantee of democratic outcomes or error-free political judgments. This is as true of Armenia with respect to Azerbaijan as it is of Israel in relation to Lebanon. This is a hard lesson for all of us working in genocide studies: politics trumps history.

Now that the issue of genocide is on the international docket of ideas, we need studies in a variety of fields to settle old issues and lead the way to new paradigms. Among the highest and thorniest issues in my opinion are the following, in no particular order of importance: (1) The relationship of warfare to genocide. (2) The relationship of civil strife and ethnic conflict to genocide, i.e., the systematic elimination of one part of those involved in strife in favor of another. (3) A more exact sense of the distinction between major genocides and whether they can also be described as "Holocausts," i.e., what sort of numbers are involved in each. (4) Why is it that certain forms of totalitarian regimes are non-genocidal and others genocidal, i.e., Italy under Mussolini in relation to Germany under Hitler? Are these differential outcomes the consequence of differential cultural inputs? (5) What price does one place on a life after the fact, namely payments to families of those destroyed in genocidal conditions? (6) What is the degree to which international law is an operational reality or a fiction with respect to the punishment of those who carry out specifically heinous forms of destruction? (7) Does the introduction of notions of cultural genocide enhance or degrade the study of mass physical murder? (8) And finally, is there is a continuum of means and ends in terminating genocidal regimes? More specifically, can the bombing and decimation of an "evil" regime be viewed as a good, without regard to the damage inflicted on the innocents of the offending nation?

These are just some themes that might lend themselves to social scientific analysis. There are other questions, such as the degree to which it is permissible or impermissible to save oneself at the expense of others in situations of ultimate desperation, the type of issues with which religious and secular law must wrestle. Even framing concerns in these terms makes it evident that the study of genocide entails an examination of the dark side of human nature as well as unbridled State power. The issues can never be fully resolved or even addressed to universal satisfaction. Even if we can develop a broad consensus at the general level, students of genocide will need to account for specific variations in grounded conditions. Alas, with Cambodia, Rwanda, Bosnia, and, most recently, Kosovo as "case studies" in the present period, we do not lack for confirmation of general propositions or for individual differences in concrete historical settings. But we can move on a variety of fronts: educational, cultural, and analytical to heighten an awareness of the preconditions of genocide. As others have pointed out, we need early warning signals and systems in place, and we need the policy resolve to address and redress such situations. However, by no means, does this imply that every situation will or can admit of solution through direct intervention. Nor can it be asserted that every situation will be resolved in a pacific manner. To appreciate the limits of analysis is to understand the finite capacities of human nature as such. And that is why the voices of silence will always have their say in the study of genocide. We stand in awe of our staggering accomplishments over the course of the twentieth century, and in the abyss of deeper despair over our failures to create a humane society. Having said this, we must also deal with quotidian events that do not admit of easy distinctions between good regimes and evil states. At the end of the day is a sense that ours is a tragic century in moral terms and an exhilarating one in technological terms. But we still have yet to learn how to match ethics and engineering. Until we do, the danger of genocide is haunting, while the policy tasks ahead are daunting.

References

Horowitz, Irving Louis (1990). *Daydreams and Nightmares: Reflections of a Harlem Childhood*. Jackson and London: University Press of Mississippi.

Horowitz, Irving Louis (1974). *Israeli Ecstasies and Jewish Agonies*. New York and London: Oxford University Press.

7

CUBAN COMMUNISM AND CUBAN STUDIES

. . . .

This discussion on the occasion of the publication of the eleventh edition of *Cuban Communism is* held at the University of Miami for several reasons. It is the home turf of my estimable coeditor, Jaime Suchlicki, and the Institute of Cuban and Cuban American Studies that he has so assiduously directed from its inception. He has adroitly and unflinchingly responded to the vitriol that pours forth from Castro's propaganda mills in Havana, as well as the only slightly less strident assaults from propaganda agencies in Washington. As the Institute of Cuban and Cuban American Studies demonstrates, the schism between honest information and tortured ideology is clearly exemplified in the field of Cuban Studies.

Cuban Communism is now in its eleventh edition: It is often graciously referred to as the "Bible of Cuban Studies." This is less testimony to the virtues of the compendium than the survival and strength of Castro's rule over Cuba for the past 45 years. For that reason, celebration of this 11th edition is a mixed blessing. Longevity is no indicator of virtue—especially in matters of political systems and empires. At fortyfive, the communist system in Cuba is one of the oldest surviving relics of the Third International. With the possible exception of North Korea, it is assuredly the only secular dynasty where the original revolutionary leadership—at least those who have lived to tell the tale-remains in power.

The eleven editions of *Cuban Communism* tell the story of this past halfcentury's odyssey of a movement that started life in 1953. It began as a liberating force from a military dictatorship and progressed to a far more embracing state promoting a variety of the same curse of military dictatorship. There are other projects over time that have attempted to tell the long story of Cuban communism. *Cuba Studies,* the Journal of the University of Pittsburgh, and the earlier *Cuba Annual* at the Radio Martí division of the U.S. Information Agency, are perhaps the most noteworthy. In this connection, the *Cuba Transition Project,* with its optimistic forward look to a Cuba free of the dictatorship may be the most ambitious scenariobuilding activity.

Cuban Communism began life as a 1969 symposium in *Society* magazine. It must be admitted—confessed would be a better word—that at the time it reflected more the hopes and aspirations of the liberal and leftist academic communities than those who early on felt the heavy boot of the Castro regime. Given the plain fact that so many Cubans who left the island in deep despair began life with involvement in the revolution and also with high expectations, one can only hope that my initial positive responses are not viewed too harshly. Whether politically astute or otherwise, Vietnam and Cuba were yoked in the imagination of the sixties, as two watersheds for American foreign policy to overcome.

The conversion of the symposium into a book was similarly less an act of inspiration than of desperation. At the time Transaction needed a solvent commercial basis for survival. We initiated relationships with commercial publishers for a series of "fastbacks" aimed at a college audience. First with Aldine Publishers, then with E.P. Dutton, and later, with several introductory texts with Harper & Row and Van Nostrand, *Society* successfully launched a book program. Indeed, *Cuban Communism* was one of the first twelve titles in our paperback series. From admittedly pedestrian commercial needs, rather than grand ideological schemes, the series and this volume in particular can be traced. By the same token, we can attribute its continuation to the incredible survival of a 45-year-old dictatorship. Material conditions rather than spiritual impulses explain most varieties of human behaviors—high and low.

Cuban Communism underwent various stages of disaffection inspired by the Castro regime. The first edition displayed respect for the guerrilla's courage, appreciation for the removal of the decadent and ineffective Batista regime, and enthusiasm for the goals of an island society liberated from the colonial ghosts of the 1894-1898 war no less than those of despotic caciques of 1953-1958. But even with the first edition there was an undercurrent of suspicion. Heavy-handed rule from the top down, anti-Americanism as a cornerstone of ideology, unpaid labor time as a critical component of the economy, and active participation in the overthrow and destabilization of other nations in the region were all noted. Over time, optimism sharply receded and pessimism regarding where the Cuban Revolution was heading became transparent. In this, the various editions of the book reflect the movement of people themselves into exile and a new life elsewhere.

As in all such projects, there are personal no less than professional reasons for editing such a volume. My initial involvement with, or better said, interest in, Cuba came about during my second (1958) stay at the University of Buenos Aires. It was a time of stirring against military politics in post-Peron Argentina—a rekindling of socialist theory amongst the students, a revival of sociology as a science rather than a footnote to Peronist ideology. The emergence of the guerrilla movement of Castro, Guevara, and their mountain-based allies, was widely reported. French currents especially influenced the students in the Faculty of Philosophy, where the new sociology was based, especially the rise of a new blend of existentialism and Marxism preached by JeanPaul Sartre and later Regis Debray. Sartre and Debray provided a *de facto* handbook of insurrectionary politics. Indeed, during the early 1960s, many fine young students—boys and girls really—saw the nascent Cuban Revolution as a prototype of what could take place in Argentina. It is among this group that many of the "disappeared" of later years were drawn. The success of the Cuban Revolution in 1959 sparked all sorts of combinations and permutations among radical internationalists and conservative nationalists, Marxists and Peronists. The intellectual wine was heady, the activist outcome brutally predictable. But that is another story for another time.

I had maintained contact with C. Wright Mills of Columbia University during this early period. By the time of my return home to North America, his manifesto, *Listen Yankee!* had become something of a literary sensation in the United States. Its publication by Ballantine as a mass paperback probably did more than any other single text of the times to introduce Castro and the Revolution to an American audience. Mills had become a literary lion— celebrated among an emerging radical intelligentsia throughout Latin America and Europe—as the true voice of academic sociology. Needless to add, such a characterization inspired as much animus as support within the profession. But Wright thoroughly delighted in the praise and adulation, accepting appointments to lecture far and wide. Much of this is described in my biography, C. *Wright Mills. An American Utopian.*

One consequence of Mills becoming a public figure of note was that he was invited to debates. A particularly attractive event was to be a special NBC television show featuring Adolph A. Berle— longtime ambassador to Latin American countries, as well as an important figure in the formation of the Liberal Party politics in the United States—debating C. Wright Mills. While the event, at least in the form envisioned, never took place (Mills suffered one of several heart attacks prior to the scheduled broadcast, his place being taken by Robert J. Alexander, a well schooled economic historian at Rutgers University), the Mills' preliminary research for the broadcast brought us into personal contact. He asked that I research the writings of Ambassador Berle, and in particular locate weaknesses, "soft spots," that could be hammered in the debate. I did, in fact, research the writings of Berle, but found myself in the presence of a towering and impressive scholar of the region—one who both appreciated the needs of Latin America and did so in the context of American liberal, postNew Deal, interests. I gave Mills my notes on Berle, including a warning that such a debate on Castro's Cuba would not be a cakewalk. He may not have welcomed the warning, but he was not dismissive. Indeed, Mills never lacked for courage, but neither was he as bombastic in behavior as he was in rhetoric.

I sometimes wonder how Mills would have responded to a serious expert critic and scholar like Berle. In particular, I wondered whether Mills' position on Cuba would have become modified—with Fidel being one more example and illustration of a Marxist pluralism—or hardened into the sort of ideologue that became all too prevalent in the New Left posturing of the 1960s. Mills' death in March of 1962 put to a close any such speculations. It also put to an end one of the very few figures in social science with the ability to put a human face on the Castro revolution. Others who followed him were far less interested in creating a myth of Castro as a pragmatic politician, than in constructing a far greater myth of Castro as a democratic socialist who would carry the message of revolution to the entire Third World. It says something about the potency of the founding father of Cuban Communism that both the soft and hard sells remain on the intellectual table 45 years after the guerrillas first seized power.

During the next several years I concentrated on the completion of my own work ranging from *Radicalism and the Revolt against Reason* to *Three Worlds of Development*. But the 1962-1965 period was also one of fermentation in Brazil, where the peasant movement in the Northeast and the political movement in coastal urban regions, were crushed by Brazil's armed forces with relative ease. To be sure, despite the facade of civilian rule, the military of Argentina also revealed considerable effectiveness in resisting, and where needed, ruthlessly suppressing, nascent radical movements. During this period, the Cuban regime hardened its control over the island. It became the undisputed outpost of the USSR in the region, and the source of support for insurrectionary movements throughout Latin America. The choice of national consolidation (Castro) versus international agitation (Guevara) took on the "classic" form of the rivalry between the ideologies of the Third and Fourth Internationals—otherwise known as Stalinism and Trotskyism respectively.

It was this internal development in Cuba that provided the basis for my 1964 essay in *New Politics* "The Stalinization of Castro". It was clear to me that such an article would be perceived as a public break with, indeed a betrayal of, the Millsian legacy. I chose as a place of publication an impeccable leftsocialist publication, albeit one that displayed evident roots in Trotskyism. I viewed the piece as a source for possible dialogue within the Left, but in point of fact, it led more to ostracism and assault than anything resembling dialogue. In retrospect, not even the moderate liberal wing of the Democratic Party was prepared for such a strong characterization of the Cuban regime. The Republicans for their part, saw the USSR in such rigid geopolitical terms, that the subtleties of Trotskyism vs. Stalinism never entered into their hemispheric thinking.

Even at this point, when a variety of scholars reluctantly now assign the label of Stalinism to Castro's regime, they often do so in emotive rather than analytic terms. The sheer absence of human rights or voting rights is scarcely some special hallmark of Stalinism. From my own viewpoint, Stalinism was a highly specific variant of totalitarian rule in the twentieth century. It features the fusion of civil and party functions, the militarization of economic activities, the exploitation of human labor and its reduction to a subsistence status, the steady elimination of all political parties other than the Communist Party, hierarchical leadership propensities, dynastic concentration of power in the hands of select families and cronies, and the cult of personality. It is a universe in which the leader can make no mistake and certainly cannot be criticized by others for making any. It became apparent to me, and to anyone who cared to look at the Cuban situation with their eyes wide open and their minds intact, that Castro's assertion of being a dedicated communist was not an idle boast but a proven fact.

The fact that I took great pains to indicate differences between the Soviet and Cuban styles of totalitarianism, not least of which were the absence of mass murder as a political tool, and a dependent economic status in global terms, spared me from criticism. In the subsequent issue of *New Politics,* a lengthy diatribe was launched with the usual canards: a failure to realize all the good that Castro had done for his people. Everything from crop diversification, mass education, to the morality of free labor dedicated to the nation was trotted out. Perhaps the most incriminating (and also the most typical) argument from my critic, who was a professor of economics at a major Canadian university, was that even should I be proved right in my criticisms, they should be kept to myself. To do otherwise was to aid and abet the cause of the common enemy—American imperialism. I realized then, five years into the regime, that the struggle was on two fronts: against the new totalitarianism in Cuba and, for me at least, against the growing expansion of New Left thinking in the United States. My strong opposition to the US involvement in Vietnam muted some of the concerns of my old friends. However, drawing the line between opposition to military adventurism and support for a despotic regime in North Vietnam only served to remind such critics that I was not to be trusted on Cuba—I had crossed the line from a weak comrade to enemy of the people.

The next effort I made to understand the Cuban Revolution was done on my own terms, and not within those parameters set by Mills and his ardent supporters. It took place three years later, in 1967. I was a visiting professor at the University of Wisconsin for a semester and had the chance to spend what is euphemistically called "quality time" with a friend, Maurice Zeitlin. We shared a deep concern for the Jewish people, for Israel, and for Middle East problems as seen from a left perspective. Indeed, Maurice had written a work on social class in the new Cuba that had been well received. We also shared disquiet that Cuba was clearly becoming a dangerous place for Jews: Nearly ninety percent of the 12,000 or so Jews in Cuba had left within the first eight years of the Revolution and the ten percent who remained were generally too old to form or maintain a viable religious community. The totalitarian dream of substituting scientific socialism for an ancient faith seemed manifest to Castro's followers. That Castro was wrong about Jews, and even more ignorant about the depth of the Catholic tradition, was to become apparent many years later, when Pope John Paul II came to Cuba and in his very presence stripped away the tattered curtain of secular worship of the state of Cuba.

The Horowitz-Zeitlin article on Castro appeared in *Judaism,* the official publication of Conservative Judaism. It was written in a measured way, out of deference to Zeitlin, more a plea for justice than a criticism of the regime. To be sure, the article did point out the wide uses of gross antiSemitic caricatures in official publications like *Granma,* the embrace of the most extreme, fanatic wing of Islamists in the Middle East, and the sharp curbing of freedom of religious practice. But it was all couched with a plea to Castro to take measures to rectify the situation, and to return to the fundamentals of socialism. As a dedicated graduate of *Hashomer Hatzair,* the strong Left Kibbutz movement in Israel, such a view made perfect sense to Zeitlin. It became clear that our appeal would fall on deaf ears when Castro sent active support to Syrians in their campaign against Israel during the Six Day War of 1967.

All that our article achieved was to expose the soft support among the American Left for any change in Cuba. Increasingly, the unity of Middle East dictatorships and their alliance with the Castro regime became a mark of bold pride. Jewish intellectuals in the academy were faced with the terrible *cul-de-sac:* they either offered support to the tyrant in Cuba, and hence to his support for terrorists in the Middle East, or they broke with Castro and the Cuban Revolution. The latter option was an act that few New Age acolytes were prepared to undertake—just as many of their parents doggedly supported Soviet tyranny despite the slaughter and imprisonment of millions of innocent Russians.

Indeed, the Cuban regime, no less than its advocates, had to come to terms with the degree to which Castro had either the will or the capacity to actively engage in insurrectionary movements in the Middle East and Africa, no less than Latin America. The necessity of choice served as the basis for the third article I wrote prior to beginning work on the first edition of *Cuban Communism.* The hard truth is that letting go of tyranny, especially tyrants who engaged in acts of perfidy in the name of the people, is a difficult act to perform—now as well as earlier in earlier times.

It is important to appreciate the fact that these three articles appeared several years before the first edition of *Cuban Communism* was even an idea. They were written in the belief that something resembling a social revolution could be still be forged in Cuba and that it would enhance rather than destroy democratic institutions and individual rights. Increasingly, it became apparent to me that political freedom and economic reorganization could not be brought together without paying a price: that price was the surrender of dictatorial forms of rule. It was a price that Castro, as a nationalist revolutionary, was unwilling then or now to concede and it was a price that his political allies, dedicated to international revolution, were even less willing to pay. It is with the abandonment of my illusions that the birth of this special anthology took place.

What assisted in the birth of the book was encouragement received from people like Carlos Alberto Montaner, Jaime Suchlicki, Frank Calzon, Carmelo Mesa-Lago, and Ernesto Betancourt, in particular. Each in their own special way offered me support, but also a forum to express my opinions. Needless to say, this may reflect less on any achievement or expertise I had in the area than on the paucity of academics willing to take even mildly critical stances. As the community of Cuban exiles evolved, so too did a new generation enriching university life in places ranging from Miami to Pittsburgh, as well as government affairs centered in Washington, DC. It was no small irony that a cadre of well-trained, thoughtful, Cuban social scientists, historians, and policymakers emerged at a time when the ranks of American academia were being depleted by growing ideological agendas operating at the expense of intellectual integrity. While these shifts were often deeply felt by honorable people, the demand of the 1960s was for a choice of allies rather than a choice of research topics.

Over the years, at a formal level, *Cuban Communism* moved from a series of relatively random essays to an integrated text. The book was increasingly aimed at the basic education of young people interested in Latin America in general and Cuban affairs in particular. The division of the book into historical, political, economic, social, military, and policy sections seemed natural enough. They drew upon the ways in which social research was departmentally divided. They made no presumption as to which element in Cuba was more "basic" than the next. Perhaps the most controversial decision was to emphasize events in Cuba as such, and not to deal extensively with the overseas Cuban communities established in places such as Miami, Madrid, and San Juan. When events such as the Mariel boatlift occurred, they were covered as part of the internal situation within Cuba. While one might argue that this was an artificial limitation on the text, I think it was and remains fully justified. There is a sense in which all books, other than the Bible and H.G. Wells have some kind of constraints built into their execution.

At the ideological level, with each edition *Cuban Communism* became a more potent tool in the struggle of ideas. I early on decided not to allow the book to become an artificial "pro" and "con" series of essays. An anthology is not a manual for electing officials. Nor is it the place where the student simply makes up his or her own mind among a choice of positions. This was to be—and indeed became—a living proof that social science has something to say about the condition of a nation and its system based on hard evidence and clear research designs. There were then and remain now enough texts celebrating Castro, Guevara, and their respective acolytes and apologists and the causes they espouse. I count several new readers and at least two books on Guevara in the year 2003 alone. In its pristine purity, *Cuban Communism,* as a work of social science, laid bare the character of the Castro regime from 1959 to the present. The work does so without bile or guile, and with a minimum of extremist rhetoric. Each selection has been chosen on the basis of its contribution to exact information, reasonable hypothesis, and where appropriate, sensible policy recommendations.

As there was a dwindling amount of available outlets for a growing amount of factual information being generated overseas (that is outside of Cuba), and a paucity of exact information from within Cuba, *Cuban Communism* increasingly provided statistical and historical information that shed light on internal events. With the discontinuance of the Radio Marti Quarterly Reports, and also its annual volumes on events in Cuba on a year-by-year basis, this aspect of the work became critical. Indeed, the Marti Annual Reports between 1985-1989 were crucial and irreplaceable. That said, only very recently with the work of the Institute for Cuban and CubanAmerican Studies at the University of Miami and the efforts of the Center for a Free Cuba in Washington, DC has the type of exact data needed by policy community become available. Other agencies have filled in many of the missing pieces. Nonetheless, our anthology in a series of appendices provided data on who's who in the Cuban political hierarchy, a brief rundown of major events in each year since the founding of the dictatorship, and activities of the regime with respect to such items as terrorism, overseas military engagements, and internal repression. Information of this sort is otherwise difficult, if not impossible, to come by.

In this regard, the active collaboration of Jaime Suchlicki in this enterprise for the past three editions, starting with the ninth, has been a vital force in my own sensitivity to the pedagogic requirements of a living text. The support of his Institute for Cuban and Cuban-American Studies has allowed for the inclusion of greater data-gathering resources than would have been otherwise possible. Without reservation, but with pride, I can point to the incredibly wide variety of people whose contributions have helped make this work central, and whose organizational frameworks have provided the informal base that both keeps up with events and anticipates prospects for future developments.

While *Cuban Communism* largely centers on the specifics of life in Cuba, much of my own writing by necessity—is focused on American policy toward Cuba. As a result, the evolution of the anthology has been in that direction. Given the interest in the best and the brightest of scholars no less than policymakers on the restitution of legitimacy and the normalization of development in Cuba, it should be of little wonder that such issues have come to play an increasingly prominent role in successive editions. I did have the great fortune of delivering the Bacardi Lectures in 1992 at the University of Miami. They provided me with an opportunity for examining in depth, a problem in the sociology of knowledge; in particular, the various strands of people drawn to Cuban Studies, and how in turn, they have impacted the social sciences and humanities of our universities. It should surprise no one that the study of contemporary Cuba provides a microcosm, not only of a society, but also of those who study that society. *Cuban Communism* has not left that double vision of objective system and subjective beliefs out of the reckoning.

I see this anthology as part of the consciousness of the Cuban people in search of mechanisms to move beyond totalitarianism as a unitary phenomenon. It is but one part, one spoke, of the revolt against tyranny. The Cold War may have ended the hub of the big wheel, the Soviet empire, but the phenomena as such did not pass into oblivion. With places like North Korea, Vietnam, China, with military politics of the sort currently practiced in Venezuela, and varieties of cruel dictatorships that repress their own people rife throughout Africa, the dangers of the Castro regime, while modulated by events and a realization of its own limitations, remain in need of steady examination and exploration.

If the Totalitarian Temptation is unitary and global, so too is the Democratic Project. Part of that project is the capacity of social science to go about conducting its business of researching and theorizing without intrusion or interruption. It is within that frame of reference that *Cuban Communism* finds its place. When this unhappy epoch in Cuban affairs comes to an end—as surely it must and will—then too this anthology will have run its course and also come to an end. At that point, the various editions of the book will serve as a warning, rather than an information resource, as to what can befall a people and a nation when one man, one party, one movement, one system, one plan, and one ideology, are granted absolute power.

8

THE LOGIC OF TRANSACTION
· ·

For Transaction, like all decent publishing activities that aim both to serve a professional public and to succeed as a commercial enterprise, the demands of the marketplace serve as a check and a reminder that the aims or policies of a chairman are circumscribed by what is euphemistically called the "real world." They range from the literary performance of authors, the shifting habits of buyers and users who shop the retail outlets and frequent the libraries, the ideological as well as emotional proclivities of those who make actual purchases or decisions as to what to buy, the fancies of sales personnel and booksellers, whose concerns may be less the quality of our list than the amount of discounts provided, to the character of human interaction within the publishing house as such. In short, as Herbert Blumer, my dear deceased colleague in sociology, and the first chairman of Transaction, might have said: it is not the action of a single person that matters nearly as much as the interaction among people that defines a situation. Publishing social science may be a mission but, at the same time, it is a grounded situation. It offers an interaction among people as well as perspectives.

Too often, hortatory proclamations emphasize the uniqueness of a publishing house. Indeed, after forty-one years as "publisher of record in international social science," a claim that Transaction works hard to justify, one is entitled to whisper such a bold statement. For our uniqueness is in the mix, not the purity. We owe a great debt to others: forerunners like Jeremiah Kaplan, who defined the original purposes of The Free Press; Martin Kessler, who amplified social science to include public policy; and Irving Kristol and Nathan Glazer, who early on understood that unfettered social science publication must be free not just of the usual conventions but, no less, liberated from professional organizations for which boundary maintenance is more important than boundless vision. And yet, it is also the case that a firm like Transaction follows with admiration in the footsteps of great houses such as Oxford University Press, Cambridge University Press, Harvard University Press, University of Chicago Press, and the Johns Hopkins University Press. Without their pioneering role (and here one must also add the extraordinary efforts of the founders of Routledge & Kegan Paul and George Allen & Unwin in the United Kingdom) the social sciences would still be scrambling to find a proper set of homes. That we refer to publishing firms as "houses" may seem curious to the outsider, but to those of us who have spent a lifetime at this business, it is quite natural. It conveys a sense of people as well as purpose, of intimacy as well as function.

Indeed, my decade of service as social science advisory editor for Oxford University Press in the United States (following in the footsteps of Robert Nisbet) arguably was my most important training for the tasks later to be undertaken by Transaction. Under the quiet and unassuming tutelage of Sheldon Meyer, I came to appreciate the sense and nonsense of scholarly and professional publishing. To start with, Transaction's targeted mission-oriented activity cares little about whether a book is defined as a commercial book, a textbook, or a trade book. Such categories may prove useful for in-house administrative rationalization, but they are of little merit in title-by-title decision-making. In a nutshell, the key to "our" kind of publishing is to determine and define whether the book being published or the serial being launched is a good work. Sheldon Meyer helped me appreciate the fact that the ultimate category with which we work as publishers, whether in the sciences, history, or arts, or any specific category, is the quality of the end product. A title is defined by how well it is written, how clearly it addresses a unique theme, how honestly it presents its information, how precisely it draws its conclusions from what has come before, and how good is the work in the ethical sense of fulfilling some human goal beyond the vanity of the well turned phrase or fame of the author.

Seen in this way, a certain essential modesty is incumbent on those who aspire to lead through the power of words. The editorial director and chairman of a professional publisher, such as Transaction, is much like a conductor. We direct music written and played by others. And these "others" whom we select to publish form, over time, a community that in turn defines quality and goodness. The sum and substance for the result of these efforts is the "list"— the seasonal catalogue, the complete catalogue, the subject area brochures, the book announcements—all of these define the company of players and hence the company as such. The conductor that orchestrates these parts should do so with a sense of modesty, no less than grandeur of purpose. If he proceeds in this way, he has an opportunity to be successful. But even then, we remain at the mercy of larger, impersonal forces: the will of the university at which we reside as well as the whim of the economic market that determines just how much discretionary capital is available for books and journals and serials. In short, even the decent conductor, or in our vernacular, head of house, is not assured rousing success. The next day at the office, or the next letter of complaint, may disturb an equilibrium established over the course of years.

My great good fortune is having come to publishing from a life of scholarship and university teaching. It has sensitized me, and I hope continues to do so, to the centrality of the author to the process of publishing. The scholar in social science, as in all else, must face the blank page and put something on it that is compelling. He or she must anticipate a nameless critic who decries that something, must confront the wrath of academic colleagues who must pass judgment on that individual's right to a permanent post, and must face himself or herself with the horrible question: was the effort worthwhile? Worse, does anyone really care? The social scientist, for the most part, is closer to the poet in our age than to the crime story writer: he or she must come facetoface with the search for immortality, while always recognizing that such a search is undertaken by mortals in a world of six billion others each with a claim on this thing called the Earth. The scholarly publisher can scarcely offer a sufficient fiscal incentive, but this community can offer friendship and the protection of a community of excellence that can at least cushion the inevitable blows identified with the world of research and ideas.

New technologies have actually taught us what we should have recognized long ago and more clearly: that such material entities like books, serials, and journals are simply vehicles for the transmission of ideas. They have no more intrinsic merit than other media do: reading ideas on a screen, booting them from a CD-ROM, or reading aloud in an auditorium. Indeed, costs vary and durability is different. But while St. John had it right when he declared that "In the beginning was the word," he was wise enough not to declare whether that word was to be written or oral, divinely inspired, diabolically imposed, or shipped in packets to be digitally reassembled on arrival. The world of publishing brings us back to First Principles, including those that presumably guide our civilization as such. And all permanent things are ultimately about First Principles. They guide us in our actions as publishers and they are revealed by what we publish. It has been my great good fortune to spend a lifetime in social science—what I fervently believe to be the most distinctive and unique feature of intellectual life of the twentieth, and now the twentiethfirst, century. Like publishing itself, the longrange goals of social science research may be unwavering, but the forms of social research constantly change to meet the needs of the human race. The purpose of Transaction is to serve with honor and distinction both the eternal aims of the human race, and the endless variety of ways of anticipating and achieving such goals.

9

A PROLOGUE TO ACADEMIC FREEDOM

. . . .

"There are good arguments for retaining appointments on permanent tenure, but they have to be strengthened against challenges by the recognition that permanent tenure is a bilateral matter. It entails costs and weighty obligations on both sides." (Edward Shils, *The Order of Learning*, 1997, page 259)

Let me preface the following with an apology for its propositional form. When writing for myself, I sometimes take recourse in the logical mysticism of Wittgenstein's Tractatus, and try to figure just what a subject area is all about. And this assignment has been undertaken to explain to myself, in propositional form, what I am talking about when dealing with the theme of academic freedom.

I make no claim to any great breakthrough or enlightenment in a theme that has occupied the best as well as the most impaired minds in academic life. But by sharing my private thoughts on a highly publicized matter, perhaps others can be encouraged to provide their own definitions and frameworks for discourse on academic freedom. The positivist dictum that one must remain silent in the face of ignorance may be too much to expect, but we can enlarge upon specifics and reduce generalities that pervade this area.

[In this brief effort I seek formal frames of reference, that offer some hope for a broad reconsideration of academic freedom. These must be made within a context that recognizes both a process of human interaction as well as a structure of juridical codes.]

1   Academic Freedom is comprised of two words, not two worlds.

1:1   Academic pertains to a member of university or a similar institution of higher learning, or to a person or groups of persons engaged in excelling in scholarly pursuits.

1:1:1   Historically, the term derives from the Platonic "academy" or a place where the higher learning took place.

1:1:2   Since the Platonic academy was also a place where the counter-revolution against Athenian democracy was forged, the academy was from time immemorial saturated with political intrigue.

1:2   Freedom at its most elementary form is the opposite of being enslaved, or the quality of being able to avoid the arbitrary control of others.

1:2:1   There are two elements recognized to being free: acting without hindranceÿor restraint; and the ability to perform at recognized levels of excellence.

1:2:1:1 In the former or "positive" sense of being free are sharing fully in the privileges of citizenship and immunities from arbitrary punishments.

1:2:2   Another element in positive freedom is the capacity to act without restraint and not be punished for excessive or mistaken views.

1:2:2:1 In the "negative" sense of freedom we are governed by laws commonly arrived at, and behave in accordance with the restraints imposed by such laws.

1:2:3   A second element of freedom is mastery; the capacity to perform on an instrument or play a game at high levels that endow the actor with freedom as achievement of goals.

1:2:3:1 Freedom as equity and freedom as mastery often entail different dimensions on a human rights scale. The right to free speech is common to all people in a democratic society, the mastery of research activities is restricted to a community of knowers.

2   Academic Freedom thus pertains to the explanation of and search for freedom in the context of those peculiar set of institutions dedicated to learning and teaching that have emerged in Western culture.

2:1   Freedom in the academy has been specially valued since professionals and intellectuals are uniquely capable of defining its contents.

2:2   In addition, it is widely held that "the life of the mind" has a special need to be unfettered and unimpeded.

2:2:1   But since "the mind" in its nature cannot be fettered or impededõoutside of raw assault on the body as such, discourse on academic freedom is in effect discourse on the actual limits of actions or performances.

2:2:2   Actions and performances can take place within classrooms, as they pertain to direct impact on students under the control of grading systems; or they can take place in the larger canvas of college and university life.

2:3:2   Monitoring actions and performances is simpler in relation to the latter broad context than in the intimate setting of the classroom, often held as sacred and off grounds to visiting surveyors or police authorities.

2:4:1   Academic freedom or academic license within the classroom are indirectly observed and examined: through comments of students, written works of teachers, syllabi and reading lists distributed, authorized visitations, etc.

2:4:1:1 Academic freedom or academic license outside of the classroom are directly observed, examined and reported upon: in the media, in campus organi-zations and legal agencies such as faculty senates, and even in community-wide groups.

2:5:1 Given the availability of a plethora of monitoring devices, calls for higher surveillance and greater discipline usually amount to displeasure with the course of political ideology within an academic or even a general context.

3:1:1 We are thus led into examining the status of freedom and its components in a given setting. Academic freedom takes places in contexts, therefore definitions of its contents are subject to modification over time.

3:2:1 The principle is freedom is a general category while the academy is a specific location for its exercise.

3:3:3 Acceptable behavior in one social and political climate may be construed as unacceptable in others.

3:3:3:1 Example: Demands for racial equality at one point in time and one institution in place may be viewed as routine expressions of academic freedom, while at another time and place may be viewed as subversion of institutional norms.

3:4:1 As a consequence, there is an intrinsic relativism in defining academic freedom. This argues for maximum tolerance and minimum interference in the conduct of learning.

3:5:1 Polarizations and dualisms between acceptable limits of academic freedom are inherently unstable. What is heretical in one context may prove to be subversive in another. What is responsible in one context may prove to be irre-sponsible in another.

3:5:1:1 Contextual accountability therefore argues for the widest possible latitude in the definition and exercise of academic freedom.

4:0:1 Academic freedom translated into freedom within the academy is historically as well as contextually bound to the principle of tenure.

4:1:1 Tenure—whether land tenure or school tenure—is a system of rights and obligations, but also a system of property relationships.

4:1:1:1 The original meaning of academic tenure, or tenure in a university context is that the professor endowed has an ownership stake in the school and its func-tioning.

4:1:2 In this way, academic freedom was fused in the past to academic tenure. Claims continue to be made that this remains the case.

4:2:1 With the division of labor and the powerful separating of functions in the modern university, tenure lost its original meaning with respect to proprietary considerations, and became strictly speaking, a doctrine of lifelong secularized peerage.

4:2:2 While such a peerage system served remarkably well to protect the academic freedom of its holders, it does little for those outside the pale of that protection.

4:2:2:1 It might be claimed that the 'class struggles' between the haves and have-nots shifts in the modern university from those who do and do not hold tenured appointments.

4:3:1   In the modern context, therefore, relatively new mechanisms for the protection of academic freedom arise. These are adopted from the large societies of the West.

4:4:1   As the modern university becomes capitalized and sheds its feudal pastōfor better or worseōit becomes subject to pressures of union or quasi union organizations (such as the American Association of University Professors) and de-mands that the laws of the land be held applicable in campus settings.

4:4:2   In such modernizing circumstances, new forms of status emerge, i.e., the worth of being a student, the value of student teaching fellowships, etc. These become the fulcrum for advancing the notion of academic freedom to make it more inclusive and operational.

4:5:1   In such a modern environment, there is a virtual fusion of academic freedom and expressions of free speech as such. This makes punishment for tenure violations as a unique transgression extremely difficult.

4:5:1:1   The testing of civil rights has traditionally involved extremist beliefs and acts. So too is the testing of academic freedom in a modern context. Extremist views on everything from political alignments to sexual behavior become issues, or testing points for an expanded notion of academic freedom.

4:6:1   As a result, the same concerns expressed over First Amendment Rights emerge with respect to Academic Freedom, i.e., the relationship of rights and responsibilities, learning and license. These cannot be mandated apriori.

4:7:1   The merging of academic life to civil society thus leads to a looser approximation of the two in the conduct and affairs of personnel who make a living or go to school on a campus

5:0:1   The interpenetrating of content and context leads to a search for codification, to the search for the legal as well as moral foundations of academic freedom at century's end.

5:0:2   Codification in Western contexts has tended over time to expand the area of rights and narrow the area of responsibilities.

5:0:3   In a sense, this is nothing other than the course of democratic society as such, which leaves to the discretion of the individual all matters explicitly not retained by institutional authority.

5:0:4   The codification of tenure rules in 1940, while essentially serviceable in 1997ōas long as the social order itself remains essentially stable in its commitments to democratic normsōis subject to modification.

5:0:5   Some of the modifications have come about as a result of extending to the public domain what was formerly held to be private (or worse, outrageous) i.e., sexual behavior and preferences being the prime example.

5:0:5:1   Other modifications have come about as a result of shifting powers of faculty and students vis a vis administrative bodies,. i.e, academic trade unions and their equivalents among graduate students being examples.

5:0:5:2   Still other modifications have resulted from changes in the size and mission of the academy; colleges as such were limited in 1940 to the

97

talented tenth (and far less than that among minorities; in 1997, college may be viewed as high school by other means—broad based but without its compulsory features.

5:0:6   Matters of how legal definition of academic freedom have been or should be changed must always begin with actual changes in the social system, and not simply annoyances at the way the legal codes presently operate.

6:0:1   Academic freedom, considered apart from empirical content and historical context is a slogan—no better and no worse than flag waving and other patriot or anti-patriot games.

6:1:1   The best way to support academic freedom is through the character of intellectual work done. The performance and assessment of such work is itself the stuff of academic freedom.

6:2:1   As with all slogans, e.g., freedom of the press or civil rights, institutions are needed to provide the support and protection necessary for individuals to create and to act.

6:3:1   Institutional supports are required for students and administrators no less than teachers. The academy is essentially rooted in this triad—each with justifiable claims, each with complaints of abrogations of freedom.

6:4:1   Each segment of the academy like each segment of a democratic society as such, must have safeguards to guarantee freedom of assembly and rights to press for interest-driven claims.

6:5:1   In the process of such external and internal interactions, academy freedom is protected because it is constantly being asserted—not as slogan, but as act.

6:5:1:1   In the course of national events, when the penumbra of specific institutions are threatened by assaults on the general institution of the Republic itself, there will be legitimate retrenchments of academic freedom.

6:5:1:2   When such external menaces to the Republic cease to exist, such as the defeat of fascism or the collapse of communism, definitions of academic freedom are likely to expand.

6:5:1:3   The explanation for the extension of academic freedom into formerly perceived private realms, such as sexual conduct, is a function of expanding opportunities and declining threats.

6:6:1   Enlarging the scope of democracy entails potential for exaggeration, mannerism, excess—phenomena that are often identified with the young, and hence with those who teach the young.

6:7:1   Since the academy is a place for experimentation it is also most likely to be the place for exaggeration. Those who would curb academic freedom must be prepared to limit experimentation.

6:7:1:1   Those who would protect and defend the academy and its traditions must be equally prepared to limit and curb freedom—in the name of corporate responsibility.

6:7:1:2   Those who would protect and defend freedom and its tradition must be prepared to accept and acknowledge broader definitions and visions of the academy—and risk a narrower view of responsibilities.

7:1:1   We thus arrive at the core reason for the dilemma confronting academic freedom: they are two words that lean in profoundly opposite epistemic directions.

7:2:1   Making the two words work together in the empirical world requires a substantial amount of bargaining, adjudication, and compromise ōtalents not in heavy supply to the human raceōespecially where differential sets of interests and limited amounts of cash are involved.

7:3:1   Academic freedom is thus the mirror image of civil rights and responsibilities. It is a concept, a phrase, a slogan, that changing meanings over time to meet the internal needs of university life and the external needs of social existence.

7:4:1   Having arrived at this point, the real story of academic freedom can begin, but only by empirical analysis and historical research of sanctions and constraints on the conduct of scholars and the course of scholarship. The rest is speculation.

99

Lecture delivered at the third meeting of the National Association of Scholars, October 3, 1998. Minneapolis, Minnesota.

10

THE AIMS AND PRINCIPLES
OF SOCIAL RESEARCH

. . . .

There were few more penetrating commentators on professional life in America than the late Everett Cherrington Hughes. In a series of articles, capped by one in *The American Psychologist* precisely a half century ago, in 1952, he discussed the relationship between science and profession and their impact on psychology. His observations remain central to the current agenda of social research, and they merit direct quotation. "The question of competence is discussed in complete separation from the outcome for the client. In protecting the reputation of the profession and the professional from just criticism, and in protecting the client from incompetent members of the profession, secrecy can scarcely be avoided. Secrecy and institutional sanctions thus arise in the profession as they do not in the pure science."

Hughes was not launching a broadside against professional life so much as noting that its imperatives and directives depart substantially from the norms of scientific method. In his time, he fought mightily to expand the responsibility of professions to publics. He was in favor of increasing the scope and size of occupations, thereby broadening the opportunity for participation. The problem became that these occupations gave rise to new professions. And while this plurality, this multiplicity, accorded with Hughes' sense of the free and open marketplace, he could hardly anticipate the next step in the evolution of professionalism in America: the developing effort of the professions to serve as imperial vanguards for the "science" they were supposedly serving. This is the current focus of struggle between scientific research and professional organization—whether to service the professional or to serve the public. Changes in the life of the academy will occur rapidly, or not at all, depending on what takes place in the field of scientific struggle.

The lacuna in Hughes' analysis was his failure to see that the struggle over the nature of science in society takes place largely within professional life. It does not emerge simply as some antinomial relationship with occupational roles. Each profession reflects a discipline with a unique inner history. In economics the struggle is between monetarist and institutionalist claims about reaching the nirvana of equilibrium. In sociology the struggle is between functional-positivist and cultural-subjectivist modalities. In anthropology it is a struggle between the traditional notion of empirical work in the field and those for whom the field is no longer overseas, but occurs rather in the forces of oppression at home. In political science, the gulf between normative theorizing and empirical description could hardly be wider. In psychology, the key rift, indeed rupture, is between clinical uncovery and experimental discovery as methods for determining evidence. In short, professional life is closely allied to pivotal conflicts and movements within each of the social science professions. Hughes saw largely external forms of combat, those in which the administrative apparatus of professions act pre-emptively, not infrequently behind the backs of its own membership. But the play of forces on a professional level involves interior dynamics that must be identified by those who want to understand the superstructure of social science.

This may appear to be an elliptical, even quarrelsome, way to open a review of forty years of *Society*, but we think otherwise. As a publication that must serve the public if it hopes to survive, much less to extend its position in the social science world, *Society* and its readers must come to grips with a new militancy on the part of professions. This is especially the case with social science organizations that consider themselves keepers of the flame, special interest group missionaries and political activists. Along with this view of their role comes the need to extend their grip on their membership, but also to weaken all other rivals for control of public organizational efforts. Hughes certainly appreciated that for better or worse we share an open society premised on free enterprise. Some professional organizations make no bones as to their own preference for planned and regimented social systems. Especially now, as the communication of ideas, facts, and information becomes not only a competition for attention but also a distribution of influence, the defensiveness of leadership in professional organizations is all the more appalling. In such an ideological climate, it is inevitable that these organizations seek to dominate not only membership scrolls, but also struggle to control communication outlets of the sciences. And that is where the issue is joined on the ground— between the pursuit of science and the self-interest of professions.

It has been often said, that imitation is the sincerest form of flattery. This year both the American Sociological Association and the American Political Science Association have announced new publications that are aimed at a larger public. It seems to be a particularly propitious moment to review where *Society* stands in relation to the social sciences in general. It is equally appropriate to review those organizations that represent a substantial segment of professional practitioners of the social sciences.

While *Society* remains open to a wide variety of viewpoints and methods of research, it does not endorse anarchy. *Society* continues to provide a framework for struggle: for the human sciences and against anti-human ideologies. The commitment to this link is a hallmark of the social sciences, one that distinguishes them from the physical sciences. Integral to the very nature of the social science enterprise is the effort to demystify the world. This requires a sustained struggle against other methods to fix belief, which either escalate beyond all reason one aspect of conflict (e.g., class struggles) or diminish to the point of complacency those relics of authority and tradition that fester as disappointments against a dynamically changing world. It also requires finding a place for people under a scientific umbrella that attempts to build and not to destroy.

The character of social science changed dramatically in the past century. From the traditional "big five" emerged a much larger group of disciplinary activities: communication studies, demography, urban affairs, policy and evaluation research, criminology, and many others. Social theory is common to all social science, new and old. Methodology is equally common to all of the social and behavioral sciences. The concept of a "general theory," or an imperial vision of any one social science over all others, is a useful fiction whose end has clearly arrived. Even a cursory review of such attempts also suggests a futility about what a post-imperial vision would look like. But the imperial vision was never simply a catching-up to modernity; it was born of a deeply conservative impulse to discover what makes life meaningful and worth living. In its transformation into a variety of utopian meandering, the theories of totality have finally given way to more modest endeavors that seek to give an account of and to predict social change. This is why it is all the more disconcerting that professional organizations have failed to learn the lessons of failed theorizing on the grand scale. Such organizations have become empires themselves.

The very effort to reach out to a larger public compels breaking the boundaries of disciplines set in abstract categories. We are in an age in which social science is driven by issues and events, not ideologies—by concrete human and global needs rather than inherited systems. This is not to say that the social sciences are now Balkanized, positivistic, or immune to general theory. It is to say that the basic mission of the social sciences is now more clearly demarcated and delineated than it was in the past.

It is dangerous for old doctrines to claim superior wisdom over and against new formulations of a more modest sort. We find such self-serving claims gratuitous and self-defeating, even if in the short-term they appear to be self-sustaining. We can recognize the achievements of the past without developing inhibiting icons that presume decay in the professional culture. It is true enough that the parameters of social science have changed significantly in the past forty years—and they doubtless will in the next forty as well. It is always better to avoid ethical labels and focus instead on identifying and developing the best of the present. That is an essential task of *Society*.

It is also essential to ensure that our publications help scholars, younger ones in particular, think outside the box in which they were presumably trained. Associations are jealous, and often unforgiving, animals. They want to serve as the reservoir of all learning, and to convince their members that all truth resides within a single mansion. The alarming tendency of professional societies to pace their own stamp on societies publications is at the same time an effort to delegitimate publications beyond their direct control. This has become a critical struggle of the moment, for professional associations today are far more insidious and powerful than they were forty years ago. They give rewards and convey status, and they do not wish others to do so. Although there are a plethora of journals in each of the social sciences, those publications that carry the stamp of officialdom are generally favored with respect to tenure and promotion.

That there is a broad recognition of the risks and dangers of professional imperialism is made evident by the rise of new scholarly groups in psychology, history, economics, and culture, all of which have emerged, from older disciplines. Beyond that, we need to factor in the rise of new disciplines whose fund of knowledge and inspiration comes mainly from the social sciences. *Society* fosters all such movements toward free and independent thought— even though its editors sometimes hold persuasions that differ from the impulses that give rise to such breakaway associations. The path of democratic struggle is not a perverse insistence on a particular interpretation of events. It serves as an exemplar to general forces of academic and policy life that advance the open society.

There are essentially three ways in which a better balance between professional desires and public needs can be brought into some sort of equilibrium. In each instance, the courage and fortitude that individuals have had in the past, or will have in the future, will make this worthy outcome take place.

First, new fields of research and theory, such as those already mentioned, continue to evolve. Such new combinations and permutations will prevent old-line societies from hardening of the arteries. Areas such as criminology, for example, boast seven different organizations. Forty years ago this field was nascent, and part of sociology or psychology departments. The explosion of social science knowledge has brought about associations that dwarf in size, and even in importance, older academic formations.

Second, a consequence of this knowledge explosion has been a parallel emergence of new journals. These enlist a whole new cluster of editors and contributors, taking place throughout policy organizations and university departments in Europe and Asia no less than North America. Such journals often acquire a status and importance to specialist audiences that dwarfs the stifling conformity of old-line journals. Indeed, in international relations, journals such as *Foreign Affairs, Foreign Policy, Orbis,* and *National Interest* easily outshine, in terms of professional significance, the publications of academic organizations grounded in international and regional associations.

Third, even within old-line organizations a "twigging effect" is taking place. In areas as distinct as psychology, history, and cultural studies, new societies have emerged to challenge—sometimes directly, other times elliptically—established organizations. Indeed, the five major organizations that represent anthropology, political science, sociology, economics, and psychology were all formed roughly one hundred years ago, at least in the United States. The wonder of it all is how these big five have managed to hold sway for as long as they have. But again, in basic social science fields, reality has overtaken sloth to the point that professional life can ill afford to ignore, much less disparage larger public concerns. Such fields as evaluation and policy, criminology and penology, communication and information, are not simply new national structures but international associations. These also challenge the parochial and insular quality of established traditional societies.

To speak of the parochial and insular character of older professional societies takes us into the realm of ideology and utopia. In violation of the Weberian distiction between the calling of science and the conduct of politics, too many of these old-line agencies act as if proclamations about the desirable are the same as statements about the actual. So we are offered hortatory proclamations on race, nationality, and sexuality ranging from demands for statehood of the District or Columbia, support for recognition of Saddam Hussein's Iraq, to assurances of new standards of the nuclear family. Some of these proposals may prove to be feasible political goals. But instead of opening up discourse concerning vital issues, they have the effect of closing down discussions. Instead of the scientific examination of abrasive social problems, we are offered smooth-talking palliatives that can barely be taken seriously as analytic claims, and even less seriously as professional platforms. Such tendentious postures serve only the cause of alienation from professional life and cynicism about the scientific calling.

This is not a call to arms, nor an effort to undo all the good that professional life has accomplished over the years in creating a scientific base and public trust in the work of social researchers. It is a call to attention that knowledge is organizationally defined and promoted. New research organizations have emerged from one end of the land to the other, and new centers of authority in universities formerly not considered part of the avant-garde have emerged. The collectivity of these developments has ensured the growth no less than the survival of *Society* over the last forty years, and it will continue to do so. Not only private will or private imagination assures continuity. Larger developments are an integral part to our human efforts.

If this cursory review of Transaction/*Society* at forty lacks the sort of elegiac note that might have been expected on so special an occasion, it is simply that self-satisfaction is a risky bit of emotional baggage to parade forth when so much is at stake and so much more still needs to be done. General theory may be in disrepute, but subjectivist anti-theory is a medication far worse than the disease. The vineyards are many; the field workers remain few. Perhaps forty years from now, our successors will be better able to stand back and survey the achievements of this publication. But for that great day to occur, we must first make sure that we do not become part of the wreckage of the past forty years. The triumph of social science and democracy over the forces of darkness is by no means assured in the book of life. We still require human intelligence and imagination to make good on such a bold vision. In a nutshell: after volume 40, number 1, comes volume 40, number 2. Making good on grand pledges for the future is, after all, an ongoing affair.

We close with a statement from Robert S. Lynd's *Knowledge for What?* It is a coda for what *Society* is all about. "Social science is confined neither to practical politics nor to things whose practicality is demonstrable this afternoon or tomorrow morning. Nor is its role merely to stand by, describe, and generalize, like a seismologist watching a volcano. There is no other agency in our culture whose role is to ask long range and if need be, abruptly irreverent questions of our democratic institutions, and to follow these questions with research and the systematic charting of the way ahead. The responsibility is to keep everlastingly challenging the present with the question: What is it that we human beings want and what things would have to be done, in what ways and in what sequence, in order to change the present so as to achieve it?"

11

SOCIOLOGY AND THE
COMMON CULTURE

· ·

In the first stanza of *The English Flag*, the great Rudyard Kipling defended worldliness against parochialism by asking—"And what should they know of England who only England knows?" I elect, with a small modification, to paraphrase Kipling in this farewell sermon to my colleagues at Rutgers. "And what should they know of Sociology who only Sociology knows?" Arguably, one could as easily ask this for political science, communication studies, psychology, or any number of subject areas in the human sciences. The point is simple enough: the world we inhabit is far more expansive to us than the fields in which we profess to possess expertise.

I sense that many if not most of us are keenly aware that ontology is greater than epistemology. The world about us is always larger than our slice of knowledge about that world. We are less aware of how to translate that sense of the world into the work we perform; or more critically, why so often our professional efforts fall dramatically short of expectations. What is it about our disciplines that shuts out the light to so much of our culture, and in so doing makes us impervious to the grand sweep of events, and more urgently, incapable of reaching an audience, much less the stars, with our work?

This would be a challenge to explain in an encyclopedia much less in a few minutes of your time. But I will cut to the quick and try my hand at a response. For I believe deeply that if we are to have an instauration, a Baconian rebirth of social scientific learning, a move beyond the parochialism of our moment, we need to address just this point. To some extent, the answer is found in the very notion of a common culture, that to which we are all privy, but choose to ignore, or even worse, denigrate, in the name of specialization, specificity, and stratification. While these are necessary attributes of social science today, without the shared passions of a common culture, specialization and specificity are simply limited exercises in futility and displeasure—our own.

Stratification, that great beast of sociology, permits us to make, nay encourages, distinctions predicated on race, class, gender, ethnicity, religion, language, tribe, neighborhood, city, state, nation, region, and even civilization. But to understand is not necessarily to resolve, or even to make a little better. Indeed, some efforts at distinction make things worse. For example, a distinguished psychologist, Professor Richard Lynn, informed the British Psychological Society on Friday, March 27th, 1998 (not 1898) that genetic engineering and natural trends would make a divided world a distinct possibility. "The two kinds of people would be so dissimilar that it would almost be like having two separate specimens of humankind." And for those obtuse enough to fail to get the point, he concludes by inventing the idea of an "intelligence gene pool," in which "the net effect is that IQ in wealthier countries was increasing at the rate of about 3 IQ points a decade. But in developing countries, the lowering of genetic intelligence was not compensated by [any corresponding] increase in environmental intelligence." With such thinking, with such a categorical denial of the commonality of the human race, could we have anything in store to look forward to other than a race war, and schisms even more hideous than those with which we have been faced this century? This is a rhetorical question only to those who prefer to walk about this planet with their eyes shut tight.

The daring restoration of racial modes of analysis, whatever their phylogenetic sources, indicates that our larger task can only be performed by an awareness and appreciation of what the human race has in common. Before the clever retort is made that I am falling into the trap of utopianism in order to escape the perils of reality, let me assure you that my life and work is such that bland optimism is remote from my mode of observation. I do not imagine for a moment that the common culture can wash away centuries of distinctions, discriminations and disasters. But it can at least move us away, however haltingly, from the widespread belief that armed struggle, mass violence, and the war between civilizations, are the only mechanisms left at our disposal in conflict resolution. Indeed, the common culture is the central instrument against the acceptance of impotent psychological, chemical, and medical placebos; pleas for togetherness based on common suffering, selfpity, and collective egotism, rather than core values.

In order to avoid confusion it should be said plainly that the common culture is not always nor uniformly comprised of great works of art, music or cinema—although they might help. But a common culture does have to cut deep into the consciousness of a society. For all of its historical flaws and ideological dispositions, the film *Titanic* well illustrates this. At one and the same time, the film explores issues of life and death, the power of nature over technology, love and hate, courage and cowardice, good and evil— the full range of philosophical polarities— while at the same time, the film also examines specific issues of social class on board the ship; ethnic relations between passengers and workers, male-female mores, generation gaps in such mores, and the mixed motives of people on board the fated vessel. Whether the film constitutes great art is a quite separate matter. Indeed, I think not. Its ability to reach people the world over, and in so doing, touch shared moral sentiments is beyond question.

I am not making a case for the mystical nor the metaphysical. Nor for that matter, would I urge upon you subjectivism, as if feelings can substitute for facts. We already have too much of that tendency prevalent in the social sciences. But, there is a type of knowledge so embedded in the culture, so profound, that it casts a bright light on all that it touches. Without that universal component, locating that which is universally true is virtually impossible. Whether expressed in art, music, poetry, whatever, the core values derived from the common culture inspire us the more because they provide grounds for shared communication and understanding. T.S. Eliot captured this sentiment well in his essay on Christianity and Culture: "The culture of an individual is dependent upon the culture of a group or class, and the culture of the group or class is dependent upon the culture of the whole society to which that group or class belongs. Therefore it is the culture of the society that is fundamental." To make this point more concrete, or at least less abstract, I should like to illustrate how the common culture underwrites my work. And if it seems that I am engaging in shameless namedropping, I hasten to note that these are my giants. You have every right, indeed, every obligation, to select your own gallery of saints, and to make your own statement not just of what you write or teach, but who you are. Ultimately, the need of the moment is to connect the learning we so freely impart to others with the deepest images we have of ourselves and who we aspire to be.

What is so strange, as we close this millennium, is not just a lack of culture, but a revolt against culture. In its place we find a series of canards about Reconstruction, relativity of values, and the racial or ethnic bases of judgment itself. In these various guises inheres the denial that classical values in the common culture even exist. The social carriers of such nihilist rubbish have even managed to betray the best in the Marxian tradition, what was referred to by Raymond Williams as the long tradition, a major source which in decades past was an engine infusing culture into sociology. With the collapse of the Soviet Empire, and the near universal rejection of communist tyranny, has come a revolt against history itself, and with it, a rebellion against the cultural tradition that nourished the "illusions" of radicals and reactionaries alike. A wave of instantaneous and immediate gratification has affected sociology in particular, making it subject to a crude empiricism that serve the ends of know-nothingism. Put another way, as Richard Rorty recently noted in *Achieving Our Country*, we are victims of "a spectatorial, disgusted, mocking [cultural] Left, given over to semiconscious anti-Americanism." In a less impassioned way, what needs to be said is that the conservative cause fears egalitarianism as subversive of liberty; while the liberal cause far too frequently see egalitarianism as a stepping stone to supremacy. It remains the essential task of an honest sociology of knowledge, to look at both unflinchingly in the spirit of Karl Mannheim, and expose as well as explore the self-interest of ideology and the illusion of utopia alike.

The cultural thread is at one and the same time universal and national. In a democratic society such as ours, the breakdown of the former results in the loss of the latter. America is at odds with itself in a cultural shuffle. A transvaluation of liberal values took place between the midtwentieth century and the end of the century. We had F.O. Matthiessen's *The American Renaissance*; Daniel J. Boorstin's *An American Primer*; Henry Steele Commager's *The American Mind*; a plethora of outstanding books on Irish ethnicity, Jewish identity, Boston community, and Max Lerner's seriously underrated summing up *American As A Civilization*. Indeed, the idea of an American century generated by Henry Luce lurked behind some of these works, and celebration became a common and not always pleasant denominator. Patriotism, ethnic identity, and pluralistic religion became ascriptive touchstones for a nation triumphant in two world wars. But all of this seemed to add up to a wholesome unity of sentiment and purpose.

By the close of this century, diversity remained a theme, but unity of means and ends did not. Instead, the measurement of liberal values was conflated into a pseudodemographic counting of race, gender and class (running a distant third with the demise of Marxism as a universal faith). The slightest deviance from am imaginary egalitarian norm became a cause for moaning and groaning. Aesthetic judgment and scientific worth yielded to social variables of a spurious sort. For example, as soon as issues of women in the workplace was resolved in wage terms, the goals shifted to harassment in the workplace. The slightest undercount from census to professional panel representation became the subject of a new ideological cause, a new social movement, a new contention concerning political gerrymandering. In the process, the sense of the whole, the sense of America dissolved, and with it, the notion of a common culture. All this took place in the lofty environment of academic life. Happily, untouched was the ordinary American sense of personal balance, respect for law, and measurement of worth by performance not color or sex or ethnic background. The failure of new movements to reposition stratification within a properly egalitarian mode is such that animosity has become a permanent part of the American psychological experience. At the same time, the extremism of such new movements within the academy reflect the inner history of university expansion more than any common thread. Indeed, the animus of the new stratification advocates reveals more in common with the old elitism than the new populism. The classic liberal assumption that a person, whatever his or her race, religion or national origin should count as one—not more than and not less than one—dissolved into a rush to repair historic injustices by the imposition of current injustices. Conservatism did not emerge triumphant, but liberalism suffered a stunning collapse of nerve. And in this new climate of division, revolutionary advocates of fanaticism, secessionism, subjectivism and relativism rode in like the four horses of the apocalypse to stake their claims.

This end-of-century situation must be spoken of frankly if we are to move beyond the current dualism between culture and sociology, one that is far more polarized and pervasive, than the two cultures of which C.P. Snow spoke more than thirty years ago. At stake is not just the soul of American liberal thought, but the heart of sociology itself, or that wing of it given over to the study of large systems and whole societies. The present status of the field reveals polarization between those performing bookkeeping functions that do not require a theoretical grounding much less a culture, and those engaged in a mysticism that requires for evidence little else than one's own personal proclivities, biases and experiences. This condition cannot long endure. Sociology is already badly shredded. In the present cocoon-like atmosphere inhabited by our profession's administrative directorate, one finds joyous disregard for the cares of the larger world, and concern only for victims which sociology preemptively declares to be morally virtuous.

The concern for a common culture is neither a flight into elitism nor a trip into anti-intellectualism. Nor is it a vague regard for esoterica of past centuries. The common culture is a concern for those shared values that make possible innovation and understanding in our own work. To hear the final round of works of Dmitri Shostakovich is not just to hear tough music. It is to share with the Russian people a revolt against its tyranny in one of the few forms permissible during the final stage of Stalinism—pure music. In the ripping and tearing of a David Oistraikh on the Violin Concerto or Matislav Rostropovich wailing on the Cello Concerto we find the reason for Russia itself.

In language as well as music, in the rich literary heritage extending from Anton Chekhov to Aleksandr Solzhenitsyn we find answers to social riddles. What Vladimir Lenin understood about Czarist bureaucracy as expressed in *Ward Number 6*, his adversaries came to appreciate about Communist bureaucracy as expressed in *The Cancer Ward*. Culture is an instrument of truth, not because it seeks to perform any tendentious political role, but because it mirrors the inner life of a society with greater force than any other mode of quotidian activity. With a knowledge of the common culture we sociologists are drawn to the central considerations of this age; giving them a full play in terms we know best: patterns of stratification and hierarchy, types of interaction typifying each society.

As with Solzhenitsyn's trilogy *The Gulag Archipelago*, we have again been reminded this time by Stephane Courtois in *The Black Book of Communism* of the cost attached to the breakdown of a common culture. Whole categories of people, real or imagined—Cossacks, Kulaks, bourgeois reactionaries—were exterminated in Russia, not for anything they had done, but for who they were. Concentration camps, forced labor, and terror were elevated to a system of government. Communism invoked "class," and Nazism invoked "race." Together, these twin scourges of the century liquidated people who in the eye of the rulers had already been condemned by history at one end and genetics at another. And as Tony Judt reminds us in reviewing Courtois' work: "Mass murder was not an unintended consequence, but part of the Fascist and Communist projects from the start." It reached a crescendo when in true Orwellian fashion, the Maoist Chinese revolution within a revolution, managed to wipe out all culture—save the book of its leader. The Nazis had book burning, the Communists avoided that embarrassment by having few books—and those published by the government printing press. We are flanked by those extremists who think social science is a means to a political end. This is insidious nonsense. The social sciences are ends in themselves. They are systems of human organization which serve the ends of knowledge, not the holders of power, or for that matter, wouldbe holders of power.

American life managed to avoid the worst excesses of twentieth century European experience. The core culture has helped. Our language and literature offer a treasure chest from which themes can be drawn to enrich social science. There is Ella Kazan's appreciation of communist and fascist politics in *A Face in the Crowd*; the twin themes of greed and national betrayal in Arthur Miller's *All My Sons*, of family dissolution and drug addiction in Eugene O'Neill's *Long Days Journey into the Night*; of male brutishness and insecurities yoked to female dreams and illusions in Tennessee Williams' *Streetcar Named Desire*. And more abstractly in musical terms, there is the sense of space one finds in Aaron Copeland's *Appalachian Spring* and *Billy the Kid*; the sense of America discovering its moral soul in everything George Gershwin did, from *Porgy and Bess* to *An American in Paris*, the urban and ethnic tensions in Leonard Bernstein's *West Side Story*, the Reconstruction of patriotism in Charles Ives' national marches as well as *Three Places in New England*; the native romanticism in Samuel Barber's *Adagio For Strings and Orchestra*; the interplay of blues and joys in Scott Joplin's ragtime. These too are themes rich in content for serious ethnography. Indeed, to study Black life in America in a serious way is to spend a lifetime listening to Jelly Roll Morton and Theolonius Monk in one's so-called spare time.

Can one forget the place of film in the formation of an American consciousness, not to mention social movements? Film may not have been an American discovery, but it most certainly has become our art form par excellence. Can one honestly understand American national character without a close look at Charlie Chaplin in *City Lights* and *Modern Times*, Katharine Hepburn in *The Philadelphia Story*, Humphrey Bogart in *Casablanca*, Orson Welles in *Citizen Kane*, Marlon Brando in *On The Waterfront*, Sidney Poitier in *A Raisin in the Sun*, or Jack Nicholson in *Five Easy Pieces* or *Chinatown*? Doubtless I am revealing my preferences as well as my age. But it would not take too much for each of you to generate your own preferences. The point is that we all have share an experience of these films because we all share in a common culture. The national mosaic is about John Walker's *Halliwell's Film Guide*. and Stanley Sadie's *The New Grove Dictionary of Music and Musicians* as well as David Sills' *Encyclopedia of the Social Sciences*.

Everyone in this room can pick and choose their own favorites in all these areas. What we can hardly avoid is the impact of the visual, of sight wedded to sound, on our sense of social life. Art imitates life and life imitates art because they are essentially one and the same: aspects of the common culture. Nor is this always a pleasant or positive thought. I sometimes think that what now cements the United States of America is CBS, NBC, ABC and CNN, and what we call politics is something which takes place in a small place called "Inside the Beltway"—that view of the universe held by those who inhabit Washington DC. Even such a concentration of communications is a source of social science potential to those of who live "Outside the Beltway" in America. The struggle of the twentieth century increasingly involves those who control the channels of communication; just as assuredly as the struggle of the nineteenth century took place over control of the means of production. We participate in this struggle in our small way and on a daily basis at Transaction. That is what every scholarly publisher which attempts to transcend the parochial aims to achieve. To do otherwise is to separate sociological means from political ends; as the demographers did under Nazi Germany, as they figured out the block by block configuration of Jews and Gentiles in cities like Berlin Warsaw, and Vienna. Separating means from ends, they could do this dance of death without batting an eye as to how such data was to be used

All societies have a cultural realm, for it is in the culture that we join ranks with others. Of course there are differences of quality in these cultures. Judgments will vary on such points. But it is precisely the common culture that gives us a humanity in common, that permits us to feel the same way about the big things, about life and death, about love and hate, about lies and truths, about goods and evils—about Shakespeare and Goethe; Cervantes and Dante, Tolstoi and Melville. On such matters, being a man or a women, a black or a white, young or old, a Russian or an American, dwindle in importance. Ascription and achievement may help us to identify and predict forms of behavior at the level of social hierarchy or voting behavior. But at night we must confront our mortality and our morality. And on such matters, in the privacy of our souls, it is the common culture that trumps the stratified sample.

This is not a plea for a Eurocentric in contrast to an American vision. It would be ironic to hold up for emulation a civilization that served as a charnel house for more than one hundred million people in the course of this twentieth century. Nor is this a plea for elitism, snobbery, or even for higher education. Mozart trios and quartets were played on the way to the gas chambers for many of those millions. The forces of human destruction are at work wherever nihilism, relativism, and subjectivism gain a foothold; often disguised as a reinterpretation or "deconstruction" of the great works of civilization In this, in culture as in sociology, Europe sheds light, but also reveals the darkness of a culture divorced from the person.

Let me conclude by noting what is all too easily ignored. Our culture is common because our concerns are common; but not cheap: life and death, love and hate, friends and enemies, success and failure, virtue and vice. In short, every polarity and a wide range of emotions in between are the core concerns of us all. The sociologist will examine how different sets of people perceive such grave matters. The political scientist will examine how government addresses such polarities in search of a consensus. Psychologists will have a field day figuring out why polarities of mind are so critical in moral judgment. Economists will see these categories as evidence for or against market forces. But at the end of the day, our common culture will help us renew our shared humanity. And in this ineluctable fact, in our historical inheritance of decency and democracy, is the best hope we have for the survival and growth of the social sciences.

These things I do believe. I hope you will forgive the shuttling about in theme and topic. Personal beliefs, unlike formal systems, are not always neat and tidy. But then again, neither is the course of science or the projects of society. The university is an assemblage of diverse voices singing many songs in many tongues. It is also a place in which students vote with their feet and agencies with their money as to which areas are important. The students, are the future, the bearers of our common culture. Let us take heed. For they also tell us for whom and when the owl of Minerva strikes. To mock the young is a sure sign of our own dotage. To simply imitate the young is a sure sign of our foolishness. The vast gray area between mocking and mimesis is one that we must navigate. Armed with both the exact tasks of our disciplines and the general appreciation of the common culture, we in the social sciences have a continuing chance at survival and even growth—and helping others do likewise.

Such an outcome will take a great deal of courage as well as culture. And if I may be permitted to conclude as I began with reference to a British tradition, to which I confess an abiding life long affection, we can have no better guide than Matthew Arnold's finale to his masterful *Culture and Anarchy*: "In all directions our habitual courses of action seem to be losing efficaciousness, credit and control, both with others and even with ourselves. Everywhere we see the beginnings of confusion, and we want a clue to some sound order and authority. This we can only get by going back upon the actual constructs and forces which rule our life, seeing them as they really are, connecting them with other interests and forces, and enlarging our whole view and rule of life." I take this to be neither a pessimistic nor optimistic reading of events, simply a call to what we do best: think and behave seriously about the affairs and actions of our fellow human beings.

Remarks delivered at a retirement dinner held for the author, sponsored by the department of sociology, Rutgers University, and held at the Eagleton Institute of Politics, May 14, 1998.

12

FACTS, VALUES, AND SCIENCE
· ·

I am deeply honored to receive the first International Academy of Humanism Award in Public Service and Science offered by the Center for Inquiry. Paul Kurtz is a life long friend, a colleague who dates back to close association with such special and diverse people as Marvin Farber, Lewis Feuer, Sidney Hook, and Roy Wood Sellars. For several years now, Paul has been a member of the Board of Directors of Transaction Publishers at Rutgers University. His acute knowledge of publishing has been an invaluable guide.

This gathering also has as its most distinguished person from McGill University, the great philosopher of science, and my senior by a decade, Mario Bunge. My own relationship with Mario goes back to the mid-1950s–when we were both contributors to *Science & Society* and *Philosophy & Phenomenological Research*. Mario has served as our editor at large in the philosophy of science field. So in a sense, while this is a new chapter in the intellectual and organizational life of the Center for Inquiry, it closes the circles in some magical way on the three of us. Indeed, I accept this award, as something made possible by the courage and fortitude of Paul, Mario and countless pioneers in the philosophy of science and the open-ended approaches to volatile issues of human rights and obligations.

In this brief comment I only want to say that I have come to believe that if we are to prevail–and by "we" I mean not just academics, but public servants, and serious laborers in the world of public opinion and ideas, it must take place in a return to the Jamesian premise that the intellectual class must unite and close ranks for ends unto itself, a class with traditions and goals that are not defined by parochial loyalties or party affiliations. The world has enough servants of power; it needs careful critics of power. In so doing, we must also return to Kant's commonsensical belief that everything should be subject to the free and public examination of reason grounded on itself and confined to itself. This is not a mechanical, Weberian plea insisting upon a separation of the political and the scientific, it is rather to appreciate the degree to which the sciences must inform politics. Science cannot simply be circumscribed by politics or worse, by the limited vision of funding agencies. Its mandate includes an autonomy that moves well beyond the boot of masters who both rule and are ruled by ideology.

What this requires on the ground, in quotidian life, is fewer belligerences and greater civility; respect for views other than those we hold near and dear. Yes, there are limits to civility: The entire 20th century bore witness to a hideous round of genocides–extending across continents and as well as nations, in nations dedicated to high culture and those advocating an end to history. At such moments civility should be trumped by concerns of survival. But let us make sure that we distinguish real culprits from cultural traditions that remain vital even as they may go awry. Public policy and scientific activities require distinctions—between those with whom we differ and those whom we consider beyond redemption. There are no magic formulas, no special incantations that will allow us to make such distinctions. And yet, people like ourselves, whom we hold as colleagues, are in the business of cooling passions so that we can continue cultures.

For more than a half century: first with Paine–Whitman Publishers, then with Oxford University Press, and for the past 42 years with Transaction, I have had the task of a daily confrontation primarily with myself, and at times with others, as to what constitutes good scholarship, good policy, and good science. After more than four thousand books published, something like fifty journals and serials operating within our mandate, I must still try to make decent judgments on ultimate truths. I daresay the same is the case for many of you in this room. We will err, sometimes on the side of passion other times on the side of caution. We will, in the process, change our minds on what constitutes high quality from momentary judgment. We will regret missed opportunities due to being unduly reserved in our decision-making; and no less, mistaking the novel for the durable.

To those who have had such experience, I would recommend a Marx-like code derived from the ancient skeptics: doubt everything This should be leavened by an Oakeshott-like resolution: sit down for a decent meal, with those who views are dissimilar from your own; and see if there are grounds for resolution. If not, then carry the struggle to its conclusion. But keep in mind the costs of struggle, and at the end of the day what it may do to the victor no less than the vanquished. As Isaac Baschevis Singer once said: there are two ways of dealing with evil: to confront it head-on and without compromise. The problem is that such confrontation may also be an embrace of the very evils we seek to oppose (fanaticism, subjectivism, mysticism, dictatorship, and sheer mayhem). Under such circumstances, you might want to consider the option: walk away and live to fight another day.

In a world of polarizations, perhaps the most difficult idea to absorb is the naturalistic one: there are various gradations of good and infinite shadings of evil. The task of social science is to make some clear-eyed distinction of what sort of struggles we want to fight for and which we want to walk away from. Our human commitment is to life and not death. This is not much of a message to offer such a distinguished gathering, but at 75 years of age, I still carry on the struggle, bent, sometimes beaten, but not broken. I like the idea of living another day as evidence of the worthiness of life itself—and also the prospects of victory for what we believe is worth the struggle. But we must also recognize the need for a world in which defeat is not disgrace—and not subject to punishment by the victor. Such homiletics may offer small comfort—sermonizing rarely does. This is all the more reason to moderate our passions as we sharpen our principles. Good evening and thank you.

Remarks delivered at "Science and Ethics" conference sponsored by the International Academy of Humanism/Center for Inquiry at the Courtyard Marriott Hotel, in Toronto, Canada. May 15, 2004.

BIBLIOGRAPHY: 1951-2004

1951

001 "Cultural Reaction in Plato's Thought." *Journal of Social Studies*, Vol. 7, No. 2, 1951, pp. 28-33. [article]

1952

002 THE RENAISSANCE PHILOSOPHY OF GIORDANO BRUNO. Boston: Coleman-Ross Publishers, 1952, 150 pp. [book]

1954

003 CLAUDE HELVETIUS: PHILOSOPHER OF DEMOCRACY AND ENLIGHTENMENT. New York: Paine-Whitman Publishers, 1954, 204 pp. [book]
Republished. New York: Humanities Press, 1959.
Reissued. Ann Arbor, Mich.: University Microfilms International, 1983.

004 *Diderot and Descartes: A Study of Scientific Naturalism* (Avram Vartanian). *Science and Society*, Vol. 18, No. 2, Spring 1954, pp. 185-87. [review]

005 *John Stuart Mill* (Karl Britton). *Science and Society*, Vol. 18, No. 4, Fall 1954, pp. 282-83. [review]
Translation (German). *Deutsche Zeitschrift für Philosophie*, Vol. 6, No. 5, 1955, pp. 785-86.

006 *Giant in Chains* (Barrows Dunham). *Mainstream*, Vol. 7, No. 1, December 1954, pp. 60-62. [review]

1955

007 "On Pragmatism." *Science and Society*, Vol. 19, No. 3, Summer 1955, pp. 259-62. [article]

008 *The Pragmatic Philosophy of Charles S. Peirce* (Manley Thompson); *Peirce and Pragmatism* (W. B. Gallie). *Science and Society*, Vol. 19, No. 1, Winter 1955. [review]

009 *Pragmatism: Philosophy of Imperialism* (Harry K. Wells). *Science and Society*, Vol. 19, No. 1, Winter 1955. [review]

010 *Introduction to Philosophy* (John Lewis). *Science and Society*, Vol. 19, No. 4, Fall 1955, pp. 354-58. [review]
Translation (German). *Deutsche Zeitschrift für Philosophie*, Vol. 7, No. 4, pp. 625-27.

1956

011 "Tolstoy and Gandhi: The Pacifist Utopia." *Iscus* (New Delhi, India), Vol. 3, No. 2, Spring 1956, pp. 3-25. [article]

012 "The New Conservatism." *Science and Society*, Vol. 20, No. 1, Winter 1956, pp. 1-26. [article] †‡
Translation (Spanish). "Los conservadores de hoy." *La Gaceta*, Vol. 5, Whole No. 53, May 1975.

013 "Gandhi in Retrospect." *Dipika* (New Delhi, India), Vol. 5, No. 2, 1956, pp. 3-25. [article]

014 *Ends and Means in Education: A Mid-Century Appraisal* (Theodore Brameld). *Science and Society*, Vol. 20, No. 2, Spring 1956, pp. 155-57. [review]

1957

015 THE IDEA OF WAR AND PEACE IN CONTEMPORARY PHI-LOSOPHY (with an introduction by Roy Wood Sellars). New York: Paine-Whitman Publishers, 1957, 224 pp. [book]
Translation (Spanish, by Pablo Levin). Buenos Aires: Editorial Nueva Visión-Galatea, 1959.
Translation (Polish, by Bernard Olejniczak) Warsaw: Panstwowe Wyndawnictwo Wiedza Powszechna, 1960.

016 "East German Marxism Renaissance and Repression." *Dissent*, Vol. 4, No. 4, Fall 1957, pp. 393-401. [article]

017 "Bernard J. Stern, Anthropologist In Memoriam." *The American Socialist*, Vol. 4, No. 2, February 1957. [article]

018 "*A Propos de l'idée de guerre et de paix dans la philosophie contemporaine.*" *La Pensée Revue du Rationalisme Moderne*, New Series, Whole No. 76, November-December 1957, pp. 129-31. [article]

019 "Bertrand Russell on War and Peace." *Science and Society*, Vol. 21, No. 1, Winter 1957, pp. 30-51. [article]

020 "History and Ideology." *The Genesis of Plato's Thought* (Alban Dewes Winspear). *The American Socialist*, Vol. 4, No 3, March 1957, pp. 21-22. [review-essay]

021 *Thomas Hobbes* (Richard Peters). *Science and Society*, Vol. 21, No. 3, Summer 1957, pp. 284-86. [review]

1958

022 LA SOCIOLOGÍA CIENTÍFICA Y LA SOCIOLOGÍA DEL CONOCIMIENTO. Buenos Aires: Librería Hachette, Colección El Mirador, 1958, 148 pp. [book]

023 "Edgar Zilsel: una apreciación retrospectiva." *Cuadernos de Sociología*, Vol. 11, No. 11, 1958. Boletín del Instituto de Sociología de la Universidad de Buenos Aires, pp. 147-51. [introduction]

024 "Der Begriff der Freiheit von Hegel zu Marx." *Sammelband über das Verhaltnis des Marxismus zur Philosophie Hegels* (edited by Wolfgang Harich). Berlin: Deutscher Verlag der Wissenschaften, 1958. [article]

025 "The Moral and the Ethical." *Philosophy and Phenomenological Research*, Vol. 19, No. 1, September 1958, pp. 104-7. [article]

026 "Los fundamentos empíricos de la sociología del concimiento." *Cuadernos de Sociología*, Vol. 2, No. 8, 1958. Boletín del Instituto de Sociología de la Universidad de Buenos Aires, pp. 43-80. [article]
Translation (English). "The Empirical Basis of the Sociology of Knowledge." *La Nuova Critica Studi e Revista di Filosofia delle Scienze*, Vol. 4, No. 2, Fall 1959. [article]

027 "Toynbee, sociedad y conocimiento" (with Carey B. Joynt). *Cuadernos de Sociología*, Vol. 2, No. 12, 1958. Boletín del Instituto de Sociología de la Universidad de Buenos Aires, pp. 171-98. [article]

028 *Marxism and the Open Mind* (John Lewis). *Philosophy and Phenomenological Research*, Vol. 19, No. 2, December 1958. [review]

029 *The Revolution in Philosophy* (Howard Selsam). *Philosophy and Phenomenological Research*, Vol. 19, No. 2, December 1958. [review]

030 *Science and the Common Understanding* (J. Robert Oppenheimer); *The Open Mind* (J. Robert Oppenheimer). *Science and Society*, Vol. 22, No. 1, Winter 1958, pp. 83-86. [review-essay]

031 "Scholar's Evolution." *The Democratic and the Authoritarian State* (Franz Neumann). *The American Socialist*, Vol. 5, No. 1, January 1958, pp. 21-22. [review]

1959

032 "Fuentes y components del analisis funcional en sociología." Spanish-language edition of *Manifest and Latent Functions* (Robert K. Merton); *A Formalization of Functionalism* (Ernest Nagel). *Cuadernos de Sociología*, Vol. 12, No. 16, 1959. Boletín del Instituto de Sociología de la Universidad de Buenos Aires, pp. 297-305. (Published under the title "Problemas metodológicos del funcionalismo en las ciencias sociales," by I. L. Horowitz, R. K. Merton, and E. Nagel) [introduction]

033 "From Bergson to Sorel: The Sociological Legacy of Irrational Radicalism." *Proceedings of the Sixth Interamerican Congress of Philosophy*. Buenos Aires: University of Buenos Aires, September-October 1959. [article]

034 "Modern Argentina: The Politics of Power." *The Political Quarterly*, Vol. 30, No. 3, October-November 1959, pp. 400-10. [article]

035 "Newton and His Century." *Isaac Newton's Papers and Letters on Natural Philosophy* (I. Bernard Cohen); *Science and Religion in Seventeenth Century England* (Richard S. Westfall). *Diogenes*, No. 27, Fall 1959, pp. 125-28. [review]
Translations (French, English, Spanish, and Arabic editions).

036 *Contemporary British Philosophy* (edited by H. O. Lewis). *Science and Society*, Vol. 23, No. 1, Winter 1959. [review]

1960

037 *La filosofía de la historia en la antigüedad y en la edad media* (León Dujovne); *La filosofía de la historia desde el Renacimiento hasta el siglo XVIII* (León Dujovne). *Studium: Revista de la Universidad de Colombia*, Vol. 3, Nos. 7-8, 1960, pp. 285-87. [review article]

038 "The Intellectual as a Suicide." *The Bard-St. Stephens Journal*. Vol. 3, No. 1, Summer 1960, pp. 7-13. [article]

039 "Science, Criticism, and the Sociology of Knowledge." Philosophy and Phenomenological Research, Vol. 21, No. 2, December 1960, pp. 173-86 [article]*

040 "Observations on the Philosophy of History." *La filosofía de la historia en la antigüedad y en la edad media* (León Dujovne); *La filosofía de la historia desde el Renacimiento hasta el Siglo XVIII* (León Dujovne). *Philosophy and Phenomenological Research,* Vol. 21, No. 1, September 1960. [review]

041 "Francis Bacon and the Pre-History of the Sociology of Knowledge." *Baconiana*, Vol. 31, No. 1, 1960. [article]
Translation (Spanish). *Cuadernos* de *Sociología.* Vol. 13, No. 22, 1960. Boletín del Instituto de Sociología de la Universidad de Buenos Aires, pp. 189-214.

042 "Averroism and the Politics of Philosophy." *The Journal of Politics* (Southern Political Science Association), Vol. 2, No. 4, November 1960, pp. 698-727. [article]

043 "Carlos Vaz Ferreira: A Review of His Collected Works." *The Hispanic American Historical Review*, Vol. 40, No. 1, February 1960, pp. 63-69. [review article]

044 *John Stuart Mill and French Thought* (Iris Wessel Mueller). *Philosophy: Journal of the Royal Institute*, Vol. 35, No. 133, April 1960, pp. 181-83. [review]

1961

045 PHILOSOPHY, SCIENCE, AND THE SOCIOLOGY OF KNOWLEDGE. Springfield, Il1.: Charles C. Thomas, 1961, 169 pp. (American Lecture Series) [book]
English edition. Oxford: Blackwell Scientific Publications, 1961.
Canadian edition. Toronto: The Ryerson Press, 1961.
Translation (Czechoslovakian, by Dedrich Baumann). Prague: Czech Academy of Sciences, 1968.
Translation (Italian, by Mario Spinella). Milan: Editrice Jaca Books, 1968.
Republished. Westport, Conn.: Greenwood Press, 1976.

046 RADICALISM AND THE REVOLT AGAINST REASON: THE SOCIAL THEORIES OF GEORGES SOREL. London: Routledge & Kegan Paul, 1961, 264 pp. [book]
American edition. New York: Humanities Press, 1961.
Translation (Italian). Milan: Editori Mandadori, 1969.
Paperback edition (revised). Carbondale: Southern Illinois University Press, 1968.
Extract. "American Radicalism and the Revolt Against Reason." *Ideology and Utopia in the United States*, by Irving Louis Horowitz. New York: Oxford University Press, 1977, pp. 180-93.

047 *The Decomposition of Marxism* (Georges Sorel). Translated from the French edition of 1908, and published as an appendix to *Radicalism and the Revolt Against Reason,* by Irving Louis Horowitz. London: Routledge & Kegan Paul, 1961; New York: Humanities Press, 1961. [translation]

048 "Formalización de la teoría general de la ideología." *Proceedings of the Jornadas Argentinas y Latinoamericanas de Sociología* (Social Psychology

Section). Buenos Aires: Institute of Sociology, University of Buenos Aires, September 1961, 14 pp. Memo B-DS-1. [article]

Reprint. "Elementos de la sociología del conocimiento." *Historia y elementos de la sociología del conocimiento*, two volumes, edited by Irving Louis Horowitz. Buenos Aires: Editorial Universitaria de Buenos Aires, 1964.

049 "Estudios sobre la pre-historia de la sociología del conocimiento." *Cuadernos de Sociología,* Vol. 13, No. 22, 1961. Boletín del Instituto de Sociología de la Universidad de Buenos Aires. [article]

050 "Lessing and Hamann: Two Views on Religion and Enlightenment." *Church History*, Vol. 30, No. 3, September 1961, pp. 334-48. [article]

051 "Arms, Policies, and Games." *The American Scholar*, Vol. 31, No. 1, Winter 1961-62, pp. 94-107. [article]‡

052 *Science and the Structure of Ethics* (Abraham Edel). *Philosophy and Phenomenological Research*, Vol. 22, No. 1, September 1961, pp. 267-69. [review]

1962

053 PROCEEDINGS OF CONFERENCE ON CONFLICT, CONSENSUS, AND COOPERATION. Geneva, N.Y.: Hobart & William Smith Colleges, 1962. [edited volume]

Translation (Spanish). *Consenso, conflicto, y cooperación: un inventorio sociologíco.* Mexico City: Instituto de Investigaciones Sociales de la Universidad Nacional Autónoma de México, 1963.

Reissue. Ann Arbor, Mich.: University Microfilms International, 1978. [edited volume]

054 *Estructura y sentido de la historia según la literatura apocalíptica* (Gerardo Leisersohn Baendel); *La filosofía de la historia, de Nietzsche a Toynbee* (León Dujovne); *Teoría de la historia: introducción a los estudios históricos* (Carlos M. Rama). *History and Theory,* Vol. 11, No. 1, 1962, pp. 85-89. [review essay]

055 THE SOCIOLOGICAL IMAGINATION OF C. WRIGHT MILLS (In Memoriam). Syracuse, N.Y.: Maxwell Graduate School of Citizenship and Public Affairs, 1962, 26 pp. [monograph]

Extract. *The American Journal of Sociology,* Vol. 68, No. 1, July 1962, pp. 105-7.

056 "Social Science Objectivity and Value Neutrality: Historical Problems and Projections." *Diogenes,* No. 39, Fall 1962, pp. 17-44. Printed in simultaneous editions in French, English, Spanish, German, and Arabic. [article]*

Reprint. (Spanish, by Servicio de Documentación de Sociología, No. 228). Buenos Aires: Instituto de Sociología, Universidad de Buenos Aires, August 1961.

057 "Crime, Custom and Culture Remarks on the Functionalist Theory of Bronislaw Malinowski." *International Journal of Comparative Sociology,* Vol. 3, No. 2, December 1962, pp. 229-44. [article]*

Translation (Spanish). Introduction to the Spanish-language edition of *Crime and Custom in Savage Society* by Bronislaw Malinowski. Buenos Aires: Editorial Nueva Visión-Losange (Colección Interciencia), 1962.

058 "Formalización de la teoría general de la ideología y la utopía." *Revista Mexicana de Sociología,* Vol. 24, No. 1, January-April 1962, pp. 87-99. [article]

059 "Sociology and the Philosophy of History in Latin America." *History and Theory,* Vol. 2, No. 1, 1962, pp. 85-99. [article]

060 "Storm Over Argentina Revolt Against Political Mythology." *The Nation,* Vol. 194, No. 13, March 31, 1962, pp. 281-84. [article]
Reprint. "The Election in Retrospect." *Political Power in Latin America Seven Confrontations,* edited by Richard R. Fagen and Wayne A. Cornelius, Jr. Englewood Cliffs, N.J.: Prentice-Hall, 1970, pp. 131-34.

061 "The Jewish Community of Buenos Aires." *Jewish Social Studies,* Vol. 14, No. 4, October 1962, pp. 195-222. [article]
Reprint. *Jewish Journal of Sociology,* Vol. 4, No. 2, December 1962, pp. 147-71.
Reprint. *Community Development Planning International Review of Community Development,* Vol. 9, 1962, pp. 187-213.
Revision. *Israeli Ecstacies/Jewish Agonies,* by Irving Louis Horowitz. New York and London: Oxford University Press, 1974.

062 "Non-War and the Constitution." *The Nation,* Vol. 194, No. 23, June 9, 1962, pp. 513-15. [article]

063 "C. Wright Mills and the Dragons of Marxism." *The American Scholar,* Vol. 31, No. 4, Autumn 1962, pp. 646-52. [review article]
Reprint. *C. Wright Mills: An Anthology,* edited by Stanley Aronowitz. Oxford: The Bardwell Press/Sage Publications, 2004.

064 "The Sociological Imagination of C. Wright Mills." *American Journal of Sociology,* Vol. 68, No. 1, July 1962, pp. 105-8. [article]

065 "The Perón Paralysis." *The Nation,* Vol. 195, No. 10, October 6, 1962, pp. 191-94. [article]
Reprint (abridged). "Cómo nos ven." *La Razón* (Buenos Aires), October 24, 1962.

066 "Consensus, Conflict and Cooperation: A Sociological Inventory." *Social Forces,* Vol. 41, No. 2, December 1962, pp. 177-88. [article]*
Reprint. *The War Game: Studies of the New Civilian Militarists,* by Irving Louis Horowitz. New York: Ballantine Books, 1963, pp. 147-69. [book]
Translation (Italian). *Quaderni di Sociologia,* Vol. 12, No. 3, July-September 1963.
Translation (Spanish). *Revista Mexicana de Sociología,* Vol. 24, No. 2, May-August 1963, pp. 591-614.
Reprint. *Man and International Relations: Contributions of the Social Sciences to the Study of Conflict and Integration,* Vol. 2, edited by J.K. Zawodny. San Francisco: Chandler Publishing, 1966, pp. 228-39.
Reprint. *System, Change, and Conflict,* edited by N.J.: Demerath III and Richard A. Peterson. New York: The Free Press, 1967, pp. 265-80.
Reprint. *Community Organization and Social Planning,* edited by Ralph M. Kramer and Thomas D. Sherrard. Englewood Cliffs, N.J.: Prentice-Hall, 1967.
Reprint. *Conflict Resolution: Contributions to the Behavioral Sciences,* edited by Clagett G. Smith. Notre Dame: University of Notre Dame Press, 1970, pp. 66-70.

067 "On the Social Theories of Giovanni Gentile." *Philosophy and Phenomenological Research,* Vol. 23, No. 1, December 1962, pp. 263-68. [article]

068 "C. Wright Mills: The Scientific Imagination of a Moral Man." *Our Generation Against Nuclear War* (Montreal), Vol. 1, No. 4, Summer 1962, pp. 6-25. [article]

069 *Emile Durkheim*, 1858-1917: *A Collection of Essays*, with translations and a bibliography, edited by Kurt H. Wolff. *Philosophy and Phenomenological Research*, Vol. 22, No. 3, March 1962, pp. 419-21. [article]

070 *Philosophy and Myth in Karl Marx* (Robert W. Tucker). *American Journal of Sociology*, Vol. 67, No. 6, May 1962, pp. 711-12. [review]

071 *Determinism in History* (Ernest Nagel). *Sociological Abstracts*, Vol. 10, No. 3, 1962. [review]

1963

072 THE WAR GAME STUDIES OF THE NEW CIVILIAN MILITA-RISTS. New York: Ballantine Books, 1963, 189 pp. [book]
Translation (Italian, augmented version, second edition). Milan: Editorial Feltrinelli, 1967.
Translation (Spanish, augmented version). Costa Rica: National University Press, 1977.
Reissue. Ann Arbor: University Microfilms International, 1978.

073 POWER, POLITICS AND PEOPLE: THE COLLECTED ESSAYS OF C. WRIGHT MILLS, edited with an introduction by Irving Louis Horowitz. New York: Oxford University Press, 1963, 657 pp. [edited volume]
Paperback edition. New York: Ballantine Books, 1963, 657 pp.
English edition. London: Oxford University Press, 1963.
Translation (German). Neuwied am Rhein: Harmand Luchterhand Verlag, 1966.
Translation (Spanish). Mexico City and Buenos Aires: Fondo de Cultura Económica, 1964, 480 pp.
Translation (Italian, two volumes). Milan: Casa Editrice Valentino Bompiani, 1970, 820 pp.
Translation (Portuguese). Rio de Janeiro: Editores Zahar, 1965, 249 pp.
Translation (Swedish). Stockholm: Wahlstron & Widstrand, 1966.
Translation (Japanese). Tokyo: Misuzu Shobo Publications, 1965, 504 pp.
Translation (French). François Maspero Editeur, 1966.
Translation (Norwegian). Oslo: Pax Forlag, 1966, 118 pp.
Paperback edition. New York: Oxford University Press-Galaxy, 1967.

074 OUTLINES OF SOCIOLOGY (Ludwig Gumplowicz). Translated from the second German-language   edition of 1905 (material from the 1885 edition translated by Frederick Moore, revised). New York: Paine-Whitman Publishers, 1963, 336 pp. [translation]
Reissued with a new preface. New Brunswick and London: Transaction Books, 1980, 336 pp.

075 GAMES, STRATEGIES AND PEACE. Philadelphia: American Friends Service Committee (Beyond Deterrence Series), 1963, 64 pp. [monograph]

076 "The Profumo Affair in Merrie Olde England." *New Politics*, Vol. 2, No. 3, Summer 1963, pp. 96-100. [article]

077 "Concepciones sociológicas e ideológicas sobre el desarrollo humano." *Estudios sociológicos: Sociología del desarrollo*, edited by Mendieta y Núñez

(Decimotercer Congreso Nacional de Sociología, Sonora, 1962). Mexico City: Instituto de Investigaciones Sociales de la Universidad Nacional Autónoma de México, 1963. [article]

078 "Another View from Our Left." *New Politics,* Vol. 2, No. 2, Winter 1963, pp. 77-88. [article]
Reprint. *The End of Ideology Debate,* edited by Chaim I. Waxman. New York: Simon & Schuster, 1968, pp. 166-81.

079 "Establishment Sociology: The Value of Being Value-Free." *Inquiry: An Interdisciplinary Journal of Philosophy and the Social Sciences,* Vol. 6, No. 1, Spring 1963, pp. 129-40. [article]*

080 "Sociology and Politics The Myth of Functionalism Revisited." *The Journal of Politics,* Vol. 25, No. 3, May 1963, p.p. 248-64. [article]*

081 "Political Morality and 'Immoral' Politics." *Council of Correspondence Newsletter (The Correspondent),* No. 25, April 1963, pp. 19-23. [article]

082 "Latin America and the Sino-Soviet Split." *Liberation,* Vol. 8, No. 3, May 1963, pp. 11-15. [article]

083 "Militarism in Argentina." *New Society,* No. 39, June 27, 1963, pp. 9-11. [article]

084 "On the Morality of Détente." *The Correspondent,* No. 28, July-August 1963, pp. 39-47. [article]

085 "The Unfinished Writings of C. Wright Mills: The Last Phase." *Studies on the Left,* Vol. 3, No. 4, Winter 1963, pp. 3-23. [article]
Translation (Japanese). *Misuzu Shobo,* Vol. 6, No 5, May 1964.
Translation (Spanish). *Revista de Ciencias Políticas y Sociales,* Vol. 10, Whole No. 35, January-March 1964, pp. 91-117.
Reprint. *Fichas de investigación económica y social,* Vol. 1, No. 2, July 1964.
Reprint. *Revista de Ciencias Sociales,* Vol. 8, No. 3, September 1964, pp. 243-70.

086 "Sociology for Sale." *Social Theory and Social Practice* (Hans Zetterberg). *Studies on the Left,* Vol. 3, No. 3, Summer 1963, pp. 109-15. [review article]*
Reprint. *The Sociology of Sociology,* edited by Larry T. Reynolds and Janice M. Reynolds. New York: David McKay, 1970, pp. 279-86.

087 "Anthropology for Sociologists Cross-Disciplinary Research as Scientific Humanism." *Anthropology and Ethics* (Abraham Edel and May Edel); *The Birth and Death of Meaning (Ernest* Becker); *Human Nature and the Study of Society* (Robert Redfield). *Social Problems,* Vol. 2, No. 2, Fall 1963, pp. 201-6. [review article]*

088 *The Decline of the Intellectual* (Thomas Molnar). *American Journal of Sociology,* Vol. 68, No. 4, January 1963, pp. 495-96. [review]

089 "On Horowitz's 'The Sociological Imagination of C. Wright Mills.'" *American Journal of Sociology,* Vol. 68, No. 5, March 1963. [an exchange with Rudolf Heberle]

1964

090 HISTORIA Y ELEMENTOS DE LA SOCIOLOGÍA DEL CONOCIMIENTO, two volumes. Buenos Aires: Editorial Universitaria de Buenos Aires, 1964. [edited volumes]

091 REVOLUTION IN BRAZIL: POLITICS AND SOCIETY IN A DE-
VELOPING NATION. New York: E. P. Dutton, 1964, 430 pp. [book]
Canadian edition. Toronto: Clarke Irwin, 1964.
Translation (Spanish, augmented version, readings deleted). Mexico City
and Buenos Aires: Fondo del Cultura Económica, 1966, 254 pp.

092 THE NEW SOCIOLOGY: ESSAYS IN SOCIAL SCIENCE AND SO-
CIAL VALUES IN HONOR OF C. WRIGHT MILLS. New York:
Oxford University Press, 1964, 512 pp. [edited volume]
English edition. London: Oxford University Press, Ltd., 1964.
Paperback edition. New York: Oxford University Press-Galaxy, 1965.
Translation (Italian). Milan: Editorial Feltrinelli, 1969.
Translation (Spanish, two volumes). Buenos Aires: Amorrortu Editores,
1969, 550 pp.
Reprint (with a new introduction). New York: Oxford University Press,
1971, 512 pp.

093 THE ANARCHISTS. New York: Dell Publishing and Delta Books, 1964,
640 pp. [edited volume]
Translation (Spanish, augmented version, two volumes). Madrid: Alianza
Editorial, S.A., 1973, 1975, 738 pp.
Extract. "A Postscript to the Anarchists." *Anarchy*, Vol. 5, No. 4, Whole
No. 59, April 1965, pp. 110-26.
Extract. "The Theory of Anarchism." *Political Ideologies,* edited by James A.
Gould and William H. Truitt. New York: Macmillan, 1973, pp. 438-43.
Extract. "Natural Man and Political Man." *Foundations of Political Sociol-
ogy,* edited by Irving Louis Horowitz. New York and London: Harper &
Row, 1972.
Translation (Spanish). *Los Anarquistas: La Practica* (abridged, one vol-
ume edition). Barcelona and Buenos Aires: Ediciones Altaya, S.A., 1997,
336 pp.

094 SOCIOLOGY AND PRAGMATISM: A STUDY IN AMERICAN
HIGHER LEARNING (C. Wright Mills). New York: Paine-Whitman
Publishers, 1964, 475 pp. [edited with an introduction]
Paperback edition. New York: Oxford University Press-Galaxy, 1966.
Translation (Spanish). Buenos Aires: Editorial Siglo Veinte, 1968.
Translation (Japanese). Tokyo: Kinoduniya-Kizoshenba Book, 1968.
Translation (Italian). Rome: Editore Armando Armando, 1968, 426 pp.
Reprint. New York: Oxford University Press, 1969, 475 pp.

095 "Sociological and Ideological Concepts of Industrial Development."
American Journal of Economics and Sociology, Vol. 23, No. 4, October
1964, pp. 352-74. [article]
Reprint. "Concepts of Industrial Development." *The Substance of Sociol-
ogy: Introductory Readings,* edited by Ephraim M. Mizruchi. New York:
Appleton-Century-Gofts, 1967, pp. 469-88.
Reprint. *The Substance of Sociology: Codes, Conduct, and Consequences,*
second edition, edited by Ephraim H. Mizruchi. New York: Appleton-
Century-Crofts, 1973, pp. 504-23.

096 "Noneconomic Factors in the Institutionalization of the Cold War." *An-
nals of the American Academy of Political and Social Science*, Vol. 351,
January 1964, pp. 110-20. [article]‡

Translation (Spanish). *Revista de Ciencias Políticas y Sociales,* Vol. 10, No. 35, January-March 1964, pp. 49-64.

Reprint. War and Its Prevention, edited by Amitai Etzioni and Martin Wenglinsky. New York: Harper & Row, 1970, pp. 112-28.

097 "A Formalization of the Sociology of Knowledge." *Behavioral Science,* Vol. 9, No. 1, January 1964, pp. 45-55. [article]*

098 "The Political Sociology of Soviet Development." *Il Politico,* Vol. 29, No. 1, 1964, pp. 48-68. [article]

099 "Palace Revolutions: A Latin American Casebook." *Transaction/Society,* Vol. 1, No. 3, March 1964, pp. 32-36. [article]

100 "Professionalism and Disciplinarianism: Two Styles of Sociological Performance." *Philosophy of* Science, Vol. 31, No. 3, July 1964, pp. 275-81. [article]

101 "Unexpected Revolt in Panama: Too Many Sardines." *Liberation,* Vol. 9, No. 1, March 1964, pp. 21-22. [article]

102 "Revolution in Brazil: The Counter-Revolutionary Phase." *New Politics,* Vol. 3, No. 2, Spring 1964, pp. 71-80. [article]

Translation (Spanish). *Revista de Ciencias Políticas y Sociales,* Vol. 10, Whole No. 37, July-September 1964. [article]

Reprint. *Political Power in Latin America Seven Confrontations,* edited by Richard R. Fagen and Wayne A. Cornelius, Jr. Englewood Cliffs, N.J.: Prentice-Hall, 1970.

103 "Historical Optimism and the Game of War." *Washington University Magazine,* Vol. 34, No. 4, Summer 1964, pp. 25-29. [article]

104 "Max Weber and the Spirit of American Sociology." *The Sociological Quarterly,* Vol. 5, No. 4, Autumn 1964, pp. 344-54. [article]*

105 "United States Policy and the Latin American Military Establishment." *The Correspondent,* Whole No. 32, Autumn 1964, pp. 45-61. [article]

106 "Marxism According to C. Wright Mills." *The Marxists* (C. Wright Mills). *Philosophy and Phenomenological Research,* Vol. 24, No. 3, March 1964, pp. 402-5. [review article]

107 "Culture Against Man: A Review Article." *Culture Against Man* (Jules Henry). *The Sociological Quarterly,* Vol. 5, No. 2, Spring 1964, pp. 271-75. [review essay]

Reprint. "The Banality of Culture." *Liberation,* Vol. 9, No. 6, September 1964, pp. 29-30.

108 *On Revolution* (Hannah Arendt). *American Journal of Sociology,* Vol. 69, No. 4, January 1964, pp. 419-21. [review]

109 *Social Change* (Wilbert E. Moore). *American Journal of Sociology,* Vol. 70, No. 2, July 1964, pp. 231-33. [review]

110 *Philosophy of the Social Sciences* (Maurice Natanson). *Philosophy and Phenomenological Research,* Vol. 25, No. 2, September 1964, pp. 289-90. [review]

111 *The Behavioral Sciences Today* (Bernard Berelson). *The Sociological Quarterly,* Vol. 5, No. 2, Spring 1964, pp. 163-65. [review]

112 *Challenge to Affluence* (Gunnar Myrdal). *New Politics,* Vol. 3, No. 4, Fall 1964. [review]

113 "Cross Fertilization in Social Science." *Social Problems,* Vol. 2, No. 3, Winter 1964. [an exchange with Lewis Coser]

114　"Ludwig Gumplowicz." *American Journal of Sociology*, Vol. 70, No. 1, July 1964. [an exchange with Alexander Gella]

115　"The Future of the American Corporation." *Transaction/Society*, Vol. 1, No. 5, July 1964, pp. 13-15, 32. [an interview with Wilbert E. Moore]

1965

116　"On Learning and Teaching Sociology." *Five Fields and Teacher Education,* edited by D.B. Cowing. Ithaca, N.Y.: Cornell University Press, 1965, pp. 28-55. [article]*

117　"Party Charisma: A Comparative Analysis of Political Practices and Principles in Third World Nations." *International Social Science Council, Center for Comparative Sociology.* Buenos Aires: Di Tella Institute, DTS No. 11. [article]

Reprint (revised and expanded version). *Studies in Comparative International Development*, Vol. 1, No. 7, 1965, pp. 83-97.

Reprint (text augmented by critical analysis by Alex Simirenko). *Indian Journal of Sociology*, Vol. 7, No. 1, 1965.

Translation (Spanish). *America Latina,* Vol. 8, No. 1, January-March 1965, pp. 77-100.

118　"In Defense of the Sociology of Knowledge." *The British Journal for the Philosophy of Science,* Vol. 16, No. 63, November 1965. [commentary]

119　"The Second Soviet Revolution From Autocracy to Technocracy." *The Correspondent,* Whole No. 33, Winter 1965, pp. 4-7. [article]

Reprint. "Soviet Russia's Evolution From Charisma to Bureaucracy." *Current,* Whole No. 60, June 1965, pp. 52-53.

Reprint. "The Transition from Totalitarianism to Authoritarianism." *Three Worlds of Development,* edited by Irving Louis Horowitz. New York and London: Oxford University Press, 1966.

120　"Unilateral Initiatives: A Strategy in Search of a Theory." *Our Generation Against Nuclear War,* Vol. 3, No. 3, April 1965, pp. 112-27. [article]‡

Reprint and Translation (French, Spanish, Arabic, Russian). *Diogenes.* Whole No. 50, April-June 1965, pp. 118-33.

121　"The Dominican Crisis in Perspective." *The Correspondent,* Whole No. 34, Spring-Summer 1965, pp. 14-16. [article]

Translation (Spanish). "Decirlo todo sobre Santo Domingo." *Siempre,* Whole No. 633, August 11, 1965, pp. 12-15.

122　"Radicalism and Contemporary American Society." *Liberation*, Vol. 10, No. 3, May 1965, pp. 15-17. [article]

Reprint. *Where It's At: Radical Perspectives in Sociology,* edited by Steven E. Deutsch and John Howard. New York: Harper & Row, 1970, pp. 562-72.

123　"The Army: Mortician for the Millions" (with John Saxe-Fernandez). *Frontier,* Vol. 16, No. 11, September 1965, pp. 10-14. [article]

Reprint. "El ejército norteamericano enviará por correo las cenizas de sus soldados muertos" (with John Saxe-Fernández). *Diorama,* March 1974.

124　"The Future of Latin America: A Dialogue" (with Carlos Fuentes). *Peace News,* Whole No. 1513, June 25, 1965; Whole No. 1514, July 2, 1965; Whole No. 1515, July 9, 1965. [article]

Translation (Spanish). *Siempre* (Supplement), No. 146, November 1965.

125 "Method and Metaphor in the Study of International Tensions." *Journal of Human Relations*, Vol. 13, No. 3, Third Quarter, 1965, pp. 310-13. [article]

126 "The Life and Death of Project Camelot." *Transaction /Society*, Vol. 3, No. 1, November/December 1965, pp. 3-12. [article]*‡

Reprint. Bureau of Intelligence and Research. Department of State, July 15, 1966.

Translation (Spanish). *Revista de Ciencias Sociales*, Vol. 10. No. 2, June 1966, pp. 145-65.

Reprint. *Sociology in Action*, edited by Arthur B. Shostak. Homewood, Ill.: Dorsey-Irwin Press, 1966, pp. 324-39.

Reprint. *American Sociologist*, Vol. 21, No. 5, May 1966.

Reprint. *The Triple Revolution*, edited by Robert Perucci and Marc Pilisuk. Boston: Houghton Mifflin, 1968, pp. 153-72.

Translation (Portuguese). *Revista Civilização Brasileira*, Vol. 1, No. 8, July 1966.

Reprint. *The Social Role of the Social Sciences*, edited by Elizabeth T. Crawford and Albert Biderman. New York: John Wiley & Sons, 1967.

Reprint. *The Sociological Perspective*, edited by Scott G. McNall. Boston: Little, Brown, 1968, pp. 522-37.

Reprint. *International Education: Past, Present, Problems, and Prospects*, prepared by the Task Force on International Education, John Brademas, Chairman. Washington, D. C. House Committee on Education and Labor, U. S. Government Printing Office, 1966, pp. 289-303.

Reprint. *Research Methods: Issues and Insights*, edited by B J Franklin and Harold W. Osborne. Belmont, Calif.: Wadsworth, 1971, pp. 75-92.

Reprint. *The Values of Social Science*, edited by Norman Denzin. Chicago: Aldine, 1970, pp. 157-82.

Reprint. *Life in Society: Introductory Readings in Sociology*, edited by Thomas H. Lasswell, John H. Burma, and Sidney Aronson. Glenview, Ill.: Scott, Foresman, 1970, pp. 509-19.

Reprint. *Sociological Methods: A Sourcebook*, edited by Norman K. Denzin. Chicago: Aldine, 1970, pp. 558-76.

Reprint. *Political Science: The Discipline and Its Dimensions*, edited by Stephen L. Wasby. New York: Charles Scribner's Sons, 1970, pp. 259-72.

Reprint. *Social Scientists and International Affairs: A Case for a Sociology of Social Science*, edited by Elisabeth T. Crawford and Albert D. Biderman. New York: John Wiley & Sons, 1969, pp. 174-82.

Reprint. *The Reinforcement of Social Behavior*, edited by Elliott McGinnies and C. B. Ferster. Boston: Houghton Mifflin, 1971, pp. 456-64.

Reprint. *Old Government, New People: Readings for the New Politics*, edited by Alfred de Grazia et al. Glenview, Ill.: Scott, Foresman, 1971, pp. 303-11.

Reprint. *The Sociological Perspective*, second edition, edited by Scott G. McNall. New York: Little, Brown, 1971, pp. 565-89.

Reprint. *The Values of Social Science*, second edition, edited by Norman K. Denzin. New Brunswick, N.J.: Transaction Books, 1973, pp. 241-66.

Reprint. *Politics/America: The Cutting Edge of Change,* edited by Walter Dean Burnham. New York: D. Van Nostrand, 1973, pp. 27-36.

Reprint. *To See Ourselves: Anthropology and Modern Social Issues,* edited by Thomas Weaver et al. Glenview, Ill.: Scott, Foresman, 1973, pp. 138-47.

Reprint. *The Rise and Fall of Project Camelot,* revised edition, edited by Irving Louis Horowitz. Cambridge, Mass.: MIT Press, 1974.

Reprint. *First-Fights in the Kitchen: Manners and Methods in Social Research,* edited by George H. Lewis. Pacific Palisades, Calif.: Goodyear, 1975, pp. 465-80.

Reprint. *Basic Research Design,* edited by B. C. Smith Boston: Houghton Mifflin, 1977.

Reprint. *Anthropological Realities: Readings in the Science of Culture,* edited by Jeanne Guillemin. New Brunswick, N.J. and London: Transaction Books, 1981, pp. 476-92.

127 "The Military of Latin America." *The Military and Society in Latin America* (John L. Johnson). *Economic Development and Cultural Change,* Vol. 13, No. 2, January 1965, pp. 238-42. [review article]

128 "C. Wright Mills Sociology in the Dismal Decade." *Character and Social Structure: The Psychology of Social Institutions* (Hans Gerth and C. Wright Mills). *Frontier,* Vol. 16, No. 5, March 1965, pp. 15-17. [review article]*

129 *Men of Ideas: A Sociologist's Views* (Lewis A. Coser). *The American Journal of Sociology,* Vol. 72, No. 4, January 1965. [review]

130 "The Pervasive Influence of Georg Lukacs." *Realism in Our Time* (Georg Lukacs); *Georg Lukacs' Marxism: Alienation, Dialectics, Revolution* (Victor Zitta). *Frontier,* Vol. 16, No. 9, July 1965, pp. 16-17. [review article]

131 *Historia del movimiento obrero en América Latina* (Víctor Alba). *The American Sociological Review,* Vol. 30, No. 2, April 1965. [review]

132 *The Meaning of History* (Erich Kahler). *Philosophy and Phenomenological Research,* Vol. 26, No. 1, September 1965. [review]

133 *George Lukacs' Marxism: Alienation, Dialectics, Revolution* (Victor Zitta). *The Sociological Quarterly,* Vol. 6, No. 3, Spring 1965. [review]

134 *Applied Sociology: Opportunities* and *Problems* (Alvin W. Gouldner and S. M. Miller). *The Behavioral Science Book Service.* Issued as a separate brochure in October 1965. No date given on brochure. [review]*

135 "The Rise and Fall of Counter-Insurgency." *Internal War: Problems* and *Approaches* (edited by Harry Eckstein). *Transaction/Society,* Vol. 2, No. 5, July/August 1965, pp. 46-49. [review essay]

136 "Kirschner on Kennedy: An Assassination in Search of a Method." *Behavioral Science,* Vol. 10, No. 3, July 1965. [commentary]

137 "The Stalinization of Fidel Castro." *New Politics,* Vol. 4, No. 4, 1965, pp. 61-69. [article]

Reprint. "The Problem of Unity and Organization." *Latin American History: Select Problems of Identity, Integration, and Nationhood,* edited by Fredrick B. Pike. Boston: Houghton Mifflin, 1968.

1966

138 THREE WORLDS OF DEVELOPMENT: THE THEORY AND PRACTICE OF INTERNATIONAL STRATIFICATION. New York

and London: Oxford University Press, 1966, 475 pp. (simultaneous publication in paperback and hardback) [book]

Translation (Portuguese). São Paulo: Editora Brasiliense Soc. An., 1968.

Extract. "Three Worlds of Development." *Reader in Political Sociology*, edited by Frank Lindenfeld. New York: Funk & Wagnals, 1968, pp. 164-79.

Extract. "The World Perceptions of the United States." International *Economics* and Business, edited by Walter Krause end John F. Mathis. Boston: Houghton Mifflin, 1967.

Extract (French). "Le Tiers-monde et nous, Américains." *Terre Entière*, Whole No. 21, January-February 1967.

Extract. "Development and Developmentalists." *From Underdevelopment to Affluence: Marxist and Non-Marxist Views*, edited by Harry G. Shaffer. New York: Appleton-Century, 1968.

Extract (Spanish). "Dos tàcticas en el desarrollo social: enmendar o destruir." *Revista Mexicana de Sociología,* Vol. 27, No. 1, January-April 1965.

Extract (Spanish). "Primer Mundo del desarrollo: los Estados Unidos." *Ciencias Políticas y Sociales,* Vol. 42, October-December 1965.

Extract. "The United States and the Third World East-West Conflict in Focus." *The United Nations Systems and Its Functions,* edited by Robert W. Gregg and Michael Barkun. Princeton, N.J.: D. Van Nostrand, 1968, pp. 350-68.

Extract (Italian). "Del totalitarismo all' autoritarismo nell' Unione Sovietica." *L'Autoritarismo e la Società Contemporanea,* edited by Riccardo Campa. Rome: Edizioni Della Nuova Antologia, 1969.

Extract. "Three Worlds of Development." *The Developing Nations: What Path to Modernization?*, edited by Frank Tachau. New York: Dodd, Mead, 1972.

Extract. "What is the Third World?" *Issues in Social Inequality,* edited by Gerald W. Thielbar and Saul D. Feldman. New York: Little, Brown, 1972, pp. 637-66.

Extract. "The Third World in International Stratification." *Social Problems and Public Policy: Inequality and Justice,* edited by Lee Rainwater. Chicago: Aldine, 1974, pp. 362-74.

Extract. "Party Charisma: Political Practices and Principles." *Intercommunication Among Nations and People,* edited by Michael H. Prosser. New York: Harper & Row, 1973, pp. 225-40.

139 THE POWER ELITE: A CRITICAL COMMENTARY. New York: American R.D.M. Corporation Publishers, 1966, 67 pp. [monograph]

140 "The Conflict Society: War as a Social Problem." *Social Problems A Modern Approach,* edited by Howard S. Becker. New York: John Wiley & Sons, 1966, pp. 695-749. [article]

141 "The Ideology of Hemispheric Militarism." *Sociology in Action,* edited by Arthur B. Shostak. Homewood, Ill.: Dorsey-Irwin Press, 1966, p. 340-47. [article]

142 "The Birth of Meaning in America." *The Sociological Quarterly,* Vol. 7, No. 1, Winter 1965-66, pp. 3-20. [a discussion on *The First New Nation* with Seymour Martin Lipset]

Translation (Spanish). "El nacimiento y significado de los Estados Unidos." *Panoramas,* Whole No. 17, Vol. 3, September-October 1965.

143 "The Hegelian Concept of Positive Freedom." *The Journal of Politics,* Vol. 28, No. 1, February 1966, pp. 3-28. [article]*

144 "On Alienation and the Social Order." *Philosophy and Phenomenological Research,* Vol. 27, No. 2, December 1966, pp. 230-37. [article]*†§
Translation (Yugoslavia). "O alijenaciji i društvenom poretku." *Nase Teme,* Vol. 10, No. 3, March 1967, pp. 670-78.
Reprint. *Dialogues on the Philosophy of Marxism,* edited by John Somerville and Howard L. Parsons. Westport, Conn.: Greenwood Press, 1974, pp. 325-36.

145 "Michigan State and the CIA: A Dilemma for Social Science." *Bulletin of the Atomic Scientists,* Vol. 22, No. 7, September 1966. [article]*
Translation (Spanish). "Las peligrosas ciencias sociales explotan en la Universidad de Michigan." *Siempre* (Supplement), No. 680, duly 6, 1966.

146 "Castrologists and Apologists: A Reply to Science in the Service of Sentiment." *New Politics,* Vol. 5, No. 1, 1966, pp. 27-34. [article]

147 "La 'Sélection' de la Commission du Service Militaire." *Les Temps Modernes,* Vol. 21, No. 241, June 1966, pp. 2295-96. [article]

148 "The Red Guard: The Permanent Revolution in China" (with Alvin W. Gouldner). *Transaction/Society,* Vol. 4, No. 1, November 1966, pp. 37-41. [article]
Reprint. *St. Louis Post-Dispatch,* Vol. 88, No. 309, November 1, 1966.
Reprint. *Perspectives on Our Time,* edited by Francis X. Davy and Robert E. Burkhart. Boston: Houghton Mifflin, 1970, pp. 305-13.
Reprint. *The United States and the Asian Revolutions,* edited by Robert J. Lifton. Chicago: Aldine, 1970.

149 *The Plural Society in the British West Indies* (Michael G. Smith). *The American Journal of Sociology,* Vol. 71, No. 4, January 1966, pp. 451-53. [review]

150 "Schisms and Chasms." *The State of War* (Stanley Hoffman). *The Nation,* Vol. 202, No. 7, February 14, 1966, pp. 189-91 [review article]

151 "Toward a General Theory of Social Development." *Modernization and the Structure of Societies* (Marion J. Levy, Jr.). *American Sociological Review,* Vol. 31, No. 6, December 1966. [review article]

152 *La democracia en México* (Pablo González Casanova). *The American Sociological Review,* Vol. 31, No. 1, February 1966. [review]

153 *The Vertical Mosaic: An Analysis of Social Class and Power in Canada* (John Porter). *The American Sociological Review,* Vol. 31, No. 6, December 1966. [review]
Reprint. *Everybody's Canada: The Vertical Mosaic Reviewed and Reexamined,* edited by James L. Heap. Toronto: Burns and MacEachern, 1974, pp. 5-10.

154 "The Military Definition of Excellence." *Viet-Report,* Vol. 2, No. 4/5, June-July 1966, pp. 4-5. [article]

155 "Graded Deferment." *Liberation: An Independent Monthly,* Vol. 11, No. 4, July 1966, pp. 33-34. [article]

156 "Behavioral Science and Federal Policy" (with Herbert Blumer). State-
ment presented to the United States Senate Committee on Government
Operations, Subcommittee on Government Research. Washington, D.
C., July 20, 1966. Published in *Federal Support of International Social
Science and Behavioral Research.* Washington, D. C. United States Gov-
ernment Printing Office, 1967, pp. 239-56.*
Extract. "The Need for Dangerous Truths." *Transaction/Society*, Vol. 5,
No. 3, January/February 1968.

1967

157 THE RISE AND FALL OF PROJECT CAMELOT (edited with an
introductory essay by Irving Louis Horowitz). Cambridge, Mass. MIT
Press, 1967, 385 pp. (simultaneous publication in paperback and hard-
back) [edited volume]
English edition. London: MIT Press, 1967-68.
Translation (Portuguese, by Alvaro Cabral). Rio de Janeiro: Civilização
Brasileira, 1969.

158 "The Natural History of *Revolution in Brazil:* A Biography of a Book."
Politics, Ethics, and Social Research, edited by Gideon Sjoberg. Cambridge,
Mass.: Schenkman, 1967, pp. 198-224. [article]

159 "Mainliners and Marginals: The Human Shape of Sociological Theory."
Sociological Theory: Inquiries and Paradigms, edited by Llewellyn Z. Gross.
New York: Harper & Row, 1967, pp. 358-83. [article]*
Translation (Polish). *Studia Sociologiczno Polityczne* (special issue on soci-
ology in the sixties), 1969.
Reprint. *Sociology of Sociology,* edited by Larry T. Reynolds and Janice M.
Reynolds. New York: John McKay, 1970, pp. 340-70

160 "The Military Elites of Latin America." *Elites in Latin America,* edited by
Seymour Martin Lipset and Aldo Solari. New York: Oxford University
Press, 1967, pp. 146-89. [article]
Translation (Spanish) "Los militares de América Latina." *Elites y desarrollo
en América Latina,* edited by S.M. Lipset and A.E. Solari. Buenos Aires:
Editorial Paidos, p. 212-53.

161 "Social Science and Public Policy: An Examination of the Political Foun-
dations of Modern Research." *Transactions of the Sixth World Congress of
Sociology.* Evian, France, September 1966. Louvain, Belgium: Interna-
tional Sociological Association, 1967. [article]*†
Translation (Italian). *Quaderni de Sociologia,* 1967.
Reprint. *The Rise and Fall of Project Camelot,* edited by Irving Louis
Horowitz. Cambridge, Mass. and London: MIT Press, 1967.
Reprint. *International Studies Quarterly.* Vol. 11, No. 1, March 1967,
pp. 32-62.
Reprint. *The Rise and Fall of Project Camelot,* revised edition, edited by
Irving Louis Horowitz. Cambridge, Mass. and London: MIT Press, 1974.

162 "Electoral Politics, Urbanization, and Social Development in Latin America."
Urban Affairs Quarterly, Vol. 2, No. 3, March 1967, pp. 3-35. [article]
Translation (Spanish). "La política urbana en Latinoamérica." *Revista
Mexicana de Sociología,* Vol. 28, No. 1, January 1967, pp. 71-112.

Reprint. "The City as a Crucible for Political Action" (revised version). *The Urban Explosion in Latin America: A Continent in the Process of Modernization,* edited by Glenn H. Beyer. Ithaca, N.Y.: Cornell University Press, 1967, pp. 215-73.

Reprint. *Ekistics: Journal of Urban Settlements,* Whole No. 34, 1968, pp. 214-20.

Reprint. *Latin American Radicalism: A Documentary Report on Left and Nationalist Movements,* edited by Irving Louis Horowitz, Josue de Castro, and John Gerassi. New York: Random House, 1969.

163   WHITE COLLAR: A CRITICAL COMMENTARY. New York: American R.D.M. Corporation Publishers, 1967, 49 pp. [monograph]

164   "Social Accounting for the Nation." *Transaction/Society,* Vol. 4, No. 6, May 1967. [comment written with Lee Rainwater]

165   "Our CIA Problem and Theirs." *Transaction/Society,* Vol. 4, No. 7, June 1967, p. 2. [comment written with Lee Rainwater]

166   *Politics in Brazil, 1930-1964: An Experiment in Democracy* (Thomas Skidmore). *The Progressive,* Vol. 31, No. 6, November 1967. [review]

167   "The Search for a Development Ideal: Alternative Models and Their Implications." *The Sociological Quarterly,* Vol. 8, No. 4, Autumn 1967. [article]
Reprint. "The Search for a Development Ideal: Models and Their Utopian Implications" (revised version). *Developing Nations Quest for a Model,* edited by Willard A. Beling and George O. Totten. New York: Van Nostrand Reinhold, 1970, pp. 83-100.

168   *Men of Ideas: A Sociologist's View* (Lewis A. Coser). *The American Journal of Sociology,* Vol. 72, No. 4, January 1967, pp. 419-21. [review]

169   "Two Martyrs of the Vietnam War: Bernard Fall and A J. Muste" *Focus-Midwest,* Vol. 5, No. 36, 1967, pp. 24-26; and *Canadian Dimension,* Vol. 4, No. 4, May-June 1967, pp. 26-29. Published in an abbreviated form under the title "Vietnam Debate Loses Two Intellects." St. *Louis Post-Dispatch,* March 12, 1967. [article]

170   "Israeli Imperatives and Jewish Agonies: A Radical Appraisal" (with Maurice Zeitlin). *Judaism,* Vol. 16, No. 4, Fall 1967, pp. 387-410. [article]
"Israeli Imperatives and Jewish Agonies" (with Maurice Zeitlin). *Judaism and the Cold War in America: 1945-1990* (edited by Jacob Neusner). New York and London: Garland Publishing Co., 1993, pp. 61-84. [reprint]

171   "Cuban Communism: Revolution within a Revolution." *Transaction/ Society,* Vol. 4, No. 10, October 1967, pp. 7-15, 55-57. [article]
Reprint. *Cuban Communism,* edited by Irving Louis Horowitz. Chicago: Aldine, 1970.
Reprint. *Cuban Guerrilla Training Centers and Radio Havana,* edited by Walter J. Chambers. Washington, D. C.: Center for Research in Social Systems, 1970.
Reprint. *Social and Political Movements,* edited by Gary B. Rush and R. Serge Denisoff. New York: Appleton-Century-Crofts, 1971, pp. 214-36.
Reprint. *Cuban Communism,* second edition, edited by Irving Louis Horowitz. New Brunswick, N.J.: Transaction Books, 1972.

Reprint. *Cuban Communism,* third edition, edited by Irving Louis Horowitz. New Brunswick, N.J.: Transaction Books, 1977.

172 "Black Sociology." *Transaction/Society,* Vol. 4, No. 9, September 1967. [commentary]
Reprint. *The Values of Social Science,* edited by Norman K. Denzin. New Brunswick, N.J.: Transaction Books, 1970, pp. 77-82.
Reprint. *The Values of Social Science,* second edition, edited by Norman K. Denzin. New Brunswick, N.J.: Transaction Books, 1973, pp. 139-44.

173 "The Warring Sociologists." *Applied Sociology Opportunities and Problems* (edited by Alvin W. Gouldner and S. M. Miller). *Frontier,* Vol. 18, No. 3, January 1967, pp. 15-16. [review article]

174 Foreword to *The Power Structure Political Process in American Society* by Arnold M. Rose. New York: Oxford University Press, 1967, pp. vii-xi.

175 "Francesco deSanctis," *The Encyclopedia of Philosophy,* Vol. 2, edited by Paul Edwards. New York: Crowell-Collier and Macmillan, 1967, pp. 343-44. [article]

1968

176 "The Americanization of Conflict Social Science 'Fiction' in Action." *Bulletin of the Atomic Scientists,* Vol. 24, No. 3, March 1968. [article]*
Translation (Spanish). "La americanización del fascismo." *Revista de Ciencias Sociales,* Vol. 13, No. 4, September 1969, pp. 447-93.

177 *The Political Illusion* (Jacques Ellul). *New Politics,* Vol. 6, No. 3, Winter 1968. [review]

178 PROFESSING SOCIOLOGY: STUDIES IN THE LIFE CYCLE OF SOCIAL SCIENCE. Chicago: Aldine, 1968, 365 pp. [book]
Paperback edition (abridged). Carbondale, Ill: Southern Illinois University Press, Arcturus Paperbacks, 1976, 232 pp.

179 "Social Deviance and Political Marginality: Toward a Redefinition of the Relation Between Sociology and Politics" (with Martin Liebowitz). *Social Problems,* Vol. 15, No. 3, Winter 1968, pp. 280-96. [article]*†‡
Reprint. *Education and Social Change,* Monograph 1, edited by John B. Orr and Lydia Pulispher. Austin, Texas: Southwest Educational Development Laboratory, 1968, pp. 93-116.
Reprint. *Social Deviance in Canada,* edited by W. E. Mann, Vancouver: Copp Clark, 1971, pp. 25-44.
Reprint. *Deviance, Conflict, and Criminality,* edited by R. Serge Denisoff and Charles H. McCaghy. Chicago: Rand-McNally, 1973, pp. 125-45.
Reprint. *The Sociology of Dissent,* edited by R. Serge Denisoff. New York: Harcourt, Brace, Jovanovich, 1974, pp. 263-80.
Reprint. *The Sociology of Deviance: Book 2,* edited by Kenneth Stoddart. Richmond, British Columbia: The Open Learning Institute, 1981, pp. 111-25.

180 "The Political Ideology of Political Economy: Dilemmas in Latin American and United States Relations." *Cultural Factors in Inter-American Relations,* edited by Samuel Shapiro. Notre Dame and London: University of Notre Dame Press, 1968, pp. 285-312. [article]

Translation (Spanish). *Aportes: Revista Trimestral de Ciencias Sociales,* Whole No. 14, October, 1969, pp. 80-102.
Reprint (Spanish). *Desarrollo,* Whole No. 11, Vol. 3, September 1969, pp. 35-44.

181 "Political Legitimacy and the Institutionalization of Crisis in Latin America." *Comparative Political Studies,* Vol. 1, No. 1, April 1968, pp. 45-70. [article]
Translation (Spanish). *Foro Internacional,* Vol. 8, No. 3, January-March 1968, pp. 235-57.

182 "The Norm of Illegitimacy: Toward a General Theory of Latin American Political Development." *Soundings: A Journal of Interdisciplinary Studies,* Vol. 15, No. 1, Spring 1968. [article]
Translation (Spanish). *Revista Mexicana de Sociología,* Vol. 30, No. 2, April-June 1968, pp. 299-322.
Reprint. *City and Country in the Third World: Issues in the Modernization of Latin America,* edited by Arthur J. Field. Boston: Schenkman, 1970, pp. 25-48.
Reprint. *Latin America: The Dynamics of Social Change,* edited by Stefan A. Halper and John R. Sterling. New York: St. Martin's Press, 1972, pp. 67-93.

183 "In Defense of the Human Body." *Transaction/Society,* Vol. 6, No. 2, December 1968. [commentary]

184 "Radicalism and the Revolt Against Reason: Then and Now." Special introduction prepared for the paperback edition of *Radicalism and the Revolt* Against *Reason,* by Irving Louis Horowitz. Carbondale, Ill.: Southern Illinois University Press, 1968.

185 "Violence and the Intellectual" (a discussion with Richard Flacks and Milton J. Rosenberg). *The University of Chicago Roundtable,* Forum Publication No. 5, 1968, 16 pp. [interview]

186 "Mind, Methodology, and Macrosociology." *American Behavioral Scientist,* Vol. 12, No. 1, September-October, 1968, pp. 51-68. [article]
Reprint. *Sociological Self-Images: A Collective Portrait,* by Irving Louis Horowitz. Beverly Hills, Calif.: Sage, 1969; and London: Pergamon Press, 1970, 255 pp.

187 "The Limited Effectiveness of the United Nations. " *Stanford Journal of International Studies,* Vol. 3, June 1968, pp. 13-19.

188 "Leadership and the Left." *The Activist,* Vol. 9, No. 1, Whole No. *22,* Fall 1968, pp. 4-5. [article]

189 "Kennedy's Death: Myths and Realities." *Transaction /Society,* Vol. 5, No. 8, July/August 1968, pp. 3-4. [commentary]‡
Reprint. *SK&F Psychiatric Reporter,* No. 41, November-December 1968.
Reprint. *Modern Criminals,* edited by James F. Short. Chicago: Aldine, 1970.
Reprint. *Modern Criminals,* second edition, edited by James F. Short. New Brunswick, N.J.: Transaction Books, 1973, pp. 171-80.

190 "The Political Sociology of Counter-Revolution: The Case of Brazil." *Sociological Quarterly,* Vol. 9, No. 3, Summer 1968, pp. 410-18. [article]

191 "Political Instability in Latin America." *Latin American Research Review,* Vol. 3, No. 2, Spring 1968, pp. 68-73. [commentary]

192 "Buenos Aires" (with Danielle Salti). *Encyclopedia Americana*, 1968-69 edition. New York:, 1968. [article]
"Buenos Aires." *Encyclopedia Americana: International Edition*. New York, 1976. Vol. 4, pp. 708-712, with Danielle Salti. (Previously unlisted)

193 *The Industrial Society: Three Essays on Ideology and Development* (Raymond Aron). *The American Political Science Review*, Vol. 63, No. 4, December 1968. [review]

194 "Social Science Yogis and Military Commissars." *Transaction/Society*, Vol. 5, No. 6, May 1968, pp. 29-38. [article]*‡
Reprint. *Social Problems Persistent Challenges*, edited by Edward C. McDonagh and Jon E. Simpson. New York: Holt, Rinehart and Winston, 1969, pp. 265-76.
Reprint. *Sociological Realities: A Guide to the Study of Society*, edited by Irving Louis Horowitz and Mary Symons Strong. New York: Harper & Row, 1971, pp. 522-31.
Reprint. *Politics /America: The Cutting Edge of Change*, edited by Walter Dean Burnham. New York: D. Van Nostrand, 1973, pp. 17-26.
Reprint. *Sociological* Realities *II: A Guide to the Study of Society*, edited by Irving Louis Horowitz and Charles Nanry. New York: Harper & Row, 1975, pp. 572-79.

195 "The Divided Politics of the United Nations." *Washington University Magazine*, Vol. 38, No. 3, Spring 1968, pp. 47-51. [article]

196 "Sociological Self-Images." *American Behavioral Scientist*, Vol. 12, No. 1, September-October 1968, p. 1. [preface]

1969

197 "Young Radicals and Professional Critics." *Commonweal,* Vol. 89, No. 17, January 31, 1969, pp. 552-56. [article]

198 "The Academy and the Polity: Interaction Between Social Scientists and Federal Administrators." *The Journal of Applied Behavioral Science*, Vol. 5, No. 3, July/August/September 1969, pp. 309-35. [article]†‡
Reprint (altered and enlarged). *Human Nature and Collective Behavior: Papers in Honor of Herbert Blumer*, edited by Tamotsu Shibutani. Englewood Cliffs, N.J.: Prentice-Hall, 1970, pp. 334-53.
Reprint. "Conflict and Consensus Between Social Scientists and Policy-Makers." *The Use and Abuse of Social Science*, second edition, edited by Irving Louis Horowitz. New Brunswick, N.J.: Transaction Books, 1975, pp. 11-35.
Translation (German) "Wissenschaftliche Gemeinschaft und Politisches System: Beziehungs konflikte zwischen Sozialwissenschaftlern und politischen praktikern." *Angewandte Sozialforschung: Studies uber Vorausset Zungen und Bedingungen der Produktion, Difuson und Verwertung sozial wissenschaftlichen Wissens*, edited by Bernhard Badura. Frankfurt am Main: Suhrkamp Verlag. 1976, pp. 31-57. [previously unlisted]

199 "A Critical Self-Evaluation of Three Worlds of Development." *et al.*, Vol. 2, No. 2, Spring 1969. [article]

200 LATIN AMERICAN RADICALISM (edited in collaboration with Josué de Castro end John Gerassi). New York: Random House, 1969, 653 pp. [edited volume]

Paperback edition. New York: (Vintage Books) Random House, 1969.
English edition. London: Johnathan Cape, 1969.

201 "Deterrence Games: From Academic Casebook to Military Codebook."
The Structure of Conflict, edited by P. G. Swingle. New York: Academic
Press, 1969, pp. 277-96. [article]†

202 "United States-Cuban Relations: Beyond the Quarantine." *Transaction/
Society,* Vol. 6, No. 6, April 1969. [article]
Reprint (revised and expanded). "Deterrence, Détente, and the-Cuban
Missile Crisis." *Cuban Communism,* third edition, edited by Irving Louis
Horowitz. New Brunswick, N.J.: Transaction Books, 1977.

203 "Is American Radicalism Possible?" *The Humanist,* Vol. 29, No. 5, Sep-
tember-October 1969, pp. 9-11. [article]
Reprint. *Where It's At: Radical Perspectives in Sociology,* edited by Steven E.
Deutsch and John Howard. New York: Harper & Row, 1970.

204 "The Struggle Is the Message: New Stages in the Anti-War Movement."
'*The Center Magazine,* Vol. 2, No. 3, May 1969. [article]
Reprint. *The Troubled Conscience: American Social Issues,* edited by Irving
Louis Horowitz. Palo Alto, Calif.: James F. Freel, 1971.

205 "Sit-in at Stanford" (with William H. Friedland). *Black Pouter and Student Rebellion: Conflict on the American Campus,* edited by James McEvoy
and Abraham Miller. Belmont, Calif.: Wadsworth, 1969, pp. 122-66.
[article]

206 "Reactionary Immortality: The Private Life in Public Testimony of John
Edgar Hoover." *Transaction /Society,* Vol. 6, No. 7, June 1969. [review
article]
Reprint. *Crisis in American Institutions,* edited by Jerome H. Skolnick
and Elliott Currie. Boston: Little, Brown, 1970, pp. 411-20.
Reprint. *Catalyst,* Vol. 2, No. 1, Whole No. 5, Summer 1970, pp. 64-75.

207 "Restructuring the University" (with William H. Friedland). *Fortnight*
(Cornell University), Vol. 1, No. 10, May 7, 1969. [article]

208 SOCIOLOGICAL SELF-IMAGES: A COLLECTIVE PORTRAIT.
Beverly Hills, Calif.: Sage, 1969, 255 pp.
Paperback edition. Beverly Hills, Calif.: Sage, 1969.
English edition. London: Pergamon Press, 1970, 255 pp.

209 "Engineering and Sociological Perspectives on Development: Interdisciplinary Constraints in Social Forecasting." *International Social Science
Journal* (UNESCO), Vol. 21, No. 4, 1969, pp. 545-56. [article]

210 "Anti-War Protest." *The Politics of Protest: Violent Aspects of Protest and
Confrontation.* A Staff Report to the National Commission on the Causes
and Prevention of Violence, prepared by Jerome Skolnick. New York:
Ballantine Books, 1969; Washington, D.C.: U.S. Government Printing
Office, 1969; New York: Simon & Schuster, 1970. [review article]

211 "Further Remarks on Alienation and the Social Order." *Philosophy and
Phenomenological Research,* Vol. 29, No. 3, March 1969, pp. 439-41.
[reply]

212 "Liquidation or Liberation: The Jewish Question as Liberal Catharsis."
The Non-Jewish Jew (Isaac Deutscher); and *The Liberation of the Jew*
(Albert Memmi). *Judaism,* Vol. 18, No. 3, Summer 1969, pp. 361-68.
[review article]

213 "Student Unrest and Political Progress at Washington University." *Focus Midwest*, Vol. 7, No. 45, January/February 1969. [interviewed by Gorden F. Andrus]

1970

214 "Tax Exempt Foundations: Their Effects on National Policy" (with Ruth L. Horowitz). *Science,* Vol. 168, April 10, 1970, pp. 220-28. [article]†
Reprint. *The Use and Abuse of Social Science,* edited by Irving Louis Horowitz. New Brunswick, N.J.: Transaction Books, 1971.

215 "The Student as Jew." *The Antioch Review,* Vol. 29, No. 4, Winter 1969-70, pp. 537-46. [article]

Reprint. *Seeing Ourselves: Introductory Readings in Sociology,* edited by Peter I. Rose. New York: Alfred A. Knopf, 1972, pp. 299-312.
Reprint. *Seeing Ourselves,* second edition, edited by Peter I. Rose. New York: Alfred A. Knopf, 1975, pp. 376-88.
Reprint. *Sociology and Student Life,* edited by Arthur B. Shostak. New York: David McKay, 1971, pp. 29-41.

216 "The Brave New World of Campus Psychiatry." *Change Magazine,* Vol. 2, No. 1, January-February 1970, pp. 47-52. [article]

217 "The Culture of Civility" (with Howard S. Becker). *Transaction/Society,* Vol. 7, No. 6, April 1970, pp. 12-19. [article]
Reprint (slightly abridged). "A Cultural Civility in San Francisco." *The Washington Post,* April 26, 1970.
Reprint. *Sociological Realities: A Guide to the Study of Society,* edited by Irving Louis Horowitz and Mary Symons Strong. New York: Harper & Row, 1971.
Reprint. *Culture and Civility in San Francisco,* edited by Howard S. Becker. New Brunswick, N.J.: Transaction Books, 1971, pp. 4-19.
Reprint. *The Urban Reader,* edited by Susan Cahill and Michele F. Cooper. Englewood Cliffs, N.J.: Prentice-Hall, 1971, pp. 66-72.
Reprint. *The Emergence of Deviant Minorities: Social Problems and Social Change,* edited by Robert W. Winslow. San Ramon, Calif.: Consensus Publishers and New Brunswick, N.J.: Transaction Books, 1972, pp. 346-57.
Reprint. *Down to Earth Sociology: Introductory Readings,* edited by James M. Henslin. New York: The Free Press, 1972, pp. 316-27.
Reprint. *Cities in Change: Studies on the Urban Condition,* edited by John Walton and Donald E. Cams. Boston: Allyn & Bacon, 1973, pp. 243-51.
Reprint (slightly abridged). *Social Structure and Social Problems in America,* edited by D. Stanley Eitzen. Boston: Allyn & Bacon, 1974.
Reprint. *Life Styles: Diversity in American Society,* edited by Saul D. Feldman and Gerald W. Thielbar. Boston: Little, Brown, 1975, pp. 199-208.
Reprint. *Drugs and Politics,* edited by Paul E. Rock. New Brunswick, N.J.: Transaction Books, 1977, pp. 233-46.
Reprint. *Cities in Change: Studies on the Urban Condition,* second edition, edited by John Walton and Donald E. Carns. Boston: Allyn & Bacon, 1977, pp. 199-205.

218 *A Modern Dictionary of Sociology: The Concepts and Terminology of Sociology and Related Disciplines* (George A. Theodorson and Achilles G. Theodorson). *Journal of Marriage and the Family,* Vol. 32, No. 2, May 1970. [review]

219 *Politics and the Labor Movement in Latin America* (Víctor Alba). *Economic Development and Cultural Change,* Vol. 18, No. 2, January 1970, pp. 290-93. [review]

220 *Il Potere politico nell'America Latina* (Riccardo Campa). *Journal of International Studies,* Vol. 11, No. 4, October 1969. [review]

221 "Trade-Unionisation of the Student Seventies." *New Society,* Whole No. 406, July 9, 1970, pp. 70-71. [article]
Reprint. "The Trade-Unionization of Students." *Current,* No. 122, October 1970, pp. 55-59.

222 CUBAN COMMUNISM. Chicago: Aldine, 1970, 143 pp. [edited volume]
Translation (Spanish). *Cuba: diez años después.* Buenos Aires: Editorial Tiempo Contemporáneo, 1971.

223 THE STRUGGLE IS THE MESSAGE: THE ORGANIZATION AND IDEOLOGY OF THE ANTI-WAR MOVEMENT. Berkeley, Calif.: Glendessary Press, 1970, 175 pp. [book]‡
Extract. "The Anti-War Movement." *The Politics of Protest: A Task Force Report Submitted to the National Commission on the Causes and Prevention of Violence,* edited by Jerome H. Skolnick. New York: Simon & Schuster, 1969.
Cassette and tape recording. "The Struggle is the Message" (selections from various chapters). Santa Barbara, CA: The Center for the Study of Democratic Institutions, No. 468, 1972.

224 THE KNOWLEDGE FACTORY: STUDENT POWER AND ACADEMIC POLITICS IN AMERICA (in collaboration with William H. Friedland). Chicago: Aldine, 1970, 354 pp. [book]
Cassette and tape recording. "The Youth Class" (slightly abridged reading of chapter five: "Students as Social Class"). Santa Barbara, CA: The Center for the Study of Democratic Institutions, No. 469, 1972.
Paperback edition. Carbondale, Ill.: Southern Illinois University Press, Arcturus Books, 1972.

225 " 'Separate but Equal': Revolution and Counter-Revolution in the American City." *Social Problems,* Vol. 17, No. 3, Winter 1970, pp. 294-312. [article]‡
Reprint. *Educating the Disadvantaged: School Year 1969/1970,* edited by Russell C. Doll. New York: AMS Press, 1970, pp. 273-91.
Reprint. *The American Scene: Social Problems of the Seventies,* edited by Lloyd Saxton and Walter Kaufman. Belmont, Calif.: Wadsworth, 1971, pp. 97-118.
Reprint. *Cities in Change: Studies on the Urban Condition,* edited by John Walton and Donald E. Cams. Boston: Allyn & Bacon, 1973, pp. 466-84.

226 "Sociological Snoopers and Journalistic Moralizers" (with Lee Rainwater). *Transaction/Society,* Vol. 7, No. 7, May 1970. [a debate with Nicholas von Hoffman]

Reprint. *Readings in Sociology,* fourth edition, edited by Edgar A. Schuler et al. New York: Thomas Y. Crowell, 1971, pp. 711-19.

Reprint. *Issues, Debates, and Controversies: An Introduction to Sociology,* edited by George Ritzer. Boston: Allyn & Bacon, 1972, pp. 75-82.

Reprint. *Experimentation with Human Beings,* edited by Jay Katz. New York: Russell Sage Foundation, 1972, pp. 327-29.

Reprint. *The Values of Social Science,* second edition, edited by Norman K. Denzin. New Brunswick, N.J.: Transaction Books, 1973, pp. 151-64.

Reprint. *Social Psychology and Everyday Life,* edited by Rilly J. Franklin and Frank J. Kohout. New York: David McKay, 1973, pp. 547-57.

Reprint. *Social Realities Dynamic Perspectives,* edited by George Ritzer. Boston: Allyn & Bacon, 1974, pp. 49-56.

Reprint. *Tearoom Trade: Impersonal Sex in Public Places,* by Laud Humphreys. Chicago: Aldine, 1975, pp. 181-90.

Reprint (slightly abridged). *Sociology: A Critical Approach to Power, Conflict, and Change,* by J. Victor Baldridge. New York: John Wiley & Sons, 1975, pp. 45-47.

Reprint. *Sociological Realities II: A Guide to the Study of Society,* edited by Irving Louis Horowitz and Charles Nanry. New York: Harper & Row, 1975, pp. 46-49.

Reprint (abridged). *Sociology: Human Society,* second edition, edited by Melvin L. Defleur, William V. D'Antonio, and Lois Defleur. Glenview, Ill.: Scott, Foresman, 1976, p. 600.

Reprint. *Sociology for Our Times,* edited by Gerald L. Sicand and Philip Weinberger. Glenview, Ill.: Scott, Foresman, 1977, pp. 322-26.

227 "United States 'Policy' in Latin America." *New Politics,* Vol. 9, No. 1, Whole No. 33, Spring 1970, pp. 74-83. [article]
Reprint. "What U. S. Policy for Latin America?: The Schism between Action and Doctrine." *Current,* No. 135, December 1971, pp. 43-52.

228 "The Student Seventies Conservative Revolution in the Making." *Continuum,* Vol. 8, No. 1, Spring-Summer 1970, pp. 190-93. [commentary]

229 "Three Worlds of Development: A Critical Self-Evaluation." et al., Vol. 2, No. 3, 1970, pp. 74-87. [article]

230 "The Condition of the Working Class in the United States (1970)." *New Politics,* Vol. 8, No. 3, Whole No. 31, Summer 1969, pp. 13-27. [article]†‡
Translation (French). *Sociologie du Travail,* No. 3, July-September 1971, pp. 25-39.

231 "Comments on Frank K. McCann's Paper." *Religious and Cultural Factors in Latin America,* edited by Charles J. Fleener and Harry J. Carcas. St. Louis: Office of International Programs, St. Louis University, 1970, pp. 29-32. [commentary]

232 Foreword to *Democracy in Mexico,* by Pablo Gonzalez Casanova. New York: Oxford University Press, 1970, pp. xiii-xvii.

233 MASSES IN LATIN AMERICA. New York: Oxford University Press, 1970, 608 pp. [edited volume]

234 "Israel's Democracy of the Gun." *New Society,* Vol. 16, Whole No. 421, 1970. [article]

235 "Social Science Mandarins: Policymaking as a Political Formula." *Policy Sciences: An International Journal,* Vol. 1, No. 3, Fall 1970, pp. 339-60. [article]†
Reprint. *Social Science and Public Policy,* edited by Daniel L. Knapp and Walter F. Schafer. University of Oregon: Lina Acheson Wallace School of Community Service and Public Affairs, 1970, pp. 3-26.

236 Foreword to *Urban Power and Social Welfare: Corporate Influence in an American City,* by Richard E. Edgar. Beverly Hills, Calif.: Sage, 1970, pp. 7-8.

237 "The Divided Norms of the United Nations." *Main Currents in Modern Thought,* Vol. 27, No. 2, November-December 1970, pp. 55-59. [article]
Translation (Greek). *Ilisos/Athens,* Vol. 17, Whole No. 91, January-February 1972.

238 "The Fifth Epoch: Postscript to an Epilogue to an Unfinished Social Theory of the Living and the Dead." *Philosophy and Phenomenological Research,* Vol. 21, No. 2, December 1970, pp. 382-88. [commentary]

239 "Personality and Structural Dimensions in Comparative International Development." *Social Science Quarterly,* Vol. 51, No. 3, December 1970, pp. 494-513. [article]
Reprint. *Comparative Modernization: A Reader,* edited by Cyril E. Black. New York: The Free Press, 1976, pp. 257-77.

240 "Masses in Latin America." *Masses in Latin America,* edited by Irving Louis Horowitz. New York: Oxford University Press, 1970, pp. 3-27. [edited volume]

1971

241 "Rock on the Rocks or Bubblegum, Anybody?" *Psychology Today,* Vol. 4, No. 8, January 1971, pp. 59-61, 83. [article]
Reprint. *Mass Culture Revisited,* edited by Bernard Rosenberg and David Manning White. New York: Van Nostrand Reinhold, 1971, pp. 459-65.
Reprint. *Reading, Writing, and Rhetoric,* revised edition, edited by James Burl Hogins and Robert E. Yarber. Chicago: Science Research Associates, 1972, pp. 481-87.
Reprint. *College English: The First Year,* sixth edition, edited by Action C. Morris et al. New York: Harcourt, Brace, Jovanovich, 1973, pp. 123-26.
Reprint. *Subject and Structure: An Anthology for Writers,* fifth edition, edited by John M. Wasson. Boston: Little, Brown, 1975, pp. 121-27.

242 "Rock and Rebellion: From Modern Jazz to Hard Rock: A Sociological View." *Commonweal,* Vol. 93, No. 19, February 12, 1971, pp. 466-69. [article]
Reprint. *The Anti-American Generation,* edited by Edgar Z. Friedenberg. New Brunswick, N.J.: Transaction Books, 1971, pp. 137-60.
Reprint. *American Music From Storyville to Woodstock,* edited by Charles Nanry. New Brunswick, N.J.: Transaction Books, 1972, pp. 137-59.
Reprint. *Annual Edition: Readings in Sociology,* 72-73. Guilford, Conn.: Dushkin, 1972, pp. 239-41.

Reprint. *Annual Edition: Readings in Sociology,* 73-74. Guilford, Conn.: Dushkin, 1973, pp. 306-9.

Reprint. *Annual Edition: Readings in Sociology,* 74-75. Guilford, Conn.: Dushkin, 1974, pp. 273-76.

Reprint. "Rock and Rebellion." *Demystifying Human Behavior* (edited by Leroy Gruner). Copley Publishing Company, 1988.

"Sociological Priorities for the Second Development Decade." *Social Problems,* Vol. 19, No. 1, Summer 1971, pp. 137-43 [article]

Reprint. "Research Priorities for the Second Development Decade." *Studies in Comparative International Development,* Vol. 7, No. 2, Spring 1972, pp. 181-85.

244 "Something New, Something Blue." *Music and Politics* (John Sinclair and Robert Levin). *New Society,* Vol. 18, Whole No. 463, August 12, 1971, pp. 297-98. [review]

245 THE USE AND ABUSE OF SOCIAL SCIENCE: BEHAVIORAL SCIENCE AND POLICYMAKING, New Brunswick, N.J.: Transaction Books, 1971, 350 pp. [edited volume]

246 "The Pentagon Papers and Social Science." *Transaction/Society,* Vol. 8, No. 11, September 1971, pp. 37-46. [article]‡

Reprint. *Beyond Conflict and Containment Critical Studies of Military and Foreign Policy,* edited by Milton J. Rosenberg. New Brunswick, N.J.: Transaction Books, 1972, pp. 297-322.

Reprint (abridged). *Environments, People, and Inequalities: Some Current Problems,* edited by Harry C. Bredemeier and Judy Getis. New York: John Wiley & Sons, 1973, pp. 258-64.

Reprint. *The Values of Social Science,* second edition, edited by Norman K. Denzin. New Brunswick, N.J.: Transaction Books, 1973, pp. 267-92.

Reprint. *The Rise and Fall of Project Camelot,* revised edition, edited by Irving Louis Horowitz. Cambridge, Mass. MIT Press, 1974.

Reprint. *Social Problems in Corporate America,* edited by Helen Safa and Gloria Levitas. New York: Harper & Row, 1975, pp. 447-54.

Reprint. *Sociological Realities II: A Guide to the Study of Society,* edited by Irving Louis Horowitz and Charles Nanry. New York: Harper & Row, 1975, pp. 580-86.

247 "Discussion of 'A Minority People Becomes a Majority'" (Arthur J. Lelyveid). *Congress Bi-Weekly: A Journal of Opinion and Jewish Affairs,* Vol. 39, No. 5, March 10, 1972. [commentary]

248 "The Treatment of Conflict in Sociology Literature." *International Journal of Group Tensions,* Vol. 1, No. 4, October-December 1971, pp. 350-63. [article]

249 "The Political Sociology of Cuban Communism." *Revolutionary Change in Cuba,* edited by Carmelo Mesa-Lago. Pittsburgh, Pa.: University of Pittsburgh Press, 1971, pp. 127-41. [article]

Reprint. *Cuban Communism,* second edition, edited by Irving Louis Horowitz. New Brunswick, N.J.: Transaction Books, 1972, pp. 307-25.

Reprint. *Cuban Communism,* third edition, edited by Irving Louis Horowitz. New Brunswick, N.J.: Transactions Books, 1977.

250 "Harris: The New Populist." *ADA World Magazine,* Vol. 26, No. 10-11, October-November 1971. [article]

251 "Officialist from the Harvard Business School." *Engines of Change: United States Interests and Revolution in Latin America* (George C. Lodge). *Transaction/Society,* Vol. 8, No. 7, May 1971, pp. 61-62. [review article]

252 "Political Systems of the Middle East: Opening Remarks." *People and Politics in the Middle East,* edited by Michael Curtis. New Brunswick, N.J.: Transaction Books, 1971, pp. 216-19. [article]

253 "Social Change, Social Control, and Social Policy." *Handbook on the Study of Social Problems,* edited by Erwin O. Smigel. Chicago: Rand McNally, 1971, pp. 435-78. [article]

254 SOCIOLOGICAL REALITIES: A GUIDE TO THE STUDY OF SOCIETY (with Mary Symons Strong). New York: Harper & Row, 1971, 551 pp. [edited volume]

255 THE TROUBLED CONSCIENCE: AMERICAN SOCIAL ISSUES. Palo Alto: James E. Freel and the Center for the Study of Democratic Societies, 1971, 395 pp. [edited volume]

256 *Sociological Work: Method and Substance* (Howard S. Becker). *American Sociological Review,* Vol. 36, No. 3, 1971, pp. 524-27. [review article]

257 "Militarization, Modernization, and Mobilization." *New Statements,* Vol. 1, No. 3, 1971, pp. 4-13. [article]†
Reprint. *Protagonists of Change: Subcultures in Development and Revolution,* edited by Abdul A. Said. Englewood Cliffs, N.J.: Prentice-Hall, 1971, pp. 41-51.
Reprint. *Soldiers in Politics,* edited by Steffen W. Schmidt and Gerald A. Dorfman. Los Altos: Geron-X, 1974, pp. 3-24.
Reprint. *Militarism in Developing Countries,* edited by Kenneth Fidel. New Brunswick, N.J.: Transaction Books, 1975, pp. 301-16.

258 Preface to the *Ward-Gumplowicz Correspondence: 1897-1909*, edited by Aleksander Gella. New York: Essay Press, 1971, pp. vii-ix.

259 "Moral Incentives in Economic Development." *The Theory of Moral Incentives in Cuba,* by Robert M. Bernardo. Birmingham: University of Alabama Press, 1971, pp. xv-xix. [introduction]

1972

260 "The Jewish Vote in the 1972 Elections." *New Outlook: Middle East Monthly,* Vol. 15, No. 8, October 1972, pp. 2-8. [article]

261 "Jewish Ethnicism and Latin American Nationalism." *Midstream: A Monthly Jewish Review,* Vol. 18, No. 9, November 1972, pp. 22-28. [article]

262 "The Sociology Textbook: The Treatment of Conflict in American Sociological Literature." *Social Science Information,* Vol. 11, No. 1, February 1972, pp. 5 1-63. [article]

263 "The Environmental Cleavage: Social Ecology Versus Political Economy. pp. 125-34. [article]‡§
Reprint. *Environmental Quality and Social Responsibility,* edited by R. S. Khare et al. Green Bay: University of Wisconsin Press, 1972, pp. 125-31.

264 "United States Policy and Latin American Politics: From Alliance for Progress to Action for Progress." *Toward a Wiser Colossus: Reviewing and*

Recasting United States Foreign Policy, edited by James A. Stegenga. Lafayette, Ind.: Purdue University Studies, 1972, pp. 88-105. [article]

265 "The Morphology of Modern Revolution." *The Indian Journal of Sociology,* Vol. 3, No. 1/2, March-September 1972, pp. 3-34. [article]

266 CUBAN COMMUNISM, second edition. New Brunswick, N.J.: Transaction Books, 1972, 328 pp. [edited volume]

267 "Israel Developing." *Worldview,* Vol. 15, No. 19, September 1972, pp. 28-31. [article]

268 "Alias 'Mad Bomber Sam': A Long Lost Friend Dies at Attica." *Commonweal,* Vol. 96, No. 14, June 16, 1972, pp. 327-31. [article]
Reprint. "Reflections on Attica." *The Journal: Forum for Contemporary History,* Vol. 1, No. 1, June-July 1972, pp. 24-28.

269 "The Jewish Vote." *Commonweal,* Vol. 92, No. 2, October 13, 1972, pp. 30-33. [article]

270 "The Politics of Drugs." *Social Policy,* Vol. 3, No. 2, July/August 1972, pp. 36-40. [article]
Reprint. *Drugs and Politics,* edited by Paul E. Rock. New Brunswick, N.J.: Transaction Books, 1977, pp. 155-66.

271 "Packaging a Sociological Monsterpiece." *Society Today. Transaction/Society,* Vol. 9, No. 8, June 1972, pp. 50-54. [review article]

272 THREE WORLDS OF DEVELOPMENT: THE THEORY AND PRACTICE OF INTERNATIONAL STRATIFICATION, second edition. New York and London: Oxford University Press, 1972, 556 pp. (simultaneous publication in paperback and hardback) [book]

273 Foreword to *American Music from Storyville to Woodstock,* edited by Charles Nanry. New Brunswick, N.J.: Transaction Books, 1972, pp. ix-xii.

274 "Radical Politics and Sociological Research: Observations on Methodology & Ideology" (with Howard S. Becker). *American Journal of Sociology,* Vol. 76, No. 1, July 1972. [article]§
Reprint. *Varieties on Political Expression in Sociology,* edited by Robert K. Merton. Chicago, Ill.: University of Chicago Press, 1973, pp. 48-66.
Reprint. *Contemporary Sociological Theories,* edited by Alan Wells. Santa Monica, Calif.: Goodyear Publishing Co., 1978, pp. 227-40.
Reprint. "Radical Politics and Sociological Research." *Doing Things Together* (Howard S. Becker). Evanston: Northwestern University Press, 1986, pp. 83-102.

275 FOUNDATIONS OF POLITICAL SOCIOLOGY. New York: Harper & Row, 1972, 590 pp. [book]
Translation (German). *Grundlagen der Politischen Soziologie,* 5 Vols. Frieberg: Rombach Verlag, 1975.
Vol. 1 *Ideologie und Geschichte.*
Vol. 2 *Ideologie und System.*
Vol. 3 *Formen Gesellschaftlichen und Politischen Wandels.*
Vol. 4 *Wissenschaft und Politik.*
Vol. 5 *Interessen und Interessengruppen.*
Translation (Spanish). Madrid and Mexico City: Fondo de Cultura Económica, 1977, 671 pp.

FOUNDATIONS OF POLITICAL SOCIOLOGY (with a new introduction). New Brunswick and London. Transaction Publishers, 1997, 590 + xxiv pp.

Translation (Bengali). FOUNDATIONS OF POLITICAL SOCIOLOGY. Selections published under the title as *Studies in Social Relations* (edited by Hasanuzzaman Chowdhury) Dacca, Bangladesh: Textbook Division of Bangla Academy, 1998, 320 pp.

276 "Qualitative and Quantitative Research Problems in Comparative International Development." *Social Development: Critical Perspectives,* edited by Manfred Stanley. New York: Basic Books, 1972, pp. 6-38. [article]

277 "Israel: Remembering It Is Foreign." *Sh'ma: A Journal of Jewish Responsibility,* Vol. 2, No. 30, April 7, 1972, pp. 75-80. [article]

278 "Shouldn't Jews Transcend Their Class?" *Sh'ma: A Journal of Jewish Responsibility,* Vol. 2, No. 39, October 13, 1972, pp. 145-46. [article]

279 "Lyndon Baines Johnson and the Rise of Presidential Militarism." *The Vantage Point: Perspectives of the Presidency, 1963-1969* (Lyndon Baines Johnson). *Social Science Quarterly,* Vol. 53, No. 2, September 1972. [review article]‡

1973

280 "Authenticity and Originality in Jazz: Toward a Paradigm in the Sociology of Music." *Journal of Jazz Studies,* Vol. 1, No. 1, October 1973, pp. 57-64. [article]
Reprint. *Education,* Vol. 8, No. 1, October/November 1975, pp. 4-5, 26-27.

281 "*Transaction* Magazine: A Decade of Critical Social Science Journalism." *International Social Science Journal,* Vol. 25, No. 1/2, 1973, pp. 170-89. (simultaneous publication in English and French) [article]

282 "Socialism and the Problem of Knowledge: Three States in Marx and Three Strategies in Socialism." *Social Praxis,* Vol. 1, *No.* 3, 1973. [article]§
Reprint. *The Concept of Socialism,* edited by Bhikhu Parekh. New York: Holmes & Meier, 1975, pp. 120-33.

283 "Comments on Session III." *Frontiers of Planned Unit Development: A Synthesis of Expert Opinion,* edited by Robert W. Burchell. New Brunswick, N.J.: Center for Urban Policy Research, 1973, pp. 271-78. [article]

284 WAR AND PEACE IN CONTEMPORARY SOCIAL AND PHILOSOPHICAL THEORY, second edition. London: Souvenir Press; New York: Humanities Press, 1973, 218 pp. (original title was *The Idea of War and Peace in Contemporary Philosophy*) [book]

285 "Political Terrorism and State Power." *Journal of Political and Military Sociology,* Vol. 1, No. 1, Spring 1973, pp. 147-57. [article]
Reprint. *Political Sociology: Readings in Research and Theory,* edited by George Kourvetaris and Betty Dobratz. New Brunswick, N.J. and London: Transaction Books, 1980, pp. 263-74.

286 "Discussion." *Proceedings of the Experts Conference on Latin America and the Future of Its Jewish Communities.* London: Institute of Jewish Affairs, 1973, pp. 24-28, 141-45. [commentary]

287 "Coalition for a Democratic Majority: The Operators Make Their Play." *The Nation,* Vol. 216, No. 6, April 13, 1983, pp. 72-75. [review article]

288 "The Holocaust: Sharing in the Ultimate Act." *Judenrat: The Jewish Councils in Eastern Europe under Nazi Occupation* (Isaiah Trusk). *Commonweal,* Vol. 98, *No.* 6, April 13, 1973. [review article]

289 "El poder como medida del político." *Revista de ciencias sociales,* Vol. 17, No. 1, March 1973, pp. 5-30. [article]

290 "Israel: The Years Ahead." *Worldview,* Vol. 16, No. 5, May 1973, pp. 17-19. [article]

291 "Notes on an American Family." *The Journal of the Forum for Contemporary History,* April 23, 1973, pp. 3-4. [review]

292 "Buñuel's Bourgeoisie." *The Discreet Charm of the Bourgeoisie* (a film by Luis Buñuel). *Transaction/Society,* Vol. 10, No. 5, July/August, 1973. [review article]
Reprint. *The World of Luis Buñuel,* edited by Joan Mellen. New York: Oxford University Press, 1978, pp. 397-404.
Reprint. *Film in Society,* edited by Arthur Asa Berger. New Brunswick, N.J. and London: Transaction Books, 1980, pp. 85-92.

293 "The Hemispheric Connection: A Critique and Corrective to the Entrepreneurial Thesis of Development, with Special Emphasis on the Canadian Case." *Queen's Quarterly,* Vol. 80, No. 3, Autumn 1973. [article]

294 *The People: Growth and Survival* (Gerhard Hirschfeld). *Worldview,* Vol. 16, No. 12, December 1973, pp. 51-53. [review]

295 "Trouble in Paradise: The Institute for Advanced Study." *Change,* Vol. 5, No. 8, October 1973, pp. 44-49. [article]

296 "An Israeli Vanguard: Military or Moral?" *ACIID: A Critical Insight Into Israel's Dilemmas,* April 1973. [article]

1974

297 "Authenticity and Militarization: A Postscript on the Cuban Revolution." *Atlanta Forum on National and International Affairs.* Atlanta: Georgia Institute of Technology, pp. 7-9. [article]

298 "Sociology and Futurology: The Contemporary Pursuit of the Millennium." *Berkeley Journal of Sociology,* Vol. 19, 1974-75, pp. 37-54. [article]‡§
Reprint. "America's Pursuit of the Millennium: Between a Grandiose Past and a Utopian Future." *Bulletin of the Atomic Scientists,* Vol. 31, May 1974.
Reprint (slightly abridged). *The Globe and Mail* (Toronto), May 28, 1975.

299 "Rejoinder to Paul Joseph and David Plotke." *Berkeley Journal of Sociology,* Vol. 19, 1974-75. [a reply]

300 "Mediating Journals: Reaching Out to a Public beyond the Scientific Community" (with Paul Barker). *International Social Science Journal,* Vol. 26, No. 3, 1974, pp. 393-410. [article with discussion]
Translation (French). *Revue Internationale des Sciences Sociales,* Vol. 26, No. 3, 1974, pp. 429-49.

301 Preface to *Jewishness Rediscovered: Jewish Identity in the Soviet Union*, edited by Harris O. Schoenberg. New York: Anti-Defamation League of B'nai B'rith, 1974, pp. 3-7.

302 *Military Rule in Latin America: Function, Consequences, and Perspectives* (edited by Philippe C. Schmitter). *Contemporary Sociology*, Vol. 3, No. 4, July 1974. [review]

303 *In Search of Self Reliance: U. S. Security Assistance to the Third World Under the Nixon Doctrine* (Guy J. Pauker et al.) *Armed Forces in Society*, Vol. 1, No. 1, Fall 1974, pp. 133-38. [review article]

304 THE RISE AND FALL OF PROJECT CAMELOT, revised edition. Cambridge, Mass.: MIT Press, 1974, 409 pp. [edited volume]

305 "The Penal Colony Known as the U.S.S.R." *The Gulag Archipelago, 1918-1956: An Experiment in Literary Investigation*, Parts I-II, (Aleksandr Solzhenitsyn). *Transaction /Society*, Vol. 11, No. 5, July/August 1974, pp. 22-26. [review article]§

306 "Is the Future an Extension of the Present?" *An Inquiry into the Human Prospect* (Robert L. Heilbroner). *Business and Society Review*, No. 11, Autumn 1974, pp. 101-3. [review article]

307 ISRAELI ECSTASIES/JEWISH AGONIES. New York: Oxford University Press, 1974, 244 pp. [book]

308 "The Middle East Terror: A Global Estimate." *Sh'ma: A Journal of Jewish Responsibility*, Vol. 4, No. 66, January 25, 1974. [article]
Reprint. *New Outlook Middle East Monthly*, Vol. 17, No. 2, February 1974, pp. 7-14.
Reprint (slightly abridged). *Current*, No. 160, March 1974.

309 "Forced Coexistence: More Militant Jews in a More Possessive State." *Present Tense*, Vol. 1, No. 2, Winter 1974, pp. 64-68. [article]

310 "The Europeanization of American Politics." *Commonweal*, Vol. 100, No. 5, April 5, 1974, pp. 103-6. [article])‡
Translation (Portuguese). *Jornal do Brasil*. January 13, 1974.
Translation (Italian). *Rinascità*, Vol. 3, No. 3, January 1, 1974.
Reprint (slightly abridged). *Current*, No. 162, May 1974.
Reprint. *Watergate and the American Political Process*, edited by Ronald E. Pynn. New York: Praeger, 1975, pp. 95-102.

311 "Horowitz Responds to Gusfield's Review of Foundations of Political Sociology." *American Journal of Sociology*, Vol. 80, No. 3, November 1974, pp. 722-24. [reply]

312 "Capitalism, Communism, and Multinationalism." *Transaction /Society*, Vol. 11, No. 2, January/February 1974, pp. 32-43. [article]‡
Reprint. *The New Sovereigns: Multinational Corporations as World Powers*, edited by Abdul A. Said and Luiz R. Simmons. Englewood Cliffs, N.J.: Prentice-Hall, 1975, pp. 120-38.
Reprint. *Sociological Realities II: A Guide to the Study of Society*, edited by Irving Louis Horowitz and Charles Nanry. New York: Harper & Row, 1975, pp. 496-503.
Translation (Portuguese). "A Détente e as Multinacionais." *Dados*, Whole No. 12, 1976.
Reprint. *Conflict and Consensus in Modern American History*, fifth edition, edited by Allen F. Davis and Harold D. Woodman. Lexington, Mass.: D.C. Heath & Co., 1980, pp. 420-38.

313 "Americanism as Substitutive Socialism." *Failure of a Dream?*, edited by John H. M. Laslett and Seymour Martin Lipset. New York: Anchor Press/Doubleday, 1974, pp. 456-62. [article]

314 "Looking Ahead." The *Study of Society.* Guilford, Conn.: Dushkin, 1974, pp. 464-67. [interview]

315 Foreword to *Social Problems in Corporate America,* edited by Helen Icken Safa and Gloria Levitas. New York: Harper & Row, 1974.

1975

316 THE USE AND ABUSE OF SOCIAL SCIENCE: BEHAVIORAL RESEARCH AND POLICY MAKING, second edition. New Brunswick, N.J.: Transaction Books, 1975, 509 pp. [edited volume]

317 SOCIAL SCIENCE AND PUBLIC POLICY IN THE UNITED STATES (with James Everett Katz). New York: Praeger, 1975, 187 pp. [book]
"Brown vs. Board of Education" abridged from "Social Science and Public Policy in the United States" in *Knowledge for Policy: Improving Education Through Research* (edited by Don S. Anderson and Bruce J. Biddle). New York and London: The Falmer Press/Taylor & Francis, 1991, pp. 237-244.

318 SOCIOLOGICAL REALITIES II: A GUIDE TO THE STUDY OF SOCIETY (with Charles Nanry). New York: Harper & Row, 1975, 607 pp. [edited volume]

319 "Ernest Becker: An Appreciation of a Life that Began September 27, 1924 and Ended March 6, 1974. " *The American Sociologist,* Vol. 10, No. 1, February 1975, pp. 25-27. [commentary]

320 "Spying and Security: The American Way." *Transaction/Society,* Vol. 12, No. 2, March/April 1975. [article]‡
Reprint (slightly abridged) *Current,* No. 173, May/June 1975, pp. 3-6.

321 "Critics' Choices from University Presses." *Frame Analysis: An Essay on the Organization of Experience* (Erving Goffman). *Commonweal,* Vol. 102, No. 5, May 23, 1975. [review essay]

322 "Science and Revolution in Contemporary Sociology: Remarks to an International Gathering." *The American Sociologist,* Vol. 10, No. 2, May 1975. [article]

323 "La conexión hemisférica: crítica y correcciones a la tesis empresarial del desarrollo con énfasis especial en el caso canadiense." *Revista Mexicana* de *Ciencias Políticas y Sociales,* Vol. 81, No. 21, July/September 1975, pp. 61-98. [article]

324 "An Amnesty International of One." *Transaction/Society,* Vol. 13, No. 1, November/December 1975. [article]
Reprint. *Détente: Prospects for Democracy and Dictatorship,* edited by Aleksandr Solzhenitsyn. New Brunswick, N.J.: Transaction Books, 1976, pp. 125-34.

325 "Military Origins of the Cuban Revolution." *Armed Forces and Society,* Vol. 1, No. 4, August 1975, pp. 402-18. [article]
Reprint. *Cuban Communism,* third edition, edited by Irving Louis Horowitz. New Brunswick, N.J.: Transaction Books, 1977.

326 "For Marx/Against Engels: Dialectics Revisited" (with Bernadette Hayes). *The International Journal of Critical Sociology,* Vol. 1, No. 1, Fall.1975, pp. 33-51. [article]

327 "Ideologies and Theories about American Jazz" (with Charles Nanry). *Journal of Jazz Studies,* Vol. 2, No. 2, June 1975, pp. 24-41. [article]

328 "Head and Hand in Education: Vocationalism Versus Professionalism." *The Hand University of Chicago School Review,* Vol. 83, No. 3, May 1975. [article]

329 "United States Policies and Latin American Realities: Neighborliness, Partnership, and Paternalism." *Latin America: The Search for a New International Role,* edited by Ronald G. Hellman and H. Jon Rosenbaum. New York: John Wiley & Sons, 1975, pp. 39-56. [article]

330 "Race, Class, and the New Ethnicity." *Worldview,* Vol. 18, No. 1, January 1975, pp. 46-53. [article]‡

331 "Cuba Libre?: Social Science Writings on Postrevolutionary Cuba, 1959-1975." *Studies in Comparative International Development,* Vol. 10, No. 1, Fall 1975, pp. 101-23. [article]
Reprint. *Cuban Communism,* third edition, edited by Irving Louis Horowitz. New Brunswick, N.J.: Transaction Books, 1977.

332 *The Science of Society and the Unity of Mankind: A Memorial Volume for Morris Ginsberg* (edited by Ronald Fletcher). *Social Forces,* Vol. 54, No. 2, December 1975, pp. 475-77. [review]

333 "A More Equal World: An Interview with Irving Louis Horowitz." *Worldview,* Vol. 18, No. 12, December 1975, pp. 16-19. [interviewed by Rafael Rodríguez Castañeda]
Reprint. "Ten Questions and Answers on the State of the United States in Foreign Policy." *International Studies Notes,* Vol. 3, No. 2, Summer 1976.
"Foreword" to *Solid Gold: The Popular Record Industry* by R. Serge Denisoff. New Brunswick and Oxford: Transaction Books, 1975, pp. XI-XVI.

1976

334 GENOCIDE: STATE POWER AND MASS MURDER. New Brunswick, N.J.: Transaction Books, 1976, 80 pp. [book]
Paperback edition (with a new postscript). New Brunswick, N.J.: Transaction Books, 1977.
Reprinted in *Folkemord og politisk massevold i det 20 Arhundre: Arsaker, forlop, virkninger,* edited by Bernt Hagivet. Oslo, Norway: Universitetet I Oslo – Institutt for statsvitenskap, 2002, 228 pp.

335 "Unicorns and Terrorists." *International Terror: National, Regional* and *Global Perspectives* (edited by Yonah Alexander). *The Nation,* Vol. 222, No. 20, March 20, 1976. [review]

336 "Authenticity and Autonomy in the Cuban Experience." *Cuban Studies/ Estudios Cubanos,* Vol. 6, No. 1, January 1976, pp. 67-91. [article]
Reprint. *Cuba: The Institutionalization of the Revolution,* edited by Carmelo Mesa-Lago. Pittsburgh: Center for Latin American Studies, University of Pittsburgh, pp. 67-74.
Reprint. *Cuban Communism,* third edition, edited by Irving Louis Horowitz. New Brunswick, N.J.: Transaction Books, 1977.

337   "State Power and Military Nationalism in Latin America" (with Ellen Kay Trimberger). *Comparative Politics,* Vol. 8, No. 2, January 1976, pp. 223-44. [article]

338   *Ethnicity: Theory and Experience* (edited by Nathan Glazer and Daniel P. Moynihan). *American Journal of Sociology,* Vol. 82, No. 1, July 1976, pp. 221-25. [review article]

339   *Marx, Freud, and the Critique of Everyday Life: Toward a Permanent Cultural Revolution* (Bruce Brown); *The Ordeal of Civility: Freud, Marx, Levi-Strauss, and the Jewish Struggle with Modernity* (John Murray Cuddihy). *Contemporary Sociology,* Vol. 5, No. 6, March 1976. [review article]

340   "From Pariah People to Pariah Nation: Jews, Israelis, and the Third World." *Israel in the* Third World, edited by Michael Curtis and Susan Aurelia Gitelson. New Brunswick, N.J.: Transaction Books, pp. 361-91. [article]

341   "Energy, Equity and the Revolution of Falling Expectations." *Occasional Papers Number I,* Institute for Urban Studies and Community Services, The University of North Carolina at Charlotte, 21 pp. [article]‡

342   "A Funeral Pyre for America." *The Cultural Contradictions of Capitalism* (Daniel Bell); *The Twilight of Capitalism* (Michael Harrington); *The Dying of the Light: A Searching Look at America* (Arnold A. Rogow). *Worldview,* Vol. 19, No. 11, November 1976, pp. 45-48. [review article]

343   "Jewish Ethnicity and Latin American Nationalism." *Ethnicity in an International Context,* edited by Abdul A. Said and Luis R. Simmons. New Brunswick, N.J.: Transaction Books, 1976, pp. 92-109. [article]

343a   Reprint. *Latin American Institute* (Rutgers, the State University of New Jersey). 1980. Reprint Series, No. 10.

344   "Introduction: National Realities and Universal Ambitions in the Practice of Sociology." *Sociological Praxis: Current Roles and Settings*, edited by Elisabeth Crawford and Stein Rokkan. Beverly Hills, Calif.: Sage, 1976, pp. 11-28. [article]

345   "Pictures at an Exhibition." *The Human Image: Sociology and Photography,* edited by Derral Cheatwood and Therold Lundquist. Fredonia, N.Y.: State University of New York:, 1976, pp. 7-11. [article]

346   "Kalman H. Silvert. " *Memorial Service for Kalman H. Silvert.* New York: Faculty of Arts and Sciences, New York University, 1976, pp. 8-13. [memorial address]

347   "Looking at 'Looking Back' A Brief Critique of Melvin L. Kohn's Review and Appraisal of Social Science Problems." *Social Problems,* Vol. 24, No. 1, October 1976, pp. 113-14. [commentary]

348   "The Domestic Impact of Foreign Clandestine Operations: The CIA and Academic Institutions, the Media, and Religious Institutions." *Foreign and Military Intelligence Book 1,* Senate Select Committee to Study Governmental Operations. Washington, D.C.: U.S. Government Printing Office, 1976.

349   "Science, Security, and Politics," *Covert Action in Chile: 1963-1973* (Staff Report of the U.S. Senate Select Committee to Study Government Operations with Respect to Intelligence Activities); *Alleged Assassination Plots Involving Foreign Leaders* (An Interim Report of the United States Senate Committee to Study Governmental Operations with Respect to Intelligence Activities); *The CIA File* (edited by Robert L. Borosage end

John Marks); and *Intelligence Activities* (Hearings before the U. S. Senate Select Committee to Study Governmental Operations with Respect to Intelligence Activities). *Transaction/ Society,* Vol. 13, No. 5, July/August 1976. [review article]

1977

350 EQUITY, INCOME, AND POLICY: COMPARATIVE STUDIES IN THREE WORLDS OF DEVELOPMENT. New York: Praeger, 1977, 298 pp. [edited volume]

351 "Social Welfare, State Power, and the Limits to Equity." *Equity, Income, and Policy: Comparative Studies* in *Three Worlds of Development,* edited by Irving Louis Horowitz. New York: Praeger, 1977, pp. 1-18. [article] Reprint. *Policy Studies Review* Annual, edited by Howard E. Freeman. Beverly Hills, Calif. and London: Sage, 1978, pp. 341-58.

352 IDEOLOGY AND UTOPIA IN THE UNITED STATES, 1956-1976. New York and London: Oxford University Press, 1977, 464 pp. (simultaneous publication in paperback and hardback) [book]

353 "Science, Sin, and Sponsorship." *The Atlantic Monthly,* Vol. 39, No. 3, March 1977, pp. 98-102. [article]

354 *Who's Running America: Institutional Leadership in the United States* (Thomas R. Dye). *Political Science Quarterly,* Vol. 92, No. 1, Spring 1977, pp. 111-13. [review]

355 "Can Democracy Cope with Terrorism?" *The Civil Liberties Review,* Vol. 4, No. 1, May-June 1977, pp. 29-37. [article]§ Reprint (expanded with new title). "Transnational Terrorism, Civil Liberties, and Social Science." *Terrorism: Interdisciplinary Perspectives,* edited by Yonah Alexander and Seymour Maxwell Finger. New York: The John Jay Press, 1977; London: McGraw-Hill Book Co., Ltd., 1977, pp. 283-97. Reprint (abridged). "Dangers to Liberty in Fighting Terrorism." *The New York Times,* April 30, 1977. Translation (Portuguese). *Jornal do Brasil.* May 29, 1977. Reprint. *Taking Sides: Views on Controversial Social Issues,* second edition, edited by Kurt Finsterbusch and George McKenna. Guilford, Conn.: Dushkin, 1982, pp. 288-94. Reprint. *Terrorism: Information as a Tool for Control.* Washington, D. C.: Congressional Research Service, Library of Congress, 1978, pp. 165-72.

356 CUBAN COMMUNISM, third edition. New Brunswick, N.J.: Transaction Books, 1977, 576 pp. [edited volume]

357 *Community and Polity: The Organizational Dynamics of American Jewry* (Daniel J. Elazar). *Contemporary Sociology,* Vol. 6, No. 3, May 1977, pp. 287-89. [review article]

358 " 'When the President Does It ….' " What the Tapes Really Reveal." *The Nation,* Vol. 224, No. 24, June 18, 1977, pp. 751-53. [article]

359 "Castrology Revisited: Further Observations on the Militarization of Cuba." *Armed Forces and Society,* Vol. 3, No. 4, August 1977, pp. 617-31. [article] Reprint. *Cuban Communism,* third edition, edited by Irving Louis Horowitz. New Brunswick, N.J.: Transaction Books, 1977.

Reprint. *Current News* (Department of Defense, Washington, D. C.), Whole No. 240, September 1, 1977.

360 "Coming of Age of Urban Research in Latin America." *Current Perspectives in Latin American Urban Research* (edited by Alejandro Portes and Harley L. Browning); *Urban Latin America: The Political Condition from Above and Below* (edited by Alejandro Portes and John Walton). *American Journal of Sociology*, Vol. 83, No. 3, November 1977, pp. 761-65. [review article]

361 "Social Science and Presidential Choices." *Transaction/Society*, Vol. 14, No. 4, May/June 1977. [commentary]

362 "Death and Transfiguration in the Third World." *Worldview*, Vol. 20, No. 9, September 1977, pp. 20-25. [article]

363 "Israeli-Diaspora Relations as a Problem in Center-Periphery Linkages." *Contemporary Jewry: A Journal of Sociological Inquiry*, Vol. 4, No. 1, Fall 1977, pp. 28-38. [article]

364 "Ethnic Policies and American Foreign Policy." *Ethnicity and United States Foreign Policy*, edited by Abdul A. Said. New York and London: Praeger/Holt, Rinehart and Winston, 1977, pp. 175-80. [article]

365 "From Dependency to Determinism: The New Structure of Latin American Militarism." *Journal of Political & Military Sociology*, Vol. 5, No. 2, August 1977, pp. 217-38. [article]
Translation (Spanish). "La nueva estructura del militarismo latinoamericano." *Opiniones Latinoamericanas*, Vol. 1, No. 2, August 1978.
Reprint. *Conflict, Order, and Peace in the Americas*, edited by Michael E. Conroy and Norman V. Walbek. Austin: Lyndon B. Johnson School of Public Affairs, University of Texas, 1978, pp. 50-82.

366 "Autobiography as the Presentation of Self for Social Responsibility." *New Literary History*, Vol. 9, No. 1, Autumn 1977, pp. 173-79. [article]§

367 "War in the Darkroom." *Photomontages of the Nazi Period* (John Heartfield); "With a Camera in the Ghetto" (Mender Grossman). *Present Tense*, Vol. 5, No. 1, Autumn 1977, pp. 60-61. [review]

368 "On Human Rights and Social Obligations." *Transaction/Society*, Vol. 15, No. 1, November 1977. [introductory statement]
Reprint. *Human Rights and World Order*, edited by Abdul A. Said. New York and London: Praeger/Holt, Rinehart and Winston, 1978 (cloth edition); New Brunswick, N.J. and London: Transaction Books/Basil Blackwell (paperback edition), 1978, pp. vii-xii.

369 "The Science of Poverty or the Poverty of Science: Consideration on Malnutrition and Misnutrition." *The Asian Economic* and *Social Review*, Vol. 2, Nos. 3/4, 1977, pp. 27-36. [article]

370 "Moral Incentives in Economic Development." *The Theory of Moral Incentives in Cuba*, by Robert M. Bernardo. University: The University of Alabama Press, 1971. [introduction]

1978

371 "Taking Lives in South America," *Genocide in Paraguay* (edited by Richard Arens); *Victims of the Miracle: Development and the Indians of Brazil*

(Shelton H. Davis). *The Nation,* Vol. 225, No. 6, February 18, 1978, pp. 181-83. [review essay]

372 "The Danger of Positive Thinking." *Society,* Vol. 15, No. 3, Whole No. 113, March-April 1978, pp. 13, 16-17. [article]

373 "Politicians, Intellectuals and Other Israelis." *Reconstructionist,* Vol. 44, No. 2, March 1978, pp. 7-16. [interview with Itamar Rabinovich]

374 Foreword to *Presidential Politics and Science Policy,* by James Everett Katz. New York and London: Praeger/Holt, Rinehart and Winston, 1978, pp. vi-ix.

375 *From Georges Sorel: Essays in Socialism and Philosophy* (edited by John L. Stanley). *The American Political Science Review,* Vol. 72, No. 1, March 1978. [review]

376 SCIENCE, SIN AND SCHOLARSHIP. Cambridge, Mass. and London: MIT Press, 1978, 290 pp. [edited book]

377 "The Norm of Illegitimacy: Ten Years Later." *Legitimation of Regimes,* edited by Bogdan Denitch. London and Beverly Hills, Calif.: Sage, 1978, pp. 23-35. [essay]

378 "Observations on Soviet Sociology." *Current Anthropology,* Vol. 19, No. 2, 1978. [commentary]

379 Foreword to *Guestworkers in Germany: The Prospects for Pluralism,* by Ray C. Rist. New York and London: Praeger/Holt, Rinehart and Winston, 1978, pp. vii-x.

380 "Advertising: Truth, Propaganda and Consequences." *Proceedings of the Council of Better Business Bureaus on the Responsibilities of Advertisers to Society.* Washington, D. C. Council of Better Business Bureaus, 1978, pp. 63-70. [article]

381 "The Cuba Lobby." *The Washington Review of Strategic and International Studies,* Vol. 1, No. 3, July 1978, pp. 58-71. [article]
Translation (Spanish). "El grupo de presión en los asuntos Cubanos: Soga para una revolución hipotecada," *El Comunismo Cubano: 1959-1979,* by Irving Louis Horowitz. Madrid: Editorial Playor, 1979.
Reprint. *Cuban Communism,* 4th edition, edited by Irving Louis Horowitz. New Brunswick, N.J. and London: Transaction Books, 1981.

382 "Style and Stewardship: Sociological Considerations on the Professionalization of Music." *Journal of Jazz Studies,* Vol. 5, No. 1, Fall/Winter 1978, pp. 4-18. [article]

383 "Social Planning and Social Science: Historical Continuities and Comparative Discontinuities." *Planning Theory in the* 1980's, edited by Robert W. Burchell and George Sternlieb, New Brunswick, N.J.: The Center for Urban Policy Research, 1978, pp. 41-68. [article]§

384 "On Truth in Publishing: A Response" (with Mary E. Curtis). *The Nation,* Vol. 226, No. 21, June 3, 1978, pp. 660-61. [commentary]

385 "Small Lives for Big Words: Individualism and State Power Reconsidered." *Worldview,* Vol. 21, No. 9, September 1978, pp. 13-19. [article]

386 DIALOGUES ON AMERICAN POLITICS (with Seymour Martin Lipset). New York and London: Oxford University Press, 1978, 199 pp. [book]
Extract. "Equality." *Sociology: Contemporary Readings,* edited by John Stimson and Ardyth Stimson. Itasca, Ill.: F.E. Peacock Publishers, 1983, pp. 188-93.

387 "Care and Feeding of Overseas Researchers." *Studies in Comparative International Development,* Vol. 13, No. 3, Fall 1978, pp. 97-103. [article]

388 "Revolution, Retribution, and Redemption." *Transaction/Society,* Vol. 15, No. 6, September/October 1978. [article]§

1979

389 "Open Societies and Free Minds: The Last Testament of Hannah Arendt." *Contemporary Sociology,* Vol. 8, No. 1, January 1979, pp. 15-39. [survey essay]§

390 "On the Expansion of New Theories and the Withering Away of Old Classes." *Transaction/Society,* Vol. 16, No. 2, January/February 1979, pp. 55-62. [article]§

391 "Social Welfare, State Power, and the Limits of Equity." *Growth in a Finite World,* edited by Joseph Grunfeld. Philadelphia: The Franklin Institute Press, 1979, pp. 21-36. [article]§
Expanded and revised version. "Limits to Growth or Limits to Equity: The Contemporary American Debate on Justice." *Democracy in Two Nations: USA and India,* edited by Ramashray Roy. New Delhi/Madras: South Asian Publishers, 1982, pp. 135-56.

392 "The Church Political Religion and the Rise of the Reverend Moon." *The Nation,* Vol. 228, No. 13, April 7, 1979, pp. 365-67. [article]

393 "The Politics of New Cults: Non-Prophetic Observations on Science, Sin, and Scholarship." *Soundings: An Interdisciplinary Journal,* Vol. 62, No. 2, Summer 1979, pp. 209-19. [article]
Reprint. *In Gods We Trust,* edited by Thomas Robbins and Dick Anthony. New Brunswick, N.J. and London: Transaction Books, 1981, pp. 161-70.

394 "No Exaggeration, No Minimization." *The Last Half-Century: Societal Change and Politics in America* (by Morris Janowitz). *Commonweal,* Vol. 106, No. 14, August 3, 1979, pp. 443-44. [review]

395 "Fifteen Years of SCID: Looking Ahead." *Studies in Comparative International Development,* Vol. 14, No. 1, Spring 1979. [commentary]

396 "On Relieving the Deformities of Our Transgressions." *Transaction/Society,* Vol. 16, No. 5, July/August 1979, pp. 80-83. [film review]

397 "Institutionalization as Integration: The Cuban Revolution at Age Twenty." *Cuban Studies/Estudios Cubanos,* Vol. 9, No. 2, July 1979, pp. 84-90. [article]

398 "The Sociology of Development and the Ideology of Sociology." *Societal Growth: Processes and Implications,* edited by Amos H. Hawley. New York: The Free Press/Macmillan Publishing Co. (in conjunction with the American Sociological Association), 1979, pp. 279-89. [article]§

399 "Robert S. Lynd and Helen Merrell Lynd." *International Encyclopedia of the Social Sciences: Biographical Supplement.* New York: The Free Press/Macmillan Publishing Co., 1979, pp. 471-77. [article]

400 CONSTRUCTING POLICY: DIALOGUES WITH SOCIAL SCIENTISTS IN THE NATIONAL POLITICAL ARENA. New York and London: Praeger/Holt, Rinehart and Winston, 1979, 244 pp. [edited book]

401 THE AMERICAN WORKING CLASS PROSPECTS FOR THE
1980's (with John C. Leggett and Martin Oppenheimer). New Brunswick,
N.J.: Transaction Books, 1979. [edited book]
Extract. "Race, Class, and the New Ethnicity: The Holy Ghost of Social
Stratifiction." *Winners and Losers: Social and Political Polarities in America*,
by Irving Louis Horowitz. Durham, N.C.: Duke University Press, 1984.

402 EL COMUNISMO CUBANO: 1959-1979. Madrid: Editorial Playor/
Biblioteca Cubana Contemporánea, 1979. [book]

403 "Beyond Democracy: Interest Groups and the Patriotic Gore," *The Humanist*, Vol. 39, No. 5, September/October 1979, pp. 4-10. [article]§

404 "The Linchpin is Antisemitism." *The Russian New Right: Right-Wing
Ideologies in the Contemporary USSR* (Alexander Yanov); *The Final Fall:
An Essay on the Decomposition of the Soviet Sphere* (Emmanuel Todd).
Present Tense, Vol. 7, No. 1, Autumn 1979, pp. 60-62. [review essay]

405 "Paradigms of Political Psychology." *Political Psychology: Journal of the
International Society of Political Psychology*, Vol. 1, No. 2, Autumn 1979,
pp. 99-103. [article]

406 "Skokie, The ACLU, and the Endurance of Democratic Theory" (with
Victoria Bramson). *Law and Contemporary Problems Duke University School
of Law*, Vol. 43, No. 2, Spring 1979, pp. 328-49.
Reprint. "Skokie, the ACLU and the Endurance of Democratic Theory."
The Bill of Rights and American Legal History, Volume 3 (edited by Paul L.
Murphy). New York and London: Garland Publishing. Inc., 1990, pp.
156-178.

407 "Marketing Social Science." Transaction/Society, Vol. 17, No. 1, November/December 1979, pp. 12-19. [article]

408 *Prophecy and Progress* (Krishnan Kumar); *Post-Industrial Society* (edited by
Bo Gustafsson). *Technology and Culture*, Vol. 20, No. 4, October 1979,
pp. 848-52. [review]

409 "Methods and Strategies in Evaluating Equity Research." *Social Indicators Research*, Vol. 6, No. 1, January 1979, pp. 1-22. [article]

1980

410 "The Tripartite World of the University Press." *The Chronicle of Higher
Education*, Vol. 19, No. 16, January 7, 1980. [article-commentary]

411 "Mannheim's Wissenssoziologie und C.W. Mills' Soziologisches Wissen."
Kolner Zeitschrift für Soziologie und Sozialpsychologie, Vol. 22, No. 2, Summer 1980, pp. 360-83.

412 "Economic Equality as a Social Goal." *Journal of Economic Issues*, Vol. 14,
No. 4, December 1980, pp. 937-58.§
Reprint. *Policy Studies Review Annual*, Volume Five, edited by Irving Louis
Horowitz. Beverly Hills, Calif. and London: Sage, 1981, pp. 256-77.

413 "Commercial Advertising as a Form of Knowledge: Ten Propositions in
Search of a Theory." *Knowledge: Creation, Diffusion, and Utilization*,
Vol. 2, No. 1, September 1980, pp. 19-26. [article]

414 "Experiment Perilous: The First Years at Livingston College of Rutgers
University" (with Joshua Feigenbaum). *Urban Education*, Vol. 15, No.
2, July 1980, pp. 131-68. [article]

415 "Historical Antecedents and Intellectual Consequences of C. Wright Mills' *Power Elite.*" *Hosei University Journal* (Tokyo). Vol. 7, No. 1, Spring 1980. [article in Japanese only]

416 "Slouching Toward the Brave World: Bureaucracy, Administration, and State Power." *Marxist Perspectives,* Vol. 3, No. 1, Whole No. 9, Spring 1980, pp. 142-57. [article]§

Reprint (with altered title). "The Expansion of State Power, Post-Industrial Society and the Future of Public Administration." *Conference Proceedings of the International Conference on the Future of Public Administration.* Quebec: Ècole nationale d'administration publique, 1980, pp. 113-41.

417 "For Marx/Against Engels" (with Bernadette Hayes). *Social Praxis: International and Interdisciplinary Quarterly of Social Sciences,* Vol. 7, Nos. 1-2, Spring-Summer 1980, pp. 59-76. (revision and expansion of item number 326).

418 "A Postscript to Genocide." *Chitty's Law Journal* (Canada), Vol. 28, No. 1, March 1980, pp. 90-95.

419 "When Worlds Collide. " *North-South: A Program for Survival* (edited by Willy Brandt). *The Washington Quarterly: A Review of Strategic and International Issues,* Vol. 3, No. 3, Summer 1980, pp. 213-17. [review essay]

420 "Moral Development, Authoritarian Distemper, and the Democratic Persuasion. *"Moral Development and Politics,* edited by Richard W. Wilson and Gordon J. Schochet. New York: Praeger/CBS Educational and Professional Publishing, 1980, pp. 5-21.§

Reprint. *Ethnicity, Identity, and History: Essays in Memory of Werner J. Cahnman,* edited by Joseph B. Maier and Chaim I. Waxman. New Brunswick, N.J.: Transaction Books, 1983, pp. 211-26.

421 TAKING LIVES: GENOCIDE AND STATE POWER. New Brunswick, N.J.: Transaction Books; London: Holt-Saunders, Ltd., 199 pp. (a newly titled, greatly expanded third edition of *Genocide State Power and Mass Murder*—item number 334) [book]

Reprint. New Brunswick, N.J.: Transaction Books; London: Holt-Saunders Ltd. (an augmented and enlarged third edition)

422 "Human Rights, Foreign Policy, and the Social Sciences." *Rights and Responsibilities: International, Social and Individual Dimensions,* edited by Nelson Horn. Los Angeles: University of Southern California, Center for Study of the American Experience, 1980 pp. 167-80. [article]

423 "Social Science Publishing Defined." *Book Marketing Handbook* by Nat G. Bodian. New York and London: R.R. Bowker Co., 1980, pp. 251-52. [article]

424 "Bodies and Souls." *Accounting for Genocide: National Response and Jewish Victimization During the Holocaust* (Helen Fein). *Contemporary Sociology,* Vol. 9, No. 4, July 1980, pp. 489-92. [review essay]

425 "El éxodo: causas y efectos: Cuba, hacia dónde ahora?" *Opiniones Latinoamericanas,* Vol. 3, No. 7, October 1980, pp. 38-41. [article]

426 "The Politics of Centrism: Jews and the 1980 Elections." *Forum (on Jewish People, Zionism and Israel),* Whole No. 38, Summer 1980, pp. 31-42. [article]

Reprint. *Jewish Spectator,* Vol. 45, No. 3, Fall 1980.
Reprint. *Viewpoints: The Jerusalem Letter,* Whole No. 13, May 16, 1980, 16 pp.

427 *The Left Against Zion: Communism, Israel and the Middle East* (edited by Robert S. Wistrich). *Studies in Comparative International Development,* Vol. 15, No. 2, Spring 1980, pp. 99-105. [review]

428 *Multinational Organization Development: A Social Architectural Perspective* (by David A. Heenan and Howard V. Perlmutter). *Administrative Science Quarterly,* Vol. 25, No. 4, December 1980, pp. 695-700. [review]

1981

429 "Gino Germani: 1911-1970." *The Sociology of Modernization: Studies in Its Historical and Theoretical Aspects with Special Regard to the Latin American Case.* New Brunswick, N.J.: Transaction Books, 1981, pp. 1-8. [forward]

430 "Military Origins of Third World Dictatorship and Democracy." *Third World Quarterly,* Vol. 3, No. 1, January 1981, pp. 37-47. [article]
Reprint. *Research and Social Movements, Conflicts and Change: A Research Annual,* edited by Louis Kriesberg. Greenwich, Conn. and London: JAI Press, Inc., 1983.

431 "Ethnic Politics and U. S. Foreign Policy. " *Ethnicity and U. S. Foreign Policy,* second, revised edition, edited by Abdul A. Said. New York and London: Praeger Special Studies/CBS Educational and Professional Publishing, 1981, pp. 217-40. (completely revised version of item number 364)

432 "Jewish Soul on Ice." *Prisoner Without a Name, Cell Without a Number* (Jacobo Timerman). *The New Leader,* Vol. 58, No. 11, June 1981, pp. 16-17. [review essay]

433 "Left-Wing Fascism: An Infantile Disorder." *Transaction/Society,* Vol. 18, No. 4, May/June 1981, pp. 19-24. [article]§

434 "From the End of Ideology to the Beginning of Morality: On Daniel Bell." *Contemporary Sociology,* Vol. 10, No. 4, 1981, pp. 493-96. [article]§
Reprint. *Contemporary Issues Criticism,* edited by Robert L. Brubaker. Detroit: Gale Research Company, 1983, pp. 91-93.

435 "Corporate Ghosts in the Photocopying Machine." *Scholarly Publishing,* Vol. 12, No. 4, July, 1981, pp. 299-304. [article]
Reprint. *Library Literature* 12: *The Best of 1981,* edited by Bill Katz and Kathleen Weibel. Metuchen, N.J. and London: The Scarecrow Press, Inc., 1982, pp. 235-39.

436 "The Allensbach Affair: Labelling Data and Representing Reality." *The American Sociologist,* Vol. 16, No. 3, August 1981, pp. 148-52. [article]

437 "Social Science and the Reagan Administration." *Journal of Policy Analysis and Management,* Vol. 1, No. 1, September-October 1981, pp. 126-28. [article]
Reprint (slightly augmented). "Truth in Spending." *Transaction/Society,* Vol. 18, No. 6, September/ October 1981, pp. 18-23.

Reprint. *Policy Studies Review Annual: Volume Six,* edited by Ray C. Rist. Beverly Hills, Calif.: Sage, 1982, pp. 111-14.

438 "Many Genocides, One Holocaust?: The Limits of the Rights of States and the Obligations of Individuals." *Modern Judaism,* Vol. 1, No. 1, 1981, pp. 74-89. [article]

439 "C. Wright Mills' *Power Elite:* A Twenty-Five Year Retrospective." *The Antioch Review,* Vol. 39, No. 3, Summer 1981, pp. 373-82. [article]

440 POLICY STUDIES REVIEW ANNUAL: VOLUME FIVE. Beverly Hills, Calif.: and London: Sage, 1981, 767 pp. [edited volume]

441 CUBAN COMMUNISM, fourth edition. New Brunswick, NJ. and London: Transaction Books, 1981, 688 pp. [edited volume]

442 "International Studies and the Pursuit of the Millennium." *International Studies Notes,* Vol. 8, No. 1. Spring 1981, pp. 11-12. [commentary]

443 Introduction to *Public Policy and the Migrant Child,* edited by Cassandra Stockburger. New York: National Organization for Migrant Children, Inc., 1981.

444 "Is Social Science A God That Failed?" *Public Opinion,* Vol. 4, No. 5, October/November, 1981, pp. 10-15. [a symposium]

445 "Cuban Foreign Policy and Small-Power Myopia." *The Miami Herald,* November 15, 1981. [article]
Reprint. "Cuba y Estados Unidos: la clave es la independencia." *El Herald Miami,* November 15, 1981.
Reprint. "Proyecto Realista para Evitar Catástrofes." *El Universal de Caracas* (Venezuela), November 7, 1981.

446 "Scientific Cooperation and Human Rights: The International Development Context." *Human Rights and Scientific Cooperation Problems and Opportunities in the Americas,* edited by Eric Stover and Kathie McCleskey. Washington, D.C.: American Association for the Advancement of Science, 1981, pp. 109-21. [article]
Translation. "Cooperación Científica y Derechos Humanos: El Concepto del Desarrollo Internacional." *Revista Argentina de Relaciones Internacionales,* Vol. 6, Whole No. 18, 1981.
Translation. "La cooperación científica y los derechos humanos: El concepto del desarrollo internacional." *Los Derechos Humanos y la Cooperación Científica: Problemas y Oportunidades en las Américas,* 1982, pp. 109-21.

447 "From the Monroe Doctrine to the Betancourt Doctrine: The Western Hemisphere Alliance." *The Daily Journal* (Caracas, Venezuela), December 14, 1981. [article]
Translation (Spanish) "Recordando a un grande hombre de America." *El Miami Herald*, March 14, 1985. p. 5.

1982

448 *Who Should Know What?: Social Science, Privacy, and Ethics* (J.A. Barnes). *American Journal of Sociology,* Vol. 87, No. 4, January 1982, pp. 1006-1009. [review]

449 BEYOND EMPIRE AND REVOLUTION MILITARIZATION AND CONSOLIDATION IN THE THIRD WORLD. New York and London: Oxford University Press, 1982, 321 pp. [book]

450 "Endangered and Vulnerable Communities: Nation into Pariah." *Present Tense,* Vol. 9, No. 2, Winter 1982, pp. 33-35. [commentary]

451 "Tradition, Modernity and Industrialization: Toward an Integrated Developmental Paradigm." *Tradition and Modernity: The Role of Traditionalism in the Modern Process,* edited by Jessie G. Lutz and Salah El-Shakhs. Washington, D. C.: University Press of America, 1982, pp. 23-34. [article]

452 "The Impact of the New Information Technology on Scientific and Scholarly Publishing" (with Mary E. Curtis). *Scholarly Publishing,* Vol. 13, No. 3, April 1982, pp. 211-28. [article]
Reprint. *Journal of Information Science,* Vol. 4, No. 3, 1982, pp. 87-96.
Reprint. *Information Technology: Impact on the Way of Life,* edited by Liam Bannon, Ursula Barry, and Olav Holst. Dublin: National Board for Science and Technology/Tycooly International Publishing, Ltd., 1982, pp. 342-55.

453 "Neoliberalism: Poland Si, El Salvador, No." *The New Leader,* Vol. 65, No. 9, May 1982, pp. 10-13. [commentary]

454 "The Iconoclastic Imagination: Benjamin Nelson, A Breaker and Destroyer of Images." *Contemporary Sociology,* Vol. 11, No. 5, September 1982, pp. 524-26. [review essay]

455 "Socialization Without Politicization: Emile Durkheim's Theory of the Modern State." *Political Theory: An International Journal of Political Philosophy,* Vol. 10, No. 3, August 1982, pp. 353-77. [article]

456 "The Protestant Weber and the Spirit of American Sociology." *History of European Ideas,* Vol. 3, No. 4, Autumn 1982. [article]

457 "Language, Truth, and Politics." *The Washington Quarterly,* Vol. 6, No. 1, Winter, 1982-83. [article]§

458 "The New Fundamentalism." *Transaction /Society,* Vol. 20, No. 1, November/December 1982. [article]

459 "Winners and Losers: The Limits of Pragmatism and Moralism in Politics." *New Literary History,* Vol. 13, No. 3, Spring 1982, pp. 515-32. [article]§

1983

460 "Social Research and Political Advocacy: New Status and Old Problems in Integrating Science and Values" with Jeanne Guillemin). *Ethics, the Social Sciences, and Policy Analysis,* edited by Daniel Callahan and Bruce Jennings. New York and London: Plenum Press, 1983, pp. 187-211. [article]§

461 "The Routinization of Terrorism and Its Unanticipated Consequences." *Terrorism, Legitimacy and Power: The Consequences of Political Violence,* edited by Martha Crenshaw. Middletown, Conn. and London: Wesleyan University Press, 1983, pp. 38-51. [article] §

462 C. WRIGHT MILLS: AN AMERICAN UTOPIAN. New York: The Free Press/Macmillan Publishers; London: Collier/Macmillan Publishers Ltd., 1983, 341 pp. [book]
Paperback edition. *C. Wright Mills: An American Utopian.* New York: Macmillan/The Free Press; and London: Collier Macmillan Publishers Ltd. 1985, 341 pp.

463 "Timerman's New Country." *The New Leader*, Vol. 66, No. 3, January 24, 1983, pp. 15-17. [review essay]

464 "Talmon's Genius" (on the Myth of the Nation and the Vision of Revolution: Origins of Ideological Polarization in the Twentieth Century). *Present Tense*, Vol. 10, No. 2, Winter 1983, pp. 55-57. [review essay]§

465 "Toward A Nobel Prize for the Social Sciences." Political Science *(PS)*, Vol. 16, No. 1, Winter 1983, pp. 57-59. [commentary]
Reprint. *Anthropology Newsletter*, Vol. 24, No. 1, January 1983, pp. 1, 4.
Reprint. *Footnotes of the American Sociological Association*, Vol. 12, No. 1, January 1984, pp. 1, 8.

466 "The Contemporary American Debate on Justice: Limits to Growth or Limit to Equity." *Democracy in Two Nations: United States and India*, edited by Ramashray Roy. New Delhi and Madras: South Asian Publishers, 1983, pp. 135-56. [article]
Reprint. "The Limits of Modernity." *In Gods We Trust: New Patterns of Religious Pluralism in America* (edited by Thomas Robbins and Dick Anthony). New York and London: Transaction Publishers, 1990, pp. 63-77.

467 "From the New Deal to the New Federalism: Presidential Ideology in the U.S. from 1932 to 1982." *American Journal of Economics and Sociology*, Vol. 42, No. 2, April 1983, pp. 129-48. [article]§

468 "National Interests and Professional Ethics: Struggling for the Soul of a Discipline." *Transaction/Society*, Vol. 20, No. 5, July/August 1983, pp. 4-15. [article]

469 "Printed Words, Computers, and Democratic Societies." *The Virginia Quarterly Review*, Vol. 59, No. 4, Autumn 1983, pp. 620-36. [article]
Reprint (slightly abridged). "Views on Print: Computers and Democratic Societies." *Dialogue: Quarterly Journal of the United States Information Agency*, Whole No. 66, Issue No. 4, 1984, pp. 67-70.

470 "Universal Standards, Not Uniform Beliefs: Further Reflections on Scientific Method and Religious Sponsors" and "A Reply to Critics and Crusaders." *Sociological Analysis*, Vol. 44, No. 3, Fall 1983, pp. 179-82, 221-25. [article and reply to critics]

471 "Cuba and the Caribbean." *Worldview*, Vol. 26, No. 12, December 1983, pp. 19-22. [article]
Reprint. "Cuba and the Caribbean." *Identifying Human Values* (for The Great Decisions Program of the Foreign Policy Association by The Council on Religion and International Affairs) New York: Worldview, 1985, pp. 4-6.

472 "A Man in the Fray." *Marxism and Beyond* (Sidney Hook); *Sidney Hook: Philosopher of Democracy and Humanism* (edited by Paul Kurtz). *The New Leader*, Vol. 66, No. 10, May 1983, pp. 7-9. [review essay]

473 "Social Theory as Revolutionary Virtue." *Georges Sorel and the Sociology of Virtue* (Arthur Greil); *The Sociology of Virtue* (John Stanley). *Contemporary Sociology*, Vol. 12, No. 4, July 1983, pp. 374-76. [review essay]

474 "New technology, Scientific Information, and Democratic Choices." *Information Age*, Vol. 5, No. 2, April 1983, pp. 67-73. [article]
Reprint. "New Technology, Scientific Information, and Choices for Democratic Societies." *Representation and Exchange of Knowledge as a Basis of*

Information Processes, edited by Hans J. Dietschmann. Amsterdam and New York: North Holland/Elsevier Science Publishers, 1984, pp. 397-415.

475 "Democracy and Development: Policy Perspectives in a Postcolonial Context." *The Newer Caribbean: Decolonization, Democracy, and Development,* edited by Paget Henry and Carl Stone. Philadelphia: The Institute for the Study of Human Issues, 1983, pp. 221-34. [article]

476 *Genocide Its Political Use in the Twentieth Century* (Leo Kuper). *Modern Judaism,* Vol. 3, No. 2, May 1983, pp. 243-47. [review]

477 Foreword to *Political Terrorism: A Research Guide to Concepts, Theories, Databases and Literature,* by Alex P. Schmid and A.J. Jongman. Amsterdam: North Holland Publishing Company (published for the Centre for the Study of Social Conflicts at the University of Leiden), 1983, pp. vii-xii.

1984

478 "Librarians, Publishers, and the New Information Environment." *The Right to Information,* edited by Jana Varlejs. Jefferson, N.C. and London: McFarland & Co., 1984, pp. 20-36. [article and discussion]

479 WINNERS AND LOSERS: SOCIAL AND POLITICAL POLARITIES IN PRESENT-DAY AMERICA. Durham, N. C. and London: Duke University Press, 1984, 321 pp. [book]

480 "Moncada and the Castro Myth." *The Washington Times.* February 19, 1984, pp.1-2, section C. [article based on lecture]

481 "The Fulbright Experience: Reflections on American Innocence and Guilt Abroad." *The First Forty Years of the Fulbright's Encounters and Transformations,* edited by Arthur P. Dudden and Russell R. Dynes. Bryn Mawr, Pa.: Fulbright Alumni Association, 1984. [article]

482 CUBAN COMMUNISM, fifth edition, edited with new preface, introduction and other materials by Irving Louis Horowitz. New Brunswick, N.J. and London: Transaction Books, 1984, 804 pp. [anthology]
Translation (Spanish). "Cuba y los gusanos de la consciencia," *El Miami Herald.* May 9, 1986 Section 7. (Extracts from the Introduction to Cuban Communism).

483 "The Political Economy of Data-Base Technology." *Information and Behavior:* Vol. 1, edited by Brent D. Ruben. New Brunswick, N.J. and London: Transaction Books, 1984. [article]

484 "Religion, the State, and Politics." *Religion and Politics:* Volume 4 of *Political Anthropology,* edited by Myron J. Aronoff. New Brunswick, N.J. and London: Transaction Books, 1984, pp. 5-9. [article based on lecture]

485 "Fair Use versus Fair Return: Copyright Legislation and Its Consequences" (with Mary E. Curtis). *Journal of the American Society for Information Science* (JASIS), Vol. 35, No. 2, March 1984. pp. 67-74 (with Mary E. Curtis). [article]
Reprint. "Fair Use versus Fair Return." *Modern Copyright Fundamentals,* edited by Ben H. Weil and Barbara Friedman Polansky. New York: Van Nostrand Reinhold, 1985, pp. 218-25. [previously unlisted]
Reprint. "Fair Use Versus Fair Return: Copyright Legislation and its Consequences," *Modern Copyright Fundamentals*, edited by B.H. Weil and

B.F. Polansky. Medford, NJ: Learned Information / American Society for Information Science, 1989, pp. 216-225.

486   Preface to *Castro, Israel and the PLO,* by David J. Kopilow. Washington, D. C.: The Cuban-American National Foundation, 1984, pp. 1-2.

487   "The Role of Cuba in the Pacification of Central America." Report of the National Bipartisan Commission on Central America (Appendix). Washington, D.C.: U.S. Government Printing Office, March 1984, pp. 617-32. [An abbreviated version of this testimony appears in item 471]

488   "Genocide and the Reconstruction of Social Theory: Observations on the Exclusivity of Collective Death." *Armenian Review,* Vol. 37, No. 1, Spring 1984, pp. 1-21.
Reprint. *Genocide and the Modern Age: Etiology and Case Studies of Mass Death*, edited by Michael N. Dobkowski and Isidor Walliman. Westport, Conn.: Greenwood Press, 1984, pp. 61-80.

489   "US Power and Its Central American Policies." *The Washington Quarterly,* Vol. 7, No. 4, Fall 1984, pp. 4-12
Translation (Spanish) "El poder norteamericano y su politica en Centroamerica." *Opinion/Diario* 16 (Madrid). November 8, 1984, pp. 3-4.
Reprint. "US Power and Its Central American Policies." *Current News/ Special Edition* (Department of Defense). Whole No. 1253, 29 January 1985, pp. 1-7.
Translation (Spanish) "El poder norteamericano." *El Miami Herald.* January 26, 1985, pp. 7-8.

490   "Field Access." *Science* (AAAS), Vol. 224, Whole No. 4651, May 25, 1984, pp. 794, 796. [an exchange with Kenneth Prewitt]

491   "Review Symposium on *Beyond Empire and Revolution*" (with Claude E. Welch, Jr. and Augustus Richard Norton). *Studies in Comparative International Development.* Vol. 19, No. 2, Summer 1984, pp. 59-77.
Reprint (English) and Translation (Korean). "The Role of the Armed Forces in the Process of Third World Modernization: Toward a General Theory of Post-Industrial Development." *The Third International Conference of Korean Culture and Its Characteristics.* Seoul: The Academy of Korean Studies, 1984, pp. 3-18.

492   "The Reconstitution and Reconstruction of Social Science in America." *Social Science Newsletter,* Vol. 69, No 1 (Winter) 1984, pp. 30-33.

493   "A Pessimistic View of New Technology." Computer Power and Human Reason (review of Joseph Weizenbaum). *Information Age*, Vol. 6, No. 3, July 1984, pp. 186-87. [review essay]

494   "Fresh Havana Breezes?" *Freedom at Issue*, Whole No. 81, November-December 1984, pp. 16-19. [article]

495   "Books: Critics' Choices" *Commonweal*, Volume CXI, No. 21, November 30, 1984, pp. 666-667. [occasional piece]
Translation (Spanish) "Nuevas brisas de La Havana?" *El Miami Herald.* March 2, 1985. p. 9.

496   "On Seeing and Hearing Music." *Annual Review of Jazz Studies*, Volume 1, 1982, pp. 72-78. [article, previously unlisted]

497   "A Naive Sophisticate" (*Caveat: Realism, Reagan, and Foreign Policy*, Alexander Haig). *Cross Currents: A Quarterly Review*, Vol. XXXIV, No. 2, summer, 1984, pp. 220-224. [review essay]

498 "Elite Roles and Democratic Sentiments: The Uses and Control of Knowledge," *Transaction/SOCIETY*, Vol. 22, No. 2, January-February 1985, pp. 16-19. [commentary-article]
Translation (French) "Caveat: Realism, Reagan and Foreign Policy." *Societies: Revue des Sciences Humaines et Sociales,* Vol. I, No. 5, September 1985, pp. 30-33.

499 "The Political Economy of Data-Base Technology." *Information and Behavior, Vol. I*, edited by Brent D. Ruben. New Brunswick and Oxford: Transaction Books, 1985. [article]
Reprint. "The Political Economy of Database Technology," *Book Research Quarterly*, Vol. 1, No. 1, spring 1985, pp. 68-80.

500 "Militarism and Civil-Military Relationships in Latin America: Implications for the Third World." *Research in Political Sociology, Vol. I*, edited by Richard G. Braungart, New York: JAI Press, 1985, pp. 79-100.
Translation (Chinese). *The Chinese Intellectual*, Vol. 1, No. 1, autumn 1984, pp. 42-49.
"Militarism and Civil-Military Relationships in Latin America: Implications for the Third World." Reprinted in "Research in Political Sociology," in *The Political Sociology of the State* (edited by Richard G. Braungart and Margaret M. Braungart). Greenwich, Conn. and London: JAI Press Inc., 1991, pp. 181-201.
Translation (into Portuguese). "Militarismo e relacoes civil-militares." *Politica e Estrategia*, Vol. II, No. 3, July-Sept. 1984, pp. 373-392.

501 "Latin America, Anti-Americanism, and Intellectual Hubris." *Anti-Americanism in the Third World: Implications for US Foreign Policy*, edited by Alvin Z. Rubenstein and Donald E. Smith. New York: Praeger/Holt, Rinehart and Winston, 1985, pp. 49-66.

502 "Were the Elections a Watershed? Reluctant Peace." *Present Tense*. Vol. 12, No. 2, winter 1985, pp. 45-46. [commentary]

503 "Passion and Compassion: The Conflict in Central America." *Caribbean Review,* Vol. XIV, No. 1, winter 1985, pp. 23-25, 45. [article]
Translation (Spanish). "El conflicto de la America Central." *El Nuevo Dia* (Puerto Rico). May 23, 1985, pp. 48-49.
Translation (Spanish). "El conflicto caribeno como historia." *El Nuevo Dia* (Puerto Rico). June 6, 1985, pp. 52-133.

504 "Castro's Cuba in 1985: Waiting for the End," in *Problems of Succession in Cuba*, edited by Jaime Suchlicki, Miami: University of Miami/North-South Center, 1985, pp. 20-29.
Translation (Spanish). "La Cuba de Castro: Se acerca el final." *El Miami Herald*, May 19, 1985.
Translation (Spanish). "La sucesion en Cuba." *El Nuevo Dia*, June 2, 1985, pp. 69-73.

505 "Los obispos, dignidad e ideologia." *El Nuevo Dia* (Puerto Rico), June 8, 1985, pp. 50, 71.

506 Guide to the Bureau of Applied Social Research, edited by Judith S. Barton. *Contemporary Sociology*, Vol. 14, No. 3, May 1985, pp. 364-365. [review]

507 "At the Jerusalem Book Fair." *Congress Monthly*, Vol. 52, No. 5, July-August, 1985, pp. 13-14.

508 "Los vicios y virtudes de Norteamerica." *El Miami Herald* (United States), August 5, 1985. [review essay]

509 "Fascism with a Theological Face." *Freedom at Issue*, Whole No. 87, November-December 1985, pp. 16-18.

510 *Ethics, Politics, and International Social Science Research* (Michael P. Hamett et. al). *Contemporary Sociology*, Vol. 14, No. 5, September 1985, pp. 621-22. [review]

511 "Foreign Policy: Domestic Policy by Overseas Directives." *Policy Studies Review Annual, Vol. 7*, edited by Ray C. Rist. New Brunswick and Oxford: Transaction Books, 1985, pp. 259-265.

1986

512 "The Rashomon Effect: Ideological Proclivities and Political Dilemmas of the International Monetary Fund," *Journal of Interamerican Studies and World Affairs*. Vol. 27, No. 4. Winter 1986, pp. 37-55.
Translation (Chinese) "Ideological Proclivities and Political Dilemmas of The International Monetary Fund," *The Chinese Intellectual*, Vol. 2, No. 4, summer 1986, pp. 111-117.

513 "Human Resources and Military Manpower Requirements," *Armed Forces & Society*. Vol. 12, No. 2. Winter 1986, pp. 173-193.
Translation (Portuguese). "Recursos Humanos e Necessidades Militares," *Politica e Estratégia*. Vol. III, No. 3, July-Sept. 1985, pp. 495-512.
Reprint. "Human Resources and Military Manpower Requirements: Past Strategies and Future Policies," *Policy Studies Review Annual, Vol. 8*, edited by Ray C. Rist. New Brunswick and Oxford: Transaction Books, 1987, pp. 569-586.
Reprint. "Human Resources and Military Manpower Requirements: Strategic Considerations on Past and Future," *The Strategic Dimension of Military Manpower*, edited by Gregory Foster, Alan Ned Sabrosky, William J. Taylor. Cambridge, Mass.: Ballinger Publishers/Harper & Row, 1987, pp. 163-184. (Additional comments pp. 212-220).

514 "The Doctors and The Bomb," *Chronicles of Culture*, Vol. 10, No. 3. March 1986, pp. 26-32.

515 "American Virtues/Washington Vices" (review essay of *Capital Corruption* by Amitai Etzioni), *Contemporary Sociology*, Vol. 15, No. 2. March 1986, pp. 187-189.

516 "Government by Satrapies: The Unraveling of the Reagan Presidency," *The New Leader*, Vol. LXIX, No. 19 (December 29) 1986, pp. 5-7.
Translation (Spanish) "Los intricados laberintos del gobierno de Reagan," *El Miami Herald*. February 2, 1987.

517 "The Jews and Modern Communism: The Sombart Thesis Reconsidered," *Modern Judaism*, Vol. 6, No. 1. February 1986, pp. 13-25.

518 *The Sociological Domain: The Durkheimians and the Founding of French Sociology*, edited by Philippe Besnard. *History of European Ideas*. Vol. 7, No. 1. Spring 1986, pp. 102-104. [review]

*519   *Communicating Ideas: The Crisis of Publishing in a Post-Industrial Society.*
New York and Oxford: Oxford University Press, 1986. 240 pp.
Extract. "Gatekeeper Functions and Publishing Truths," *Chronicles: A Magazine of American Culture*, Vol. 11, No. 4 (April) 1987, pp. 19-21. From *Communicating Ideas: The Crisis of Publishing in a Post-Industrial Society.*
Translation (Italian). "Dai Mezzi di Produzione ai Modi di Communicazione: La Transformazione delle Classi Sociali in Gruppi D'Interesse. Vol. 25. No. 2 (April-June) 1987, pp. 189-196. From *Communicating Ideas: The Crisis of Publishing in a Post-Industrial Society*, pp. 189-196.

520   "Scientific Access and Political Constraint to Knowledge." *Knowledge: Creation, Diffusion, and Utilization.* Vol. 7, No. 4. June 1986, pp. 397-405.
Reprint. "Revisiting The Dilemma of Rights and Obligations" *Society.* Vol. 23, No. 5. July/ August 1986, pp. 5-8.

521   "Selected Writings of Henry Hughes: Antebellum Southerner, Slavocrat, Sociologist" (Stanford M. Lyman). *Journal of the History of the Behavioral Sciences.* Vol. 22, No. 4 (July) 1986, pp. 272-278. [review]

522   "Expropriating Ideas: The Politics of Global Publishing," *The Bookseller* (London), Whole No. 4206 August 2, 1986, pp. 528-532.
Reprint. "Expropriating Ideas: The Politics of Global Publishing" (with a discussion summary*). STM: International Publishers Association.* [monograph] 40 pp.

523   *Here the People Rule: Selected Essays* (Edward C. Banfield). *Contemporary Sociology*, Vol. 15, No. 5, September 1986, pp. 774-775. [review]

524   "The Protection and Dissemination of Intellectual Property," *Book Research Quarterly.* Vol. 2, No. 2. Summer 1986, pp. 4-13.

525   *Israel in America; The New Jewish Identity in America; and Jews in American Life and Thought. American Jewish History*, Vol. LXXV, No. 4, June 1986, pp. 457-462. [review]

526   "Government Responsibilities to Jews and Armenians: Nazi Holocaust and Turkish Genocide Reconsidered." *Armenian Review*, Vol. 39, No. 1, Spring 1986, pp. 1-9.

527   "Jews, Anti-Semitism, and Sociology." *Congress Monthly*, Vol. 53, No. 7, November-December 1986, pp. 4-7.

528   "Fidel's Stalinism." *Freedom at Issue*, Whole Nos. 92-93, November/December 1986, pp. 11-12.

529   "More Than Funny Pictures." *Chronicles*, Vol. 10, No. 11, November 1986, pp. 30-31.

530   *Talcott Parsons and the Capitalist Nation-State: Political Sociology as a Strategic Vocation* (William Buxton). *The New England Quarterly*, Vol. LIX, No. 4, December 1986, pp. 569-574. [review]

531   *The Trouble with America: Why the System is Breaking Down* (Michael Crozier). *Social Forces.* Vol. 64, No. 3 (March) 1986, pp. 799-802. [review]

1987

532   "Reflections on American Innocence and Guilt Abroad." *The Fulbright Experience, 1946-1986: Encounters and Transformations*, edited by Arthur

Power Dudden and Russell R. Dynes. New Brunswick and Oxford: Transaction Books, 1987, pp. 195-205.

533 "Genocide and the Reconstruction of Social Theory." *Genocide and The Modern Age: Etiology and Case Studies* (edited by Isador Walliman and Michael N. Dobkowski). Westport and London: Greenwood Press, 1987, pp. 61-80.

534 "Media Metaphysics and Mid-Term Results," *Chronicles: A Magazine of American Culture*, Vol. 11, No. 2 (February) 1987, pp. 17-19.

535 "Disenthralling Sociology," *Transaction/SOCIETY*, Vol. 24, No. 2, (Jan.-Feb.) 1987, pp. 48-55.
Reprint. "Disenthralling Sociology." *Deviance in American Life*, edited by James M. Henslin. New Brunswick and Oxford (UK): Transaction Publishers, 1989, pp. 61-88.

536 "The Sociology of Knowledge as a Theory of Knowledge: Observations on the Structure of Social Science," in *Pragmatics: Handbook of Pragmatic Thought* (*Pragmatik: Handbuch Pragmatischen Denkens*), edited by Herbert Stachowiak. Hamburg: Felix Meiner Verlag, 1986. (Band II, Siebenter Teil. Die Aufstieg des pragmatismus), 1987, pp. 171-201.

537 *Law and Order* (Ralf Dahrendorf). *American Journal of Sociology*, Vol. 91, No. 5, March 1987, pp. 1264-1266. [review]

538 "The ACLU and Politics: First Amendment Blues." *American Bar Foundation Research Journal*, Volume 1986, Number 3 (summer), 1987, pp. 533-545.

539 "New Technology and the Changing System of Author-Publisher Relations." *Editors' Notes: Bulletin of the Conference of Editors of Learned Journals*, Volume VI, No. 1 (spring), 1987, pp. 10-13.
"The Mission of Social Science." *Society*, Vol. 25, No. 3, March-April 1988. *A Memorial Tribute to Jeremiah Kaplan*. New York and Washington: Association of American Publishers. September 22, 1993, pp. 9-12.

540 "Between the Charybdis and Capitalism and the Scylla of Communism: The Emigration of German Social Scientists, 1933-1945" *Social Science History*, Vol. 11, No. 2 (Summer) 1987, pp. 113-139.
Translation (German). "Zwischen der Charybdis des Kapitalismus und der Szylla des Kommunismus: Die Emigration deutscher Sozialwissenschaftler," *Exil, Wissenschaft, Identitat: Die Emigration deutscher Sozialwissenschaftler, 1933-1945* (edited by Ilja Srubar). Frankfurt am Main: Suhrkamp. 1988, pp. 37-63.

541 "When Freedom to Read Suffers." *Publishers Weekly*, Vol. 232, No. 28 (July 17), 1987. p. 38.

542 "Reflections on Cuban Communism." *Linden Lane Magazine*, Vol. 6, No. 1 (Jan.-March) 1987, pp. 20-21.

543 CUBAN COMMUNISM (sixth edition). New Brunswick and Oxford: Transaction Publishers, 1987. 866 pp. [edited volume]

1988

544 "Left-Wing Fascism and Right-Wing Communism: The Fission-Fusion Effect in American Extremist Ideologies, Philosophy, History and Social Action." *Essays in Honor of Lewis Feuer*, edited by Sidney Hook, William

O'Neil and Roger O'Toole. Deventer, Holland/Boston, Kluwer Academic Publishers, 1988, pp. 245-266.

545 "Monopolization of Publishing and Crisis in Higher Education." *Academy: Bulletin of the American Association of University Professors*, Vol. 73, No. 6 (Nov-Dec) 1987, [Appeared in January 1988] pp. 41-43.

546 "In Search of an American Theology." *Congress Monthly*, Vol. 55, No. 2, (February) 1988, pp. 15-17.

547 "The Texture of Terrorism: Socialization, Routinization and Integration." *Political Learning in Adulthood: Sourcebook of Theory and Research*, edited by Roberta Sigel. Chicago: The University of Chicago Press, 1989, Ch.11, pp. 386-414.

548 "The Politics of Aids Research." *Chronicles of American Culture*, Vol. 12, No. 3 (March) 1988, pp. 20-26.

549 "External Evaluation of Professional and Scholarly Publishing: As Others See Us." *Book Research Quarterly*, Vol. 3, No. 2, (summer) 1987, [appeared in February 1988] pp. 3-32.

550 "Political Dilemmas of Scholarly Publishing." *Proceedings of the Ninth Annual Meeting of the Society for Scholarly Publishing*. Washington, D.C.: SSP, 1988, pp. 40-41.

551 "Romancing the Dictator." *The Closest of Enemies* (Wayne C. Smith). *Caribbean Review*, Vol. XVI, No. 1, spring 1988, pp. 25-27, 37. [review essay] Reprint. "Romancing the Dictator." *The Issue is Cuba*. The Cuban American National Foundation. 1988, pp. 1-8.

552 "On Legitimacy, Force and Jeane J. Kirkpatrick." *Academic Questions*, Vol. I, No. 3 (summer), 1988, pp. 60-63.
Translation (Spanish). "Fuerza y Legitimidad: El nuevo libro de Jeane J. Kirkpatrick." *El Nuevo Herald*, (February 29) 1988, p. 9A.

553 "Publishing and Prizing." *Book Research Quarterly*, Vol. 3, No. 4 (fall) 1988, pp. 18-22.

554 "Political Troubles and Personal Passions: The Sixties: Years of Hope, Days of Rage." *Contemporary Sociology*, Vol. 17, No. 6, (November) 1988. [review essay].

555 "Culture of Sociology and Sociology of Culture." Introduction to *Meaning and Authenticity* (Cesar Graña). New Brunswick and Oxford: Transaction Books, 1988.

556 *American Jewish Visions and Israeli Dilemmas*. Monograph series in Middle Eastern Studies. Miami: Graduate School of International Studies, University of Miami, 1988. 64 pp.

557 "New Foreword," in *Political Terrorism: A New Guide to Actors, Authors, Concepts, Data Bases, Theories and Literature* (edited by Alex P. Schmid and Albert J. Jongman). Amsterdam and Oxford: North Holland Publishing Company, 1988, pp. xvii-xx.

558 "New Technologies, Old Universities and Democratic Societies." *The Policy Impact of Universities in Developing Regions*, edited by Fred Lazin, Samuel Arnoni and Yehuda Gradus. London: Macmillan Publishers and New York: St. Martin's Press, 1988, pp. 42-56.

559 "The Limits of Policy: The Case of AIDS." *Knowledge in Society: The International Journal of Knowledge Transfer*, Vol. I, No. 1, spring 1988, pp. 54-65.

Reprint. "The Limits of Policy and the Purposes of Research: The Case of AIDS." *Policy Issues for the 1990s* (Policy Studies Review Annual: 9), edited by Ray C. Rist. New Brunswick and London (UK): Transaction Publishers, 1989, pp. 35-46.

560 "Socialist Utopias and Scientific Socialists: Primary Fanaticisms and Secondary Contradictions." *Sociological Forum*, Vol. 4, No. 1, (March) 1989, pp. 107-113.

1989

561 "Freedom, Planning, and Justice: Some Global Considerations Writ Small." *Planning Theory in the 1990s: Rationalism and Critical Rationalism* (edited by Robert W. Burchell). New Brunswick: Center for Urban Policy Research, 1989. [pending].

562 "In Defense of Scientific Autonomy: The Two Cultures Revisited." *Academic Questions*, Vol. 2, No.1, Whole No.5, (Spring) 1989, pp. 22-27. Translation (Spanish). "En defensa de la autonomia cientifica." *Revista del Pensamientos Centroamericano*, Vol. XLIV, Whole No. 204, (July-Sept.) 1989, pp. 26-30.

563 "Utopianism and Scientism: The Romance of False Options." *This World: A Journal of Religion and Public Life,* Whole No. 25, (Spring) 1989, pp. 104-108.

564 "New Technology and the Changing System of Author-Publisher Relations," *New Literary History*. Vol. 20, No. 2, (Winter) 1989, pp. 505-510.

565 "The Public Costs of Private Blessings: Fundamentals of the Economic Role of Government," *Studies in Comparative International Development,* Vol. 24, No. 1, (Spring) 1989, pp. 39-46.
Reprint. "The Public Costs of Private Blessings." *Fundamentals of the Economic Role of Government*, edited by Warren J. Samuels. Westport, Connecticut and London: Greenwood Press, 1989, pp. 97-104.

566 CUBAN COMMUNISM (seventh edition). New Brunswick and London: Transaction Publishers, 1989, 851 pp. [edited volume]

567 "Triumphalism in the Crucible of Tragic Politics: On Bertrand de Jouvenel." *Encounter*, Vol. LXXII, No. 5, (May) 1989, pp. 34-36.

568 "Changes in the Environment of Scholarly Publishing" Special Issue, *Book Research Quarterly*. Vol. 4, No. 4, (winter 1988-1989), 96 pp. (co-edited volume with Mary E. Curtis). Authored Introduction, pp. 3-5.

569 "A Message of Hope." *The Modern World-System III* (Immanuel Wallerstein). *The New Leader*, Vol. LXXII, No. 7, (April 3-17), 1989, pp. 18-20. [review essay]

570 "The Cuban Revolution at 30: A Response to Jaime Suchlicki and Ernesto Betancourt." *The Cuban Revolution at Thirty.* Washington, D.C.: Cuban American National Foundation (Occasional Paper No. 29), 1989, pp. 14-23.

571 "An Exchange with Claude E. Welch Jr. on Jeane J. Kirkpartick's Legitimacy and Force." *Choice: Current Reviews for College Libraries*, Vol. 26, No. 11/12, (July/August) 1989, pp. 1800-1802.

572 "Counting Bodies: The Dismal Science of Authorized Terror." *Patterns of Prejudice*, Vol. 23, No. 2, (summer) 1989, pp. 4-15.

Translation. "La ciencia del terror autorizado." *Coloquio: Publicacion del Congreso Judio Latinoamericana*, Whole No. 22, 1989, pp. 3-29.
Reprint. "Counting Bodies: The Dismal Science of Authorized Terror." *State Crime: Defining, Delineating and Explaining State Crime*, Volume 1 (edited by David O. Friedrichs). Aldershot: Ashgate Publishing Ltd., 1998, pp. 19-31.
Reprint [Enlarged]. "Science, Modernity and Terror: Reconsidering the Genocidal State." *Studies in Comparative Genocide* (edited by Levon Chorbajian and George Shirinian). Palgrave-Macmillan Publishers, 1989, pp. 46-62.

573 "When Manhattan Worked." *You Must Remember This: An Oral History of Manhattan from the 1890s to World War II* (Jeff Kisseloff). *The New Leader*, (September 18) 1989, pp. 19-20. [review]

1990

574 DAYDREAMS AND NIGHTMARES: REFLECTIONS ON A HARLEM CHILDHOOD. Jackson and London: The University Press of Mississippi. 1990, 128 pages. [Book club edition, Jewish Publications Society, 1992]
DAYDREAMS AND NIGHTMARES (Large Print edition with new Preface). New Brunswick: Transaction Large Print, 1988, 159 pp. [book]

575 "The Place of the Festschrift in Academic Life." *Scholarly Publishing*, Volume 21, Number 2, (January) 1990, pp. 77-83.

576 "Forms of Democracy: The Place of Scientific Standards in Advanced Societies." *Information Standards Quarterly*, Volume 2, Number 1, (January) 1990, pp. 8-12.
"Forms of Democracy: The Place of Scientific Standards in Advanced Societies." *A Sourcebook on Standards Information: Education, Access, and Development* (edited by Steven M Spivak and Keith A. Winsell). Boston: G.K. Hall: A Division of Macmillan Publishers, 1992, pp. 7-13.

577 "Philo-Semitism and Anti-Semitism: Jewish Conspiracies and Totalitarian Sentiments." *Midstream*, Volume XXXVI, Number 4, (May) 1990, pp. 17-23.

578 "Modernizacion, Antimodernizacion y Estructura Social: Reconsiderando a Gino Germani en el contexto actual." *Despues de Germani: Exploraciones sobre estructura social de la Argentina* (edited by Jorge Raul Jorrat and Ruth Sautu). Buenos Aires and Barcelona: Editorial Paidos, 1992, pp. 41-57.

579 "Reviewing the State of the Israeli State: A Conversation with Chaim Herzog." *Middle East Focus*, Volume 11, Number 6, Summer 1990, pp. 6-9.
Reprint. "The State of the Israeli State: An Interview with Chaim Herzog." *Middle East Review*, Volume 22, Number 3, Spring, 1990.

580 "Fidel Castro Redux: Old Revolutionaries Resisting New Revolutions." *Freedom at Issue*, Whole No. 115, July August, pp. 12-15.
Reprint. "Cuba's Insular Revolution" (originally titled "Fidel Castro Redux"). *Hemisphere: A Magazine of Latin American and Caribbean Affairs*, Volume 2, Number 3, Summer, 1990, pp. 22-24

Reprint. "Fidel Castro Redux: Old Revolutionaries Resisting New Revolutions." *Cuba in the Nineties* (edited by Frank Calzon and Charles J. Brown). Washington, D.C.: Human Rights Watch, 1991, pp. 75-80.

Reprint. "Old Revolutionaries Resisting New Revolutions: Fidel Castro Redux." *Cuba in a Changing World* (edited by Antonio Jorge, Jaime Suchlicki, and Adolfo Leyva de Varona). Miami: University of Miami/North-South Center, 1991, pp. 23-29.

581 "The Value of Theory." *Values and Value Theory in Twentieth Century America* (edited by Murray G. Murphey and Ivar Berg). *Chronicles: A Magazine of American Culture*, Vol. 14, No.5, May 1990, pp. 40-42. [review essay]

582 "A Third Way?" *Whose Keeper?: Social Science and Moral Obligation* (Alan Wolfe). *First Things*, Vol. 1, No. 3, May 1990, pp. 57-59. [review essay]

583 "Struggle Among the Cuban Exiles." *The New Leader*, Vol. LXXIII, No. 5, March 19, 1990, pp. 9-11.

584 *Stranger in Their Midst* (Pierre L. Van den Berghe). *Social Forces*, Vol. 68, No. 4., June 1990, pp. 1320-1321. [review]

585 "Frontiers in Education." *The High Status Track: Studies of Elite Schools and Stratification* (edited by Paul William Kingston and Lionel S. Lewis). *Academe: Bulletin of the American Association of University Professors*, Vol. 76, No. 5., Sept.-Oct. 1990, pp. 53-54. [review essay]

586 *Social Class and Democratic Leadership: Essays in Honor of E. Digby Baltzell* (edited by Harold J. Bershady). *Contemporary Sociology*, Vol. 19, No. 6., November 1990, pp. 811-812. [review]

1991

587 "Chance, Choice, Civility and Coleman." *Foundations of Social Theory* (James S. Coleman). *Society*, Vol. 28, No. 2., January-February 1991, pp. 80-85. [review essay]

588 "Foreword" to *Creating Sociological Awareness: Collective Images and Symbolic Representations* (Anselm Strauss). New Brunswick and London: Transaction Publishers, 1991, pp. xi-xiii.

589 "The 'Bottom Line' as American Myth and Metaphor" (with Mary E. Curtis). *Chronicles: A Magazine of American Culture*, Vol. 15, No. 4., April 1991, pp. 26-31.

590 "On Jacob L. Talmon." *Partisan Review*, Vol. LVIII, No. 1., Winter 1991, pp. 101-107.
"On Jacob L. Talmon" an Introduction to *Myth of the Nation and Vision of Revolution: Ideological Polarization in the Twentieth Century* (Jacob L. Talmon). New York and London: Transaction Publishers, 1991, pp. xv-xxii. (slightly modified version of *Partisan Review* article)

591 "Revolution and Counter-Revolution in 1989: Longevity and Legitimacy in Communist States." *Culture and Politics in China: An Anatomy of Tiananmen Square* (edited by Peter Li, Steven Mark and Marjorie Li). New Brunswick and London: Transaction Publishers, 1991, pp. 285-298.

592 "The New Generation of Soviet Intellectuals." *Freedom Review*, Vol. 22, No. 2, Whole No. 103, March-April 1991, pp. 22-26.

593 "Specialist Journals in America: Romantic Highs, Fiscal Bottoms and a Recipe for Survival." *Logos: Quarterly Journal of British Publishing*, Vol. 2, No. 1, March 1991, pp. 37-40.

"Romantic Highs and Fiscal Bottoms: The Current Status of Scholarly Journals in America." *Editor's Notes: Bulletin of the Council of Editors of Learned Journals*, Volume X, No. 1, Spring 1991, pp. 5-10 (slightly abbreviated version of *LOGOS* article).

594 "Anti-Modernization, National Character and Social Structure." *Journal of Contemporary History* (Special Festschrift Issue in Honor of Walter Laqueur's 70th Birthday), Vol. 26, Nos. 3-4, September 1991, pp. 355-369.

Translation (Italian). "Gli Attacchi alla Modernita: Caratteri Nazionali E Struttura Sociale." *Modernizzazione e Sviluppo: Quaderni del Centro Gino Germani*, Anno 2, Numero 3, 1991-92, pp. 5-12.

"Anti-Modernization, National Character and Social Structure." *The Impact of Western Nationalisms* (edited by Jehuda Reinharz and George L. Mosse). London and Newbury Park: Sage Publications, 1992, pp. 1-14. [reprint]

595 "Rediscovering Jewish Conservatism." *From Marxism to Judaism: The Collected Essays of Will Herberg* (edited by David G. Dalin). *The Jewish Quarterly*, Vol. 37, No. 4, Whole No. 140, Winter, 1990-1991, pp. 68-69. [review essay]

596 "Laud Humphreys: A Pioneer in the Practice of Social Science" (co-authored with Glenn A. Goodwin and Peter M. Nardi). *Sociological Inquiry*, Vol. 61, No. 2, Spring 1991, pp. 139-147.

597 *Guerrilla Prince* (Georgie Anne Geyer); *Fidel* (Roberto Luque Escalona); *Cuba* (Jacobo Timerman). *The American Spectator*, Vol. 24, No. 6, June 1991, pp. 35-36. [review]

598 "Beyond Polarity: Integrating Policymaking in a Post-Cold War Environment." North-South Center, University of Miami, 1991. 10 pp.

"Beyond Polarity: Integrating Policymaking in a Post-Cold War Environment." *Knowledge and Policy: The International Journal of Knowledge Transfer and Utilization*, Volume 4, Nos. 1-2, Spring-Summer 1991, pp. 7-17.

599 "Democratic Disparities: The Glass is Half Empty and Half Full." *Society*, Vol. 28, No. 5, July-August, 1991, pp. 17-23.

600 *The Higher Learning and High Technology* (Sheila Slaughter). *Contemporary Sociology*, Vol. 20, No. 4, July 1991, pp. 557-558. [review]

601 "The Armenian Nation: Old Issues, New Realities." *Freedom Review*, Vol. 22, No. 5, Whole No. 106, Sept.-Oct. 1991, pp. 25-26.

602 "The New Nihilism: Cracking the Cultural Consensus." *Society*, Vol. 29, No. 1, Nov.-Dec. 1991, pp. 27-32.

603 *A Future for the American Economy: The Social Market* (Severyn T. Bruyn). *Queen's Quarterly*, Vol. 98, No. 4, Winter 1991-92, pp. 956-959. [review]

1992

604 *Harlem Photographs: 1932-1940* (Aaron Siskind). *Commentary*, Vol. 93, No. 2, February, 1992, pp. 59-60. [review]

605 "Shadow of a Nation." *Hemisphere: A Magazine of Latin American and Caribbean Affairs*, Volume 4, Number 2, Winter-Spring 1992, pp. 6-7.

606 "Moral Theory and Policy Science: A New Look at the Gap between Foreign and Domestic Affairs." *Ethics and International Affairs*, Volume 6, 1992, pp. 81-93.

607 "Totalitarian Options in a Post-Communist World." *Freedom Review*, Volume 23, Number 3, May-June 1992 (publication pending).

608 "The Decomposition of Sociology." *Academic Questions*, Vol. 5, No. 2, Spring 1992, pp. 32-40.

609 "The Changed Role of Cuba in the International System." *Cuba: What Next?* (edited by Antonio Jorge and Henry Hamman). Miami: North-South Center of the University of Miami, 1992, pp. 19-22.

610 "The Correct Line on Castro's Cuba." *The New Leader*, Vol. LXXV, No. 5, April 6, 1992, pp. 11-13.

611 "Waiting for Perot … Not!" *Commonweal*, Vol. CXIX, No. 12, June 19, 1992, pp. 6-7.

612 "Panama: National Shadow without Political Substance." *Conflict Resolution and Democratization in Panama: Implications for U.S. Policy* (edited by Eva Loser). Washington, D.C.: The Center for Strategic and International Studies, 1992, pp. 72-80.

613 "Morris Raphael Cohen and the Classical Liberal Tradition." *Partisan Review*, Vol. LIX, No. 3, 1992, pp. 469-483.

614 "Twelve Visions on Publishing Books: A Symposium." *Media Studies Journal*, Vol. 6, No. 3, (Summer) 1992, pp. 29-30.

615 "Revolution, Longevity and Legitimacy in Communist States." *Studies in Comparative International Development*, Vol. 27, No. 1, (Spring) 1992, pp. 61-76.

616 "Moving Comfortably toward Armageddon." *The Culture of Contentment* (John Kenneth Galbraith). *The New Leader*, Vol. LXXV, No. 14, (Nov. 2-16) 1992, pp. 19-20. [review essay]

1993

617 THE CONSCIENCE OF WORMS AND THE COWARDICE OF LIONS: THE CUBAN-AMERICAN EXPERIENCE, 1959-1992. Miami: The North-South Center/University of Miami, 1993, 92 pp. [book]

618 THE DECOMPOSITION OF SOCIOLOGY AND THE RECONSTRUCTION OF SOCIAL RESEARCH. New York and Oxford: Oxford University Press, 1993, 282 pp. [book]
THE DECOMPOSITION OF SOCIOLOGY. New York and Oxford: Oxford University Press, 1994. 282 pp. [paperback edition]

619 "Past as Prologue: On Russell Kirk." *The Unbought Grace of Life: Essays in Honor of Russell Kirk*. Detroit: Sherwood Sugden & Company, 1993.

620 "The Death of Sociology?" Death at the Parasite Cafe: Social Science (Fictions) and *The Postmodern* (by Stephen Pfohl). *The Public Interest*, Whole No. 110, (Winter) 1993, pp. 132-135. [review essay]

621 "On Scheler and the Heritage of Sociology." *On Feeling, Knowing and Valuing* (edited by Harold J. Bershady). *Society*, Vol. 30, No. 3, (March-April) 1993, pp. 81-84. [review essay]

622 "C. Wright Mills." *American National Biography*. New York, North Carolina and Oxford: Oxford University Press, 1993. [encyclopedia entry, publication pending]

623 "The Politics of Physiological Psychology: Ivan Pavlov's Suppressed Defense of Scientific Freedom and its Consequences." *Integrative Physiological and Behavioral Science*, Vol. 28, No. 2, (April-June) 1993, pp. 17-25.

624 "Scholarly Book Publishing in the 1990s" (with Mary E. Curtis). *International Encyclopedia of Book Publishing* (edited by Philip G. Altbach and Edith S. Hoshino). New York: Garland Publishing Inc., 1993. [encyclopedia entry]

625 *Revolution and Genocide: On the Origins of the Armenian Genocide and Holocaust* (Robert F. Melson). *American Political Science Review*, Vol. 87, No. 2, (June) 1993, pp. 530-531. [review]

626 "Ronald Fletcher: 11 August 1921-2 May 1992." *The Psychologist*, Vol. 6, No. 2, (February) 1993, pp. 82-83.

627 "The Darker Side of the Anglo-American Connection." *The Cambridge Spies* (by Verne W. Newton) and *The Visible College* (by Gary Werskey). *The University Bookman*, Vol. XXXII, No. 4, (Winter) 1992-93, pp. 15-20. [review essay]

628 "The Phenomenal World of Kurt H. Wolff." *Human Studies*, Vol. 16, No. 3, (Summer) 1993. [pages pending]

629 *Compromised Campus: The Collaboration of Universities with the Intelligence Community, 1945-1955* (Sigmund Diamond). *Knowledge and Policy: The International Journal of Knowledge Transfer and Utilization*, Vol. 5, No. 3, (Winter 1993), pp. 77-81. [review essay]

630 "Ugly Americans, Arrogant Indians, Amazing Individuals: India Through Fulbright Eyes." *The Fulbright Difference, 1948-1992* (edited by Richard T. Arndt and David Lee Rubin). New Brunswick and London: Transaction Publishers, 1993, pp. 276-286.

631 "The Policy Framework of The Cuban Democracy Act of 1992." *Consideration of the Cuban Democracy Act of 1992*. Hearings and Markup Before the Committee on Foreign Affairs of the House of Representatives (March 25, 1992) Washington D.C.: U.S. Government Printing Office, 1993, pp. 170-182 [testimony], 192-200 [cross-examination].

632 "America and the World II—A Symposium." *Freedom Review*, Vol. 24, No. 3, June 1993, pp. 43-44.

633 *The Smithsonian Book of Books* (Michael Olmert). *Publishing Research Quarterly*, Vol. 9, No. 1, Spring 1993, pp. 87-89. [review]

634 *History and Philosophy of Social Science* (Scott Gordon). *History of European Ideas*, Vol. 17, No. 1, January 1993, pp. 121-123. [review]

635 "Hitler, History and the Holocaust." *The Jewish Quarterly*, Vol. 40, No. 2, Whole Number 150, Summer 1993, pp. 68-71.

636 "Cuba 1993: No Calm and No Storm." *Vital Speeches of the Day*, Vol. LIX, No. 18, July 1, 1993, pp. 573-576.

637 "The Middle East: Neither Peace nor War." *Freedom Review*, Vol. 24, No. 6, December 1993, pp. 9-10.

638 "Domesticating Ideology." *Society*, Vol. 30, No. 6, September-October 1993, pp. 41-45.

639 "Struggling for the Soul of Social Science." *Society*, Vol. 20, No. 5, July-August 1983, pp. 3-15. [addendum]

640 "The Mission of Social Science." *Society*, Vol. 25, No. 3, March-April 1988, pp. 5-56. [addendum]

1994

640 "Castro and the End of Ideology." *North-South*, Vol. 3, No. 4, December 1993-January 1994, pp. 6-10.
"Fidel Castro and the End of Ideology." *Cuba Survey*, Vol. 2, No. 3, October 1993, pp. 3-4. [extract]
Translation (Spanish). "Castro y el fin de la ideolgia." *Norte-Sur*, Vol. 3, No. 4, January 1994, pp. 6-9.

641 "Russell Kirk: Past as Prologue." *The Unbought Grace of Life: Essays in Honor of Russell Kirk* (edited by James E. Person, Jr.). Peru, Illinois: Sherwood Sugden Publishers, 1994, pp. 55-58.

642 "Henry R. Luce and the Future of the American Century." *Society*, Vol. 31, No. 5, July-August 1994, pp. 18-23.

643 "Responses and Replies to Critics." *The Democratic Imagination: Essays in Honor of Irving Louis Horowitz* (edited by Ray C. Rist). New Brunswick and London: Transaction Publishers, 1994, pp. 498-597.

644 "Beyond Polarity: Integrating Policy Making in a Post Cold War Environment." Third Charles M. Haar Lectureship in International Sociology. Princeton University. Delivered in the fall of 1993. Published as a monograph in the spring of 1994.

645 "Ethical and Political Consequences of the American Embargo of Cuba." *Investing in Cuba: Problems and Prospects* (edited by Jaime Suchlicki and Antonio Jorge). Conference sponsored by The Canadian Institute of Strategic Studies. New Brunswick and London: Transaction Publishers, 1994, pp. 1-16.

646 "Genocide and Governmental Responsibilities" in *Genocide and Human Rights*, edited by Roger W. Smith and Gregory H. Adamian. *Journal of Armenian Studies* [A Special Issue], Vol. IV, Nos. 1-2 (1992). Actual publication release: August 15, 1994, pp. 383-412.

647 *Forever in the Shadow of Hitler: Original Documents of the Historikerstreit* (edited by James Knowlton and Truett Cates). *History of European Ideas*, Vol. 18, No. 1, January 1994, pp. 93-96. [review]

648 "A Day in the Life of Contemporary Sociology." *Partisan Review*, Vol. LXI, No. 3, (Summer, 1994), pp. 501-510.

649 "Historikerstreit Revisited" (an exchange with Peter F. Drucker). *The Jewish Quarterly*, Vol. 41, No. 2, (Summer, 1994), pp. 1, 70-72.

650 *Tropical Diaspora: The Jewish Experience in Cuba* (Robert M. Levine). *The Americas: A Quarterly Review of Inter-American Cultural History*, Vol. 51, No. 2, (October 1994), pp. 286-288. [review]

*651 "Totalitarian Temptations versus Democratic Imaginations." Address delivered on the occasion of the 65th birthday of the author and publication of *The Democratic Imagination*, edited by Ray C. Rist. Privately printed. Scanticon, Princeton, New Jersey, September 25, 1994. 16 printed pages.

Reprint. "Totalitarian Temptations versus Democratic Imaginations." *Australia and World Affairs: Quarterly Journal*, Whole Number 24, Autumn 1995, pp. 5-14.

652　"Politics and Publishing in a Democratic Society: Technical Breakthroughs and Research Agendas" (with Mary E. Curtis). *Publishing Research Quarterly*, Vol. 10, No. 3, (Fall 1994), pp. 22-30.

1995

653　*The Sociology of Social Change* (Piotr Sztompka). *History of European Ideas*, Vol. 21, No. 3, May 1995, pp. 462-464. [review]

654　"Presidential Politics and Dynastic Pretensions." *Orbis: Journal of World Affairs*, Vol. 39, No. 1, Winter 1995, pp. 101-112. [review essay]

655　*The Political Philosophy of Hannah Arendt* (Maurizio Passerin d'Entreves). *History of European Ideas*, Vol. 21, No. 4, July 1995, pp. 595-597. [review]

656　"Summitry as Ideology." *North-South: The Magazine of the Americas*, Vol. 4, No. 3, November-December 1994, pp. 56-60.
Translation (Spanish). "La cumbre como ideologia." *Norte-Sur: La Revista de las Americas*, Vol. 4, No. 3, Nov-Dec 1994, pp. 56-60.
Translation (Spanish). "La ideologia de la cumbre." *El Nuevo Herald de Miami*, December 8th, 1994, Op-ed page.

657　"Racial Comparisons and Media Passions: The Rushton File." *Society*, Vol. 32, No. 2, Jan.-Feb. 1995, pp. 7-17.
Reprint. "Racial Comparisons and Media Passions: The Rushton File." *The Bell Curve Debate: History, Documents, Opinions* (edited by Russell Jacoby and Naomi Glauberman). New York: Times Books/Random House, pp. 179-200.

658　"Scholarly Publishing in the 1990s" (with Mary E. Curtis). *International Book Publishing: An Encyclopedia* (edited by Philip G. Altbach and Edith S. Hoshino). New York and London: Garland Publishing, Inc., 1995, pp. 303-313.

659　"Publishing, Property, and the National Information Infrastructure." *Publishing Research Quarterly*, Vol. 11, No. 1, Spring 1995, pp. 40-46.

660　*Running for President: The Candidates and Their Images, Vols. 1-2* (edited by Arthur M. Schlesinger, Jr.). *Society*, Vol. 32, No. 4, May-June 1995, pp. 93-95. [review]

661　"Decomposition or Reconstruction of Sociology?" *Schweizerische Zeitschrift fur Soziologie/Revue suisse de sociologie*, Vol. 21, No. 1, March 1995, pp. 3-7.

662　"Culture and Economy in English and Spanish America: A Symposium on the New World of the Gothic Fox." *Partisan Review*, Vol. LXII, No. 2, Spring 1995, pp. 213-233.

663　*Before The Shooting Begins: Searching for Democracy in America* (James Davison Hunter). *Social Forces*, Vol. 73, No. 4, June 1995, pp. 1615-1617. [review]

664　"Cuba's Military: Autonomy or Dependence?" *Freedom Review*, Vol. 26, No. 4, July-August 1995, pp. 13-16.

665　"The Un-American World of U.S. Communism." *Orbis: Journal of World Affairs*, Vol. 39, No. 4, Fall 1995, pp. 622-626. [review essay]

666   "Searching for Enemies—Fin de Siècle/Fin de Millenaire." *Society*, Vol. 33, No. 1, Nov-Dec 1995, pp. 42-50.

667   "The Assured Future of Specialized Publishers in the Electronic World." *Logos: Journal of the World Book Community*, Vol. 6, No. 3, Autumn 1995, pp. 158-162.

1996

668   "The Strange Career of Alienation: How a Concept is Transformed without Permission of its Founders." *Alienation, Ethnicity, and Postmodernism* (edited by Felix Geyer). Westport, Connecticut: Greenwood Press, 1996, pp. 17-22.

669   "Thomas Szasz Against the Theorists." *Chronicles: A Magazine of American Culture*, Vol. 20, No. 1, January 1996, pp. 23-27.
       "Thomas Szasz Against the Theorists." Reissued as separate by Laissez Faire Books: A Division of the Center for Independent Thought. (New York and San Francisco), Autumn 1996.

670   "Are the Social Sciences Scientific?" *Academic Questions*, Vol. 9, No. 1, Winter 1995-1996, pp. 53-59.
       "The Scientific Status of Social Research: Valuational Contexts of Contemporary Sociology." in *Human Values and Social Change,* edited by Ishwar Modi. Delhi, India: Rawat Publishers, 447 pp., 2000-2001. [title changed, text augmented]. Pp.47-58.

671   "Democracy and Development: Policy Perspectives in a Post-Colonial Context." (Festschrift in honor of Ramkrishna Mukherjee). *Sociology in the Rubric of Social Science* (edited by R.K. Bhattacharya and Asok K. Ghosh). Calcutta (India): Anthropological Survey of India. Department of Culture, Government of India, 1996, pp. 30-43.

672   "Collectivizing Death: Relative Vices v. Ultimate Virtues." *Journal of Church and State*, Vol. 38, No. 1, Winter 1996, pp. 25-35.

673   "Cuba 1996: The Last Caudillo" (with Jaime Suchlicki). *Freedom Review*, Vol. 27, No. 2, March-April 1996, pp. 18-21.

674   "Culture, Politics, and McCarthyism." *The Independent Review: A Journal of Political Economy*, Vol. 1, No. 1, Spring 1996, pp. 101-110.
       "Culture, Politics, and McCarthyism." *The William Mitchell Law Review*, Vol. 22, No. 2, Autumn-Winter, 1996, pp. 357-368.

675   CUBA: POLITICAL PILGRIMS AND CULTURAL WARS (with Mark Falcoff and Raul Castro Ruz). Washington, DC: Freedom House, 1996, 44 pp. [monograph]
       "Political Pilgrimage to Cuba, 1959-1996." *Humanitas*, Vol. IX, No. 1, 1996, pp. 52-64.

676   "The Origins of Hannah Arendt." *Society*, Vol. 33, No. 4, May-June 1996, pp. 74-78. [review essay]

677   "Solzhenitsyn's Gulag Archipelago." *Contemporary Sociology*, Vol. 25, No. 4, July 1996, pp. 452-453. [commentary]

678   "Symposium on Irving Louis Horowitz's *The Decomposition of Sociology*." *Sociological Imagination*, Vol. 33, Nos. 3-4, pp. 176-260. With a "Reply to Critics" by Horowitz, pp. 245-260.

1997

679   TAKING LIVES: GENOCIDE AND STATE POWER (fourth edition, expanded and revised). New Brunswick and London: Transaction Books, 1997, 326 pp.

680   "Losing Giants: Baltzell, Nisbet and Strauss." *Society*, Vol. 34, No. 3, 1997, pp. 47-52.

681   "British Exceptionalism." *Modern Age*, Vol. 39, No. 1, 1997, pp. 66-72.

682   "Universal Values and National Interests: The Political Vision of a Literary Scholar." (Peter Shaw, 1936-1995). *Academic Questions*, Vol. 9, No. 5, 1997, pp. 42-47.

683   "Cuba 1997." *Vital Speeches of the Day*, Vol. LXIII, No. 8, February 1997, pp. 240-243.

684   "Remembering Harold Lasswell: Appreciating the Author of The Garrison State." *Essays on the Garrison State*, by Harold D. Lasswell (edited by Jay Stanley). New Brunswick and London: Transaction Publishers, 1997, pp. 1-14. [preface]

685   "Publishing Programs and Moral Dilemmas." *Journal of Information Ethics*, Vol. 6, No. 1, Spring 1997, pp. 13-21.

686   *Cuba: Bringing the Background to the Foreground* (Ernesto F. Betancourt). Washington, DC: Freedom House, 1997, pp. i-iii. [introduction]

687   "Prophesying America's Future." *Society*, Vol. 34, No. 6, September-October 1997, pp. 72-81.

688   "Don't Rush to Halt World's Paparazzi." *The Times* (Trenton), September 14, 1997, pp. 1-3 [commentary]

689   "Hannah Arendt: Juridical Critic of Totalitarianism." *Modern Age*, Vol. 39, No. 4, 1997, pp. 397-403.

690   *Inventing Human Science: Eighteenth Century Domains* (edited by Christopher Fox, Roy Porter, and Robert Wokler). *The European Legacy*, Vol. 2, No. 5, August 1997, pp. 882-885. [review]

1998

691   "Looking, Learning and Living: A Thirty-Five Year Celebration of *Society*." *Society*, Vol. 35, No. 2, (January-February) 1998, pp. 3-7.

692   "Three Points of Light: U.S. Policy Responses to Cuba." *Cuba 1997: The Year in Review*. Washington, DC: Center for a Free Cuba, (Winter) 1998, pp. 13-16.

693   "The Politics of Psychiatry and the Ethics of a Psychiatrist." *Existentialist Psychology and Psychiatry*, Vol. XXIII, Nos. 1-3 (Special Issue), 1998, pp. 107-115. [review]

694   "Minimalism or Maximalism: Jewish Survival at the Millennium." *Jewish Survival: The Identification Problem at the End of the Twentieth Century*. Tel Aviv: Bar-Ilan University, 1997, pp. 22-23. [abstract]

* 695   "Final Thoughts, Last Hurrahs." *Society*, Vol. 35, No. 3, (March-April) 1998, pp. 14-15.

696   "Israel and the Diaspora at 50." *Judaism: A Quarterly Journal of Jewish Life & Thought*, Vol. 47, No. 2, Spring 1998, pp. 131-144.

Reprint. "Minimalism or Maximalism: Jewish Survival at the Millennium." *Jewish Survival: The Identity Problem at the Close of the Twentieth Century* (edited by Ernest Krausz and Gitta Tulea). New Brunswick and London: Transaction Publishers, 1998, pp. 1-20.

697 "Political Periodicals in Policy Formation." *Knowledge, Technology & Policy*, Vol. 11, Nos. 1-2, Spring-Summer 1998, pp. 16-24.

698 "John D. Martz: Recollections." *Studies in Comparative International Development*, Vol. 33, No. 1, Spring 1998, pp. 3-8.

699 "The Cuba Lobby: Then and Now." *Orbis: A Journal of World Affairs*, Vol. 42, No. 4, Fall 1998, pp. 553-565.
Reprint. "The Cuba Lobby: Then and Now." *Cuba Brief: A Quarterly Review*, Winter 1998-1999, pp. 1-10.

Reprint (with new data and abbreviated narrative). "Banking the Cuba Lobby: The Role of U.S. Foundations in U.S.-Cuba Policy." *CANF Issue Brief,* May 1999, 6 pp.

700 CUBAN COMMUNISM, ninth edition (co-edited with Jaime Suchlicki). New Brunswick and London: Transaction Publishers, 1998, 898 pp. [book]
Reprint (two chapters by ILH) "Military Origins and Evolution of the Cuban Revolution." *Armed Forces and the International Diversities*, edited by Leena Parmar. Jaipur, India: Pointer Publishers, 2002, pp. 34-66.

1999

701 "Ferment in Professional Associations" (with Jonathan B. Imber). *Society*, Vol. 36, No. 2, Jan-Feb 1999, pp. 5-8.

702 BEHEMOTH: MAIN CURRENTS IN THE HISTORY AND THEORY OF POLITICAL SOCIOLOGY. New Brunswick and London: Transaction Publishers, 1999, 566 pp. [book]
"Arendt's Good Society." Adapted from chapter 11 of *Behemoth: Main Currents in the History and Theory of Political Sociology. Partisan Review*, Vol. LXVI, No. 2, Spring 1999, pp. 263-280.

703 "Memory as History." *My German Question* (Peter Gay), *I Will Bear Witness* (Victor Klemperer), and *Germany: A New History* (Hagen Schulze). *Congress Monthly*, Vol. 66, No. 1, Jan-Feb 1999, pp. 12-15. [review essay]

704 "Totalitarian Origins and Outcomes of Political Orthodoxy." *Modern Age: A Quarterly Review*, Vol. 41, No. 1, Winter 1999, pp. 19-31.
Reprint (with additional material) "Totalitarian Origins and Outcomes of Political Orthodoxy: Through A Soviet Looking Glass Darkly." *Mistaken Identities: The Second Wave of Controversy over Political Correctness*, edited by Cyril Levitt, Scott Davies, Neil McLaughlin. New York: Peter Lang, 1999, pp. 97-116.

705 "Intellectual Property and Internet Publishing." *Logos*, Vol. 10, No. 1, Winter 1999, pp. 56-57.

706 "C. Wright Mills." *American National Biography,* Vol. 15, New York and London: Oxford University Press, 1999, pp. 542-543.

707 "Science, Modernity and Authorized Terror: Reconsidering the Genocidal State." *Studies in Comparative Genocide* (edited by Levon Chorbajian

and George Shirinian) London: Macmillan Press, Ltd. and New York: St. Martin's Press, Inc., 1999, pp. 15-30.

Augmented Reprint. "Science, Modernity and Authorized Terror." *Problems of Genocide*: Proceedings of the International Conference Commemorating the 80th Anniversary of the Armenian Genocide (edited by Richard G. Hovannisian). Cambridge and Toronto: Zoryan Institute for Contemporary Armenian Research & Documentation, 1999, pp. 134-152.

708 "Breaking the Boundaries of Ideology." *Right Now!*, Whole Number 24, July-Sept. 1999, pp. 4-5.

709 "The Vietnamization of Yugoslavia." *Society*, Vol. 36, No. 5, July-August 1999, pp. 3-10.

710 "Who Owns Judaism" (Symposium on American Jews and Israel Today) *Society*, Vol.36, No.4, May-June 1999, pp. 27-31.

711 "Networking America: The Cultural Context of the Privacy v. Publicity Debates." *ETC: A Review of General Semantics*. Vol. 56, Fall, 1999, pp. 305-315.

Reprint. "Networking America: The Cultural Context of the Privacy v. Publicity Debates." *The St. Croix Review*. Vol. 32, October, 1999, pp. 52-58.

"Privacy Paradox: To Divulge or Disappear?" Reprinted in a condensed form in *UTNE READER*. March-April, 2000, whole number 98. p.50.

"Networking America: The Cultural Context of Privacy v. Publicity". Reprinted in *Knowledge, Technology & Policy*. Winter 2000, volume 12, number 4. Pp. 85-91.

712 *A History of Sociological Research Methods in America. 1920-1960*, by Jennifer Platt. *The European Legacy*, Vol. 4, No. 6, December 1999, pp. 117-119.

713 "*Mein Kampf*: Book of the Century?" *The Bookseller*. 17 December, 1999, p. 27.

"Hitler's *Kampf* and Our *Frage*" Reprinted *The St. Croix Review*. February 2000, volume 33, number 1, pp.41-44.

2000

714 "Hannah Arendt" pp. 58-61; "Eichmann in Jerusalem" pp. 210-213; "Government and Genocide" pp. 280-281; "Aleksandr Solzhenitsyn's *The Gulag Archipelago*" pp. 284-286. Four entries in the *Encyclopedia of Genocide* (in two volumes), Israel W. Charny, editor-in-chief. Santa Barbara and Oxford: ABC-CLIO Publishers, 2000.

Translation and Reprinting in French of these four articles in *Le livre noir de l'humanite (Encyclopedie Mondiale des Genocides)*, Israel W. Charny, editor. Toulouse: Éditions Privat, 2001.

715 "Globalizing Social Science." *Society*. Volume 37, Number 3 (March-April), 2000. Pp.85-88.

"Mundo desbocado: Como la globalizacionm esta remodelando nuestra vidas." *Analisis Politico*. Whole Number 43 (May-August 2001), pp. 130-133.

716 "The Long Tradition and Social Science" (Special Millennium Issue on *The Conservative Scholar in the Twenty-First Century). Modern Age*. Volume 42, Number 1 (Winter 2000), pp.82-88.

717 "Whose Handmaiden? The Parochial, Chequered Career of the Social Sciences." Review of *World Social Science Report (UNESCO): 1999*, edited by Ali Kazancigil and David Makinson. *The Times Literary Supplement.* Whole Number 5058, March 10, 2000, pp.28-29.

718 "Retrieving our Heritage" [review of *The Jewish Search for a Usable Past.* By David G. Roskies]. *Congress Monthly.* Volume 67, Number 2 (March-April 2000), pp.20-21.

* 719 "Three Worlds of Development: Thirty Five Years Later." *Studies in Comparative International Development.* Volume 34, Number 2 (Summer 1999), pp.33-40. [article appeared in April 2000].

720 Review of *Max Weber's Methodology: The Unification of the Cultural and Social Sciences*, by Fritz Ringer. *The European Legacy.* Volume 5, Number 3, Spring 2000, pp.454-456.

721 "Community and State: The Case of Miami vs. Washington, DC." *The St. Croix Review* . Volume XXXIII, No.4 (August 2000), pp. 47-52.

722 Review of *The Betrayal of Liberalism: How the Disciples of Freedom and Equality Helped Foster the Illiberal Politics of Coercion and Control,* by Hilton Kramer and Roger Kimball, eds. *Academic Questions.* Volume 13, Number 3, Summer 2000, pp. 88-92.

723 "Hitler's *Mein Kampf:* When Fair is Foul." *Congress Monthly.* Volume 67, No.4 ((July-August 2000), pp. 11-13 [expanded version of item # 713].

724 Review of *Runaway World: How Globalization is Reshaping Our Lives* , by Anthony Giddens. *Society.* Volume 38, Number 1, November-December 2000, pp. 106-107.

725 "Eleven Theses on Cuba after Castro." *Studies in Comparative International Development.* Volume 34, Number 4, Winter 2000, pp.3-6.

726 "Gino Germani, 1911-1979: Sociologist from the Other America." *The American Sociologist.* Volume 31, Number 3, Fall 2000, pp. 72-79.

727 CUBAN COMMUNISM, ninth edition (co-edited with Jaime Suchlicki). New Brunswick and London: Transaction Publishers, 2000, 1008 pp. [book/anthology]

2001

728 "Daniel J. Elazar and the Covenant Tradition in Politics." *Publius: The Journal of Federalism.* Vol. 31, No.1, Winter 2001, pp. 1-8.

729 "Presidential Accountability." *Society.* Vol. 38, No.3, March-April 2001, pp. 50-55.

730 "From the Therapeutic Society to the Regulatory State: Theoretical Issues in Studying Privacy and Publicity," *Knowledge, Technology and Policy.* Vol. 13, No. 3, Fall 2000, pp. 93-103. [appeared May 2001]

731 "Ethnicity and Foreign Policy in Multi-Ethnic States," in *Encyclopedia of Nationalism*, edited by Athena S. Leoussi and Antony D. Smith. New Brunswick and London: Transaction Publishers, 2001, pp.73-80.

732 "Humanitarian Capitulation: US-Cuba Relations According to the Council on Foreign Relations." *The St. Croix Review.* Vol. XXXIV, No. 1, February 2001, pp. 46-52.
"The Council on Foreign Relations: Cuba Report" [title change only]. *Cuba Brief.* Fall-Winter 2000-2001, pp.27-30.

"An Appeasement Policy for Castro's Cuba?" [title change only]. *Miami Herald.* December 6th, 2000. editorial page.

"Humanitarian Capitulation: US-Cuba Relations According to the Council on Foreign Relations." *The Cuban American National Foundation.* January 2001. [released as a separate brochure]

"Humanitarian Capitulation: US-Cuba Relations According to the Council on Foreign Relations." *Vital Speeches of the Day.* Volume LXVII, Number 11, March 15th, 2001, pp. 329-332.

"A Flawed Cuba Policy: Where the Council on Foreign Relations Report Goes Wrong." *The World & I.* Volume 16, Number 5, May 2001, pp. 282-291.

733   "Toward a Natural History of Holocaust Studies", *Human Rights Review.* Vol. 2, No.4, July-September 2001, pp. 77-87.

734   "Walter Laqueur: Giving Cosmopolitanism a Good Name", *Aufbau.* Vol. LXVII, No. 11, May 24 2001, p.3.

735   "The New Dealers' War or War against the New Deal: Roosevelt's Conspiracy Redux," a review-essay. *Congress Monthly.* Vol. 68, No. 5, September-October 2001, pp. 19-21.

736   "Totalitarian Collision: The Complete Black Book of Russian Jewry," *Midstream.* Vol. 47, No. 6, November-December 2001, pp. 13-17.

737   "Social Science and Scholarly Communication in the New Century," *The St. Croix Review.* Vol. 34, No.5, October 2001, pp.57-60.

2002

738   "One Hundred Years of Ambiguity: U.S. – Cuba Relations in the 20th Century," *The National Interest.* Whole Number 67, Spring 2002, pp. 58-64.

* 739   "Gauging Genocide: Social Science Dimensions and Dilemmas," in *Pioneers of Genocide Studies,* edited by Steven L. Jacobs and Samuel Totten. New Brunswick and London: Transaction Publishers, 2002, pp. 253-266.

740   "National Consequences of International Terrorism," *Society.* Vol. 39, No. 2, January-February 2002, pp. 6-11.

"September 11th, 2001" [abbreviated version, title change], *First of the Month.* November 2001-January 2002. Pp. 7-8.

"Terror and its Consequences: The Endings that Began September 11th, 2001," *The St. Croix Review.* Vol. 34, No. 6, December 2001. Pp.58-64.

741   VEBLEN'S CENTURY: A COLLECTIVE PORTRAIT. New Brunswick and London: Transaction Publishers, 302 pp. [edited volume].

742   "Social Science as Cultural Formation: A View from America," *Starting the Twenty-First Century: Sociological Reflections & Challenges,* edited by Ernest Krausz and Gitta Tulea. New Brunswick and London: Transaction Publishers, 2002, Pp.37-52.

743   "Jewish Agonies/Israeli Ecstasies: A Measured Optimism," *Congress Monthly.* Vol. 69, No. 1, January-February 2002. Pp. 6-8.

744   "Seeing Through a Manchild's Eyes," *The Chronicle of Higher Education [The Chronicle Review].* Vol. XLVIII, No. 31, April 12, 2002, p.B5.

Reprinted as "Never Grow Old," *1st of the Month.* Vol. IV, No.1, May, 2002. Pp.16-17.

745 Review of *Wittgenstein's Poker: The Story of a Ten-Minute Argument Between Two Great Philosophers*, by David Edmonds and John Eidinow. *Knowledge, Technology & Policy.* Volume 14, Number 3, Fall, 2002, pp. 152-156.

746 ELI GINZBERG: THE ECONOMIST AS A PUBLIC INTELLEC- TUAL. New Brunswick and London: Transaction Publishers, 264 pp. [edited volume].
"The Theory of Policy: Eli Ginzberg as Social Scientist" in *Eli Ginzberg: The Economist as a Public Intellectual.* New Brunswick and London: Transaction Publishers, 2002. Pp.195-206.

747 "Strange Bedfellows: The Radical Assault on Israeli Legitimacy," *Human Rights Review.* Vol. 3, No. 3, April-June, 2002, pp.3-18.
Reprint. "Strange Bedfellows: The Radical Assault on Israeli Legitimacy," *St. Croix Review.* Vol. 35, No. 4, October 2002, pp.38-50.
Reprint. "Strange Bedfellows: The Radical Assault on Israeli Legitimacy," *Midstream.* Vol. 48, No. 5, October 2002. [pending].
Translation [French]. "Strange Bedfellows: The Radical Assault on Israeli Legitimacy," *Bulletin de la Fondation Auschwitz,* Spring 2003 [pending].

* 748 "Scientific Endeavor, Professional Aims, and Public Interests," *Society.* Vol. 40, No. 1, November-December 2002, pp. 7-10.

749 Review of *Who Owns Academic Work? Battling for Control of Intellectual Property*, by Corynne McSherry. *Publishing Research Quarterly.* Volume 18, Number 2, Summer, 2002, pp. 56-60.

750 Review of *The Jews of Europe after the Black Death,* by Anna Foa. *Congress Monthly.* Volume 69, Number 5, September-October 2002, pp. 20-21.

751 "Reflections on Riesman," *The American Sociologist.* Vol. 33, No. 2, Sum- mer, 2002, pp. 118-123.

2003

752 "Facts, Policies, Morals: The Free Spirit of Aaron Wildavsky," Introduc- tion to new edition of *The Revolt Against the Masses: And Other Essays on Politics and Public Policy* by Aaron Wildavsky. New Brunswick and Lon- don: Transaction Publishers, 2003. Pp.ix-xvii.

753 "Introduction," *Philosophy, Science and Higher Education* by Mason W. Gross, edited by Richard P. McCormick and Richard Schlatter. New Brunswick and London: Transaction Publishers, 2003. Pp. vii-xv.

754 "The Indifference of Intelligence to Ideology" (Review Essay of *Lives of the Mind* by Roger Kimball, and *Freedom and its Betrayal* by Isaiah Ber- lin). *Society.* Vol. 40, No. 2, January-February 2003, pp. 89-91.

755 CUBAN COMMUNISM, eleventh edition (co-edited with Jaime Suchlicki). New Brunswick and London: Transaction Publishers, 2003, 747 pp. [book/anthology]

756 "The American Consensus and *The American Conservative.*" *Partisan Review.* Vol. 70, No.2, 2003. Pp. 298-304.

757 "In Memoriam Meyer Reinhold (1909-2002)." *International Journal of the Classical Tradition.* [co-authored with Wolfgang Haase] Vol.9, No.1, Summer 2003. Pp. 3-9.

758 "Post-War Iraq: The Cult of Dictatorship vs. the Culture of Modernity." *Society.* Vol.40, No. 5, July-August 2003, pp. 9-19.

759　Review of *Gulag: A History*, by Anne Applebaum. *Society.* Vol.41, No.1, November-December 2003, pp. 84-87.

760　"Seymour Martin Lipset: The Social Uses of Anomaly." *The American Sociologist.* Vol. 34, Nos. 1-2 [special commemorative issue on Civil Society and Class Politics] Spring-Summer 2003, pp. 10-17.

761　"Vorwort zur amerikanischen Ausgabe - '*Demozid*' *der befohlene Tod: Massenmorde im 20. Jahrhundert*" by Rudolph J. Rummel. Munster-Hamburg, 2003, pp.xii-xvi.

* 762　"*Cuban Communism* and Cuban Studies: The Political Career of an Anthology." *Institute for Cuban and Cuban-American Studies: University of Miami.* September 2003, 14 pp.

2004　　　　　　　　　　　　　　189

763　"Melvin J. Lasky: An American Voice of the European Conscience" (Introduction to a new edition of *Utopia and Revolution*). New Brunswick and London: Transaction Publishers, 2003, 747 pp.

764　"Aaron Wildavsky: Conservative Populist." *Modern Age.* Vol. 46, No.1, Winter 2004, pp. 96-105.

765　"Tabloid Politics: Formatting Ideology." *The St. Croix Review.* Vol. 37, No.1, February 2004, pp. 47-57.

* 766　"Social Science as a Mission." *LOGOS.* Vol. 14, No. 4, Winter 2003, pp. 220-221.
　　　Reprint as "The Logic of Transaction." *Knowledge, Technology & Policy.* Vol. 16, No.2, Summer 2003, pp. 4-8.

767　Review of *Cuba: The Morning After* by Mark Falcoff. *Society.* Vol.41, No. 3, March-April 2004, pp. 80-82.

768　"Two Cultures of Science: The Limits of Positivism Revisited." *Journal of Policy History.* Vol.16, No.4, Fall 2004, pp. 332-347.

769　"Machiavelli on Military Morality" [review essay]. *Armed Forces & Society.* Vol. 31, No.4, Fall [at press].

770　"Gino Germani: El Espiritu de la Práctica Sociológica." Introduction to *Gino Germani: Del Antifascismo a la Sociología,* by Ana Alejandra Germani. Buenos Aires: Editorial Santillana/Taurus, 2004, pp. 11-17.

771　"Real Wars and Cultural Wars: Domesticating the Iraq Conflict." *Society.* Vol. 41, No.5, July-August, pp.17-24.

772　"Coming Out of the *Editorial* Closet: From Feminist Issues to Gender Issues." *Gender Issues.* Vol. 21, No.2, Spring, pp.77-83.

* 773　"Science, Civility and Value Judgments." *Free Inquiry.* Vol.16, No.6, November-December 2004 [pagination pending].

2005

774　Does Social Science Need Reform?—Putting Science Back into Social Science". *Critical Review.* Vol. 16, Nos. 2-34, Summer-Fall 2004, pp. 258-288.

775　"The Cultural Contradictions of Sociology." *Michigan Quarterly Review.* (University of Michigan) Vol. 43, No. 2, Spring 2005 [pagination pending].

776 "Feuding with the Past, Fearing the Future: Globalization as Cultural Metaphor for the Struggle between Nation-State and World-Economy." *Social Philosophy & Policy.* Vol. 23, No. 1, Winter 2006 [publication pending].

777 "The Context of Policy and the Policy of Context: American Resolve and Israel Legitimacy." *St. Croix Review.* Vol. XXXVII, No. 10, October 2004. pp. 57-64.

778 "Two Cultures of Science: The Limits of Positivism." *International Social Science Journal.* Whole No. 181, September 2004, pp. 429-437. [Also published in Spanish, French, Arabic, Russian, Chinese editions] [093f - Reprint] THE ANARCHISTS. New Brunswick and London: Aldine Transaction, 2005, 660 pp. (edited volume with new introduction).

779 Review of *The Case for Democracy: The Power of Freedom to Overcome Tyranny and Terror* by Natan Sharansky. *Society.* Vol. 42, No. 4, May-June 2005 [publication pending].